Thirty-Fiv
Sunland-Tujunga
7771 Foothill Blva
Tujunga, CA 91042

P9-DGL-197

ELEVENTH EDITION

NEW MEXICO

OFF THE BEATEN PATH ®

DISCOVER YOUR FUN

NICKY LEACH

2018

978.9T
S775

Globe Pequot

Guilford, Connecticut

233876920

All the information in this guidebook is subject to change. We recommend that you call ahead to obtain current information before traveling.

Globe Pequot

An imprint of Rowman & Littlefield
Off the Beaten Path is a registered trademark of Rowman & Littlefield.

Distributed by NATIONAL BOOK NETWORK

Copyright © 2018 Rowman & Littlefield
Maps: Equator Graphics © Rowman & Littlefield

All rights reserved. No part of this book may be reproduced in any form or by any electronic or mechanical means, including information storage and retrieval systems, without written permission from the publisher, except by a reviewer who may quote passages in a review.

British Library Cataloguing in Publication Information available

ISSN 1536-6189
ISBN 978-1-4930-3073-6 (paperback)
ISBN 978-1-4930-3074-3 (e-book)

∞™ The paper used in this publication meets the minimum requirements of American National Standard for Information Sciences—Permanence of Paper for Printed Library Materials, ANSI/NISO Z39.48-1992

Printed in the United States of America

In fond memory of my longtime friend, colleague, fellow explorer, and New Mexican Richard K. Harris (October 22, 1947–November 22, 2011), who did the legwork to create the original guidebook and is now journeying through the stars.

Contents

About the Author

Longtime Santa Fe resident and former teacher **Nicky Leach** moved from her native England to the American West over 35 years ago. She has been exploring the region and writing and editing books, articles, and essays about it ever since. Nicky is the award-winning author of more than 55 travel guides, including *Insider's Guide: Santa Fe* and *Day Trips from Albuquerque* for Globe Pequot. She is also a trained bodyworker and has maintained a part-time craniosacral therapy practice in Santa Fe since 2004.

Acknowledgments

This eleventh edition of *New Mexico Off the Beaten Path* builds on the strong foundation of the original guide created by the late Richard K. Harris in 1991. I am honored to once again update and add to it. I want to acknowledge first and foremost my longtime friendship and professional respect for my colleague and friend of more than two decades. I was fortunate to know Richard and work with him on several guides, and to share our publishing community here in Santa Fe—a town that Richard, for all his wanderlust, loved deeply. We all miss you, Richard.

I'd like to thank my New Mexico community, many of whom help keep me up to date daily on what's happening here and generously share resources and, most important, support and friendship at key times. Among them: Steve Lewis and the Santa Fe CVB; Shelley Thompson and Steve Cantrell at New Mexico Department of Cultural Affairs; National Park Service interpreter Christine Beekman; Indian trader Frank Hill and his musician wife Amy Bianco; Albuquerque foodie Dawn Singh; local journalist Candelora Versace; Vicki Pozzebon, Delicious New Mexico; cookbook author and New Mexico food blogger Cheryl Alters Jamison; the late Silver City author Richard Mahler; artists Lynne Windsor and Barry McCuan; novelist Jo-Ann Mapson; Jo Fisher, Lensic Center of the Performing Arts; travel writer Nancy Zimmerman; poet Jeanie C. Williams; and publisher Ellen Kleiner, Richard's longtime partner.

Last, but first in my heart, my beloved 13-year-old feline companion Molly died during the final busy weeks of the last update in 2013. I still miss her "help" very much, particularly on deadline days.

Introduction

Renowned New Mexico artist Georgia O'Keeffe once said, "If you ever go to New Mexico, it will itch you for the rest of your life." Millions of folks from all over the world have come to know exactly what she meant. The people, the culture, the landscape, the climate—New Mexico just gets under your skin and takes hold. Whatever form it takes, the New Mexico mystique is a powerful force to reckon with. It may hit you when you're hiking among the ruins of an ancient civilization, strolling along the narrow streets of Santa Fe, or just silently soaking up the smells and sounds of the forest. Frequently, visitors become so seduced by the Land of Enchantment that they're compelled to make it their home. When asked why, they can't always explain it. But on a broad scale it has a lot to do with space and freedom and pure light. The ever-present blue skies and spectacular sunsets are addicting.

Tucked into the southwestern US, New Mexico itself is essentially "off the beaten path." Our state is often confused with Arizona on maps and is even mistaken for the country of Mexico. But most residents cherish this anonymity and obscurity about the place they call home. New Mexico's wide-open spaces, unique history, rich cultural diversity, and endless natural wonders combine to create an ideal atmosphere in which to escape and explore—or even get lost, if that's what you're after.

This is by no means a comprehensive guidebook to New Mexico; there are plenty of good ones around. Rather, it's a selective guide to the state's out-of-the-way treasures—some well-known, some not—all of which are unique and offer something special to the adventurous traveler. Geographic diversity and vastness are paramount in New Mexico's 121,336 square miles. The state will delight you with its hidden charms as you explore its ghost towns, quaint bed-and-breakfast inns, quirky cafes, ancient Indian ruins and present-day Indian pueblos, isolated museums, and all the breathtaking scenery you can bear.

While sating your wanderlust in our expansive state, remember that although New Mexico is the fifth-largest state in area (after Alaska, Texas, California, and Montana), it ranks 36th in population—a scant 2 million people, of whom approximately one-third reside in the Albuquerque metropolitan area. The point: lots of space, few people. Because everything is so spread out, plan on taking some time to get around. And always carry a detailed, current map (call the New Mexico Department of Tourism, 505-827-7400, for a free one).

Politically, New Mexico is one of the youngest states in the continental US—it didn't achieve statehood until 1912. Santa Fe may be the oldest capital in the nation, thanks to its Spanish history, but this is a land of ancient civilizations. The Ancestral Puebloans (formerly known by their Navajo name of Anasazi) were ancestors of the state's modern Pueblo people, and were themselves successors to earlier hunter-gatherer and paleohunter cultures, such as the Folsom and Clovis, dating back to around 10,000 BC, shortly after the Ice Age. From modest origins living in scattered pit-house hamlets made up of extended families, Ancestral Pueblo farmers began to coalesce in larger *pueblos* (villages) beginning around AD 700. Community living and traveling and trading with other groups led to rapid innovations in architecture, the arts, and communal wealth, and by AD 1000 Ancestral Pueblo people were living in impressively built, large-scale multistory pueblos.

The great houses and great kivas in Chaco Canyon in northwest New Mexico; Pecos (Cicuye), just east of Santa Fe in the Pecos Valley; and Gran Quivira, the largest and farthest south of the three Salinas Pueblo Missions in south-central New Mexico—all were important trading and spiritual centers on a cultural frontier. They were used by Apache, Comanche, and other native groups, and all except Chaco were still thriving when Spanish conquistadores arrived here in 1540.

Today, New Mexico has 19 autonomous pueblos (the term encompasses the tribe, the land, and the political boundaries of the designated Indian reservation) inhabited by the descendants of the Ancestral Pueblo people. The state is also home to the Diné (the Navajo Nation, the largest Indian reservation in the US) and the Chiricahua and Jicarilla branches of the Apache. Both Diné and Apache are Athabascan cultures that arrived here from northwest Canada about 1,000 years ago, according to recent evidence, toward the end of the Ancestral Pueblo era.

American Indian culture remains a vital part of life in most of our state. Although several pueblos are included as entries in this book, many are not. It's important to realize that the pueblos and other American Indian lands do not exist for tourists, even if many pueblos welcome visitors and host such events as feast days, arts and crafts shows, and ceremonial dances that are open to the public. Indian reservations are, first and foremost, sovereign nations within the US, recognized by the federal government as political entities, with their own laws and policies (and languages, although most American Indians now speak English). When you visit a pueblo, you are essentially visiting another country, with all that implies, so do call ahead before you visit, and find out what is permissible and what is not. A list of the Indian pueblos and tribes of New Mexico begins on page 228.

An aside is appropriate here. During the past decade or so, Indian tribes across the US have entered the lucrative field of operating gaming casinos, many connected to professionally run, high-end resorts with luxurious guest rooms, spas, gourmet restaurants, golf, and other activities. New Mexico tribes are no different in this respect. And while many, if not most, of New Mexico's tribes now operate casinos, other than a few exceptions they are not included in this edition. If you are interested in such gambling opportunities, however, rest assured that you'll see the often elaborate casino resorts (and/or their billboards) that have, for better or worse, cropped up along New Mexico's highways.

New Mexico also boasts a strong Hispanic heritage. The Spanish arrived here with Coronado's Entrada expedition to North America in 1540, and Spanish conquistador Don Juan de Oñate established the first Spanish colony near present-day Española, on Ohkay Ohwingeh (San Juan Pueblo) land, in 1598. Waves of new Spanish settlers came north on El Camino Real ("The Royal Road" connecting Mexico City to Santa Fe), and the Spanish influence took hold. Hispanic traditions and culture go deep in New Mexico. Among other things, this heritage is responsible for New Mexico's designation as the oldest wine-growing region in the US, starting with the missionaries' vineyards in the 1600s. A few of the state's well-reviewed and increasingly numerous contemporary wineries are included in this book. Refer to pages 229–30 for a complete list.

New Mexico is also a land of newcomers. Other than a few early adventurers, Anglo settlers didn't begin arriving until Spain ceded the territory to Mexico in 1821 and the Santa Fe Trail opened for cross-country business. By 1880 the railroad had connected New Mexico to the population centers on the East Coast, connecting this once-remote outpost with the rest of the world, for better or worse. During the early 1900s, as World War I effectively blocked travel to Europe, American tourists increasingly began exploring the West and its natural and cultural treasures on rail trips that inspired and awakened them to their own American heritage.

It wasn't just tourism. Among the new arrivals in Santa Fe were Anglos from cities back east who, on their doctor's advice, headed to a sanitorium to recuperate from tuberculosis in the arid desert air. These new arrivals were often talented artists, architects, archaeologists, poets, writers, and others, who ended up staying and creating the New Mexico institutions we know today. New Mexico is famous for its arts and culture. The northern New Mexico community of Taos is a picturesque arts enclave. Santa Fe is firmly established as an art capital of international prominence. And more recently Albuquerque, too, has become known as a major art center. Galleries are concentrated in these three cities, but you will find artists, writers, and other creatives living and working and sharing their work in small towns throughout the state. From Roswell and Ruidoso in the southeast to Silver City and Truth or Consequences in the southwest, and even a few semi–ghost towns, there are dozens of quality museums and galleries waiting to be discovered.

You can travel all over the world and never find a place that has a lasting effect on you. But after your first visit to New Mexico, expect to feel the urge to come back. It was Georgia O'Keeffe's itch, and soon it will be yours as well.

Key to lodging prices
(average double occupancy in season, exclusive of tax):
Inexpensive: Under $75   Expensive: $125–$200
Moderate: $75–$125   Very expensive: More than $200
Key to restaurant prices (price per average entree):
Inexpensive: Under $12   Expensive: $18–$30
Moderate: $12–$18   Very expensive: More than $30

Climate Overview

A clue to New Mexico's climate: Before "Land of Enchantment" became the state slogan, New Mexico went by the nickname "the Sunshine State," based on the fact that every part of New Mexico receives at least 70 percent sunshine year-round. However, as with most states, New Mexico's weather depends on the region and season.

Autumn weather is the most pleasant and predictable, usually sunny and warm in the daytime and cool at night. Early spring, while often quite warm, usually brings strong, dusty winds and a lot of pollen from juniper and cotton-wood trees and other plants; it is not unusual for there to be wet snowstorms. June is the hottest and driest month, often reaching the upper 90s (higher in the southern part of the state), with early July to mid-September temperatures hot but cooled down most days by afternoon cloudbursts, known incorrectly but charmingly as "monsoons." Winters are very cold, especially in the mountains of northern New Mexico. Nighttime temperatures can reach down to the single digits, even in southern New Mexico's lower elevations, where temperatures are mild in the daytime. Plan accordingly, if you are camping.

Keep in mind that even during summer it can get quite cool during the evenings, often requiring a sweater or jacket, especially in communities at higher elevations, which tend to be cooler throughout the year. Winter is a mixed bag because, while it is usually sunny and relatively mild, the state does receive snowfall, which ranges from less than 2 inches annually in the lower Rio Grande Valley to as much as 300 inches in the mountains of north-central New Mexico.

Helpful Information

NEW MEXICO TOURISM

New Mexico Department of Tourism, 491 Old Santa Fe Trail, Santa Fe, NM 87501; (505) 827-7400; newmexico.org.

USEFUL WEBSITES

Note: Other useful websites are scattered throughout this edition.

State of New Mexico: state.nm.us.

New Mexico State Parks: emnrd.state.nm.us/spd.

New Mexico's national parks and monuments: nps.gov/state/nm.

Ski New Mexico: skinewmexico.com.

New Mexico museums and other cultural offerings: newmexicoculture.org.

MAJOR NEWSPAPERS

Albuquerque Journal
7777 Jefferson St. NE
Albuquerque, NM 87109
(505) 823-4400
abqjournal.com

Santa Fe New Mexican
202 E. Marcy St.
Santa Fe, NM 87501
(505) 983-3303
santafenewmexican.com

Las Cruces Sun-News
256 W. Las Cruces Ave.
Las Cruces, NM 88005
(575) 541-5400
lcsun-news.com

Farmington Daily Times
203 W. Main St.
Farmington, NM 87401
(505) 325-4545
daily-times.com

Gallup Independent
500 N. 9th St.
Gallup, NM 87305
(505) 863-6811
gallupindependent.com

Roswell Daily Record
2301 N. Main St.
Roswell, NM 88201
(575) 622-7710
rdrnews.com

Taos News
226 Albright St.
Taos, NM 87571
(575) 758-2241
taosnews.com

PUBLIC TRANSPORTATION

Amtrak
320 1st St. SW
Albuquerque, NM 87102
(505) 842-9650
(800) 872-7245
amtrak.com

Albuquerque International Sunport
2200 Sunport Blvd. SE
Albuquerque, NM 87106
(505) 244-7700
abqsunport.com

Greyhound
320 Si Rat-Outer Ring Rd. Express Way
Albuquerque, NM 87102
(505) 243-4435
greyhound.com

New Mexico Rail Runner Express
809 Copper Ave. NW
Albuquerque, NM 87102
(866) 795-7245
nmrailrunner.com

Fast Facts about the Land of Enchantment

- **Area (land):** 121,336 square miles; rank: 5

- **Capital:** Santa Fe

- **Largest city:** Albuquerque, population—city: 559,277; metro: 909,906 (est. 2014)

- **Number of counties:** 33

- **Highest elevation:** 13,161 feet, Wheeler Peak, Taos

- **Lowest elevation:** 2,840 feet, Red Bluff Lake, along the Texas border south of Carlsbad

- **Population:** 2,081,015 (est. 2016); rank: 36

- **Statehood:** January 6, 1912—the 47th state

- **Nickname:** Land of Enchantment

- **State song:** "O, Fair New Mexico"

- **State motto:** Crescit Eundo ("It grows as it goes.")

- **State slogan:** "Everybody is somebody in New Mexico."

- **State flower:** yucca

- **State tree:** piñon

- **State grass:** blue grama

- **State bird:** roadrunner

- **State fish:** New Mexico cutthroat trout

- **State animal:** black bear

- **State reptile:** New Mexico whiptail

- **State amphibian:** New Mexico spadefoot toad

- **State vegetables:** chile and beans

- **State fossil:** Coelophysis dinosaur

- **State insect:** tarantula hawk wasp

- **State butterfly:** Sandía hairstreak

- **State gem:** turquoise

- **State cookie:** biscochito (or bizcochito)

- **State poem:** "A Nuevo Mexico" by Luis Tafoya

- **State Spanish-language song:** "Asi es Nuevo Mexico" by Amadeo Lucero

- **State ballad:** "Land of Enchantment" by Michael Martin Murphy

- **State bilingual song:** "New Mexico—Mi Lindo Nuevo Mexico"

- **State colors:** red and yellow

- **State question:** "Red or green?" (the color chile you want on your meal; "Christmas" means both)

- **State aircraft:** hot-air balloon

- **State neckwear:** bolo tie

Famous New Mexicans

Those who were born in, worked in, or are closely associated with the state:

- **Black Jack Ketchum,** notorious train robber

- **Gen. John (Blackjack) Pershing,** cavalry officer in the 1880s

- **Gen. Douglas MacArthur,** World War II hero

- **Manuel Lujan Jr.,** secretary of the interior during the George H. W. Bush administration

- **Bill Mauldin,** Pulitzer Prize–winning cartoonist

Traditional Foods of New Mexico

Some of the most enjoyable moments during any vacation are mealtimes, especially when you find yourself someplace with a unique cuisine. New Mexico is one such place. The traditional food of New Mexico—*la comida de Nuevo México*—is centered on the crops that American Indians were growing in this area when Spanish explorers arrived in the late 1500s: corn, beans, and squash ("the three sisters") and chile (always spelled with a final "e" in New Mexico, Spanish style).

New Mexico cuisine is very different from the Tex-Mex cuisine of our neighbor to the east, where chile is spelled "chili," and rather than denoting a vegetable (the chile pepper), it connotes a spicy bean-and-beef concoction. New Mexican cuisine can be as basic as a plate of red or green chile enchiladas (rolled or stacked corn tortillas filled with cheese, beef, or chicken and topped with red or green chile and cheese and sometimes in New Mexico, a fried egg), which can be found almost anywhere in the state, or as elaborate and experimental as an entree of piñon-laced corn crepes filled with chipotle chiles and topped with squash blossoms, which can be found only in a trendy Santa Fe bistro.

While dishes such as enchiladas or posole (a chile-infused hominy stew) are omnipresent in New Mexico restaurants, they can be time-consuming yet richly rewarding to prepare at home. Scattered throughout this edition are simple recipes for some favorite traditional (and adapted) New Mexico dishes and accompaniments—everything from green chile stew to a classic margarita. We hope you enjoy this little taste of the Southwest!

- **Miguel Trujillo,** Isleta Pueblo activist who campaigned to win Indians' right to vote

- **Ezequiel C. de Baca,** nation's first Hispanic governor

- **Conrad Hilton,** founder of the Hilton Hotel chain

- **Ernest Thompson Seton,** author, naturalist, artist, cofounder of the Boy Scouts

- **Harrison J. Schmitt,** astronaut, moonwalker, former US senator

- **Clyde Tombaugh,** astronomer who codiscovered the dwarf planet Pluto

- **J. Robert Oppenheimer,** head of the Manhattan Project, which developed the atomic bomb

- **Robert H. Goddard,** developer of world's first liquid-fuel rocket

- **Edgar D. Mitchell,** Apollo 14 astronaut

- **Nancy Lopez,** Hall of Fame golfer with LPGA
- **Al, Al Jr., and Bobby Unser,** famous race-car-driving family
- **Don Meredith,** former Dallas Cowboy
- **Trent Dimas,** Olympic gold medal–winning gymnast
- **Sam Donaldson,** ABC News anchor

Southwestern New Mexico

This rugged region of the state is often referred to as Old West Country. Its wild-and-woolly past echoes in the remains of ghost towns, in museums, and in the memories of many old-timers. Mining and ranching have traditionally dominated the landscape and have given residents their fiercely independent nature.

This is also the only region in New Mexico that borders a foreign country—our state's namesake to the south, Mexico. In southwestern New Mexico you'll find the 558,014-acre Gila Wilderness, the nation's first designated wilderness area, set aside in 1924, as well as New Mexico's largest lake, Elephant Butte Reservoir, near Truth or Consequences. And on a more somber note, this region was the site of the world's first nuclear bomb explosion, near White Sands National Monument.

Gila Wilderness is part of Gila National Forest, which spans much of Grant and Catron Counties. This region is New Mexico's birders' paradise. Some 400 bird species arrive seasonally or make their home here year-round, most popular among them 17 species of migratory hummingbirds, which arrive in the early spring from their wintering grounds in Mexico and fascinate both old and young alike. Hummingbird

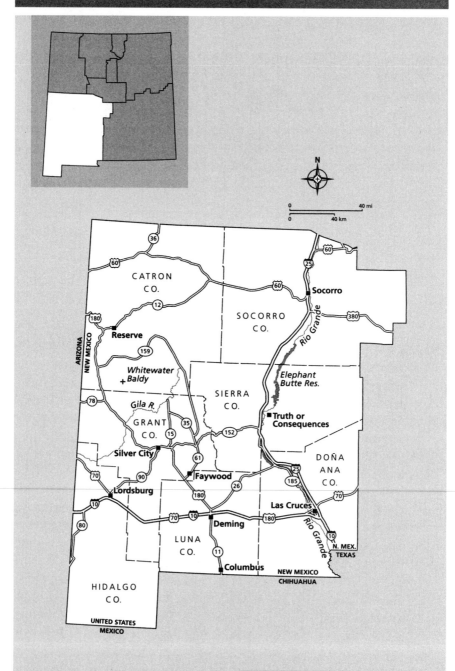

watching is immensely pleasurable and a mainstay for several birder-friendly bed-and-breakfasts in the Silver City area.

Socorro County

As you approach the **Very Large Array (VLA)** from Socorro, 50 miles to the east on US 60, you'll start to see a pattern of massive white dishlike objects interrupting the grassy plains of the horizon. As you get closer, the picture focuses a bit—"Looks like rows of huge sci-fi ray guns aimed at distant otherworldly enemies," you muse. But at this point, little do you know that the Plains of San Agustin are alive with the sounds of outer space.

You can't get more basic or accurate in the naming business than whoever came up with the name of this oft-photographed, high-tech haven.

The Very Large Array is a very big deal. Really. The VLA is an astronomical observatory used to study not only our solar system but also distant galaxies at the edge of the universe. Consisting of 27 dish-shaped antennas, each 82 feet in diameter, that are connected to form a single radio telescope, the VLA is the most powerful of its kind in the world. Astronomers from all over the world come here to study the universe. (The acclaimed sci-fi blockbuster *Contact*, starring Jodie Foster, was filmed here.)

In the unstaffed visitor center, a 20-minute video, produced in 2013 and narrated by Jodie Foster, orients you to the history of the VLA, after which you can check out displays in the museum dedicated to radio astronomy. Next take the walking-tour trails on the grounds of the VLA. One of the first stops is the "Whisper Gallery," where two dishlike structures face each other about 50 feet apart. Have a friend stand at one while you stand at the other. By whispering into a small ball attached to the dish by a string, the two of you can communicate clearly. On a minute and simplified scale, the structure illustrates how the VLA works.

newmexicotrivia

Created in July 1850, Socorro County is New Mexico's oldest county.

To get to the VLA, drive about 50 miles west of Socorro on US 60, turn south onto Highway 52, then take a right onto Highway 66 to the visitor center; (575) 835-7000; vla.nrao.edu. It's open daily from 8:30 a.m. to sunset; gift shop is open daily from 9 a.m. to 4 p.m. Admission is $6 for adults, $5 for seniors age 65 and over, age 17 and under are free. Forty-five-minute guided tours and family-friendly hands-on activities are offered the first Saturday of each month at 11 a.m., 1 p.m., and 3 p.m. No reservations are required; just show up at the visitor center 15 minutes before each tour is due to start. The first Saturday tour event culminates in an evening of free guided night sky telescope viewing at the Etscorn Observatory at New Mexico Tech in Socorro. The evening event begins at dark and lasts two hours. In April and October, free admission and expanded first Saturday tours between 11 a.m. and 4 p.m., known as Open House Events, are offered to accommodate the larger number of visitors returning from touring the Trinity Site (see page 7) near Alamogordo.

Near the center of Socorro County, in the small community of **San Antonio** (pop. 165), you'll find not one, but two cafes serving up some of the best green chile cheeseburgers in New Mexico—chile burgers so good they both appear on New Mexico's famed Green Chile Cheeseburger Trail.

The **Owl Bar & Cafe** has been serving customers since 1945. It's a hole-in-the-wall joint with a spit-and-sawdust local vibe and has long been known for its hot green chile cheeseburgers. The bar was opened during the Manhattan Project era by Frank and Dee Chavez in Dee's family's grocery store, which was saved from a fire that destroyed the town's A. H. Hilton Mercantile Store in the early 1940s.

New Mexicans traveling in these parts make a point to pass through San Antonio around lunchtime, just to get their daily chile fix at the cafe.

Choose one of the many booths to get a good view of the old wooden bar that runs the length of the dining area, or, better yet, prop yourself on a barstool as a vantage point from which to count up all the "wise ones" that constitute the cafe's owl-deco motif.

The Owl Cafe is ¼ mile east of I-25 on US 380, near the intersection with Highway 1, about 10 miles south of Socorro; (505) 835-9946. It's open daily, except Sunday, from 8 a.m. to 9 p.m. (or 10 p.m., if they're busy).

The **Buckhorn Tavern**, also opened in the 1940s and now run by Bobby and Debby Olguin, third-generation owners, is located close by in an equally rustic building. It has its own claim to fame in the long-running New Mexico green chile cheeseburger wars. Competition ramped up in 2005, when *GQ* magazine voted its green chile cheeseburger no. 7 in *GQ*'s "The 20 Hamburgers You Must Eat Before You Die." Then, in 2009, chef Bobby Olguin, a larger-than-life character, competed with well-known chef Bobby Flay on his *Throwdown with Bobby Flay* show on the Food Network, with the results judged by a local chile expert.

The Buckhorn Tavern is at 68 US 380 in San Antonio; (575) 835-4423; buckhornburgers.com. It's open Mon through Fri from 11 a.m. to 8 p.m. and Sat from 11 a.m. to 2:45 p.m.

San Antonio's other claim to fame is as the birthplace of hotelier Conrad Hilton. It was in his father's San Antonio hotel that Conrad began as a baggage carrier, only to end up starting one of the world's largest luxury hotel chains years later.

You won't find many owls at the nearby 57,331-acre **Bosque del Apache National Wildlife Refuge**, but if you time your visit for late fall or winter, you're sure to spot lots of migratory birds in this sanctuary along the Rio Grande. Bring plenty of film—and a telephoto lens if you have one—to join the ranks of international photographers who are drawn by the beauty of the *bosque* (bottomlands) and its birds.

Established in 1939 as a "refuge and breeding grounds for migratory birds and other wildlife," the refuge also

newmexicotrivia

Chile peppers are New Mexico's top cash crop. New Mexico ranks first in the amount of chiles produced and acreage planted, double that of its nearest rival, California.

provided winter habitat for greater sandhill cranes. In 1941 only 17 cranes visited the refuge, whereas their number is now as high as 17,000. A program to breed endangered whooping cranes took place at this refuge, but unfortunately was unsuccessful; whooping cranes have not been seen here for several years now.

Staff at the visitor center can fill you in on what to expect on the driving or walking tour. The migratory patterns of different bird species are highlighted, and you can put your back against the wall, spread-eagle, in the "How Big Is Your Wingspan?" display to see how you measure up to the feathered ones. Then there's the Birdcall Game, in which you listen to a recorded call and try to match it to a list of birds.

The self-guided, 15-mile tour loop is available for driving, cycling, and walking and takes you through the birds' habitat in the *bosque*. Here's where, during peak winter migrations, you get a close view of snow geese, sandhill cranes, peregrine falcons, and bald eagles, along with 290 other bird species. Each year during the third weekend in November, the refuge hosts the **Festival of the Cranes**, which celebrates the wildlife of the Middle Rio Grande Valley and the return of the snow geese and cranes. The festival includes bird-related demonstrations as well as wildlife art exhibits and area tours.

Bosque del Apache is 8 miles south of Highway 380 (at the Owl Cafe) on Highway 1; (575) 835-1828; fws.gov/refuge/bosque_del_apache. The daily admission fee is $5 per vehicle. Visitor center hours are weekdays from 7:30 a.m. to 4 p.m. and weekends from 8 a.m. to 4:30 p.m. The tour loop is open daily from one hour before sunrise to one hour after sunset.

The mass ascensions and returns of flocks of birds in the skies over the *bosque* are famous, and a huge draw for both birders and photographers. To get there early, you'll want to stay nearby. ***Casa Blanca Bed and Breakfast Guesthouse*** in San Antonio is less than 10 miles from Bosque del Apache. The 1880s Victorian country farmhouse is owned by innkeeper Phoebe Wood; assistant innkeeper Phil Norton was manager of Bosque del Apache from 1986 to 2000, so you are in good hands if you want to learn more about the *bosque*.

Whether you're into birds or not, a stay at Casa Blanca is a relaxing experience away from the noise of the city. During fall and winter, guests enjoy the warmth of a wood-burning stove in one of three guest rooms, all with private baths, named after birds. When it's warmer, you can avail yourself of the rural serenity of Casa Blanca's large veranda, which surrounds the front of the home. In addition, the bed-and-breakfast has two sitting areas, one with a piano, and a large selection of books and board games.

Casa Blanca is located at 13 Montoya St. in San Antonio (575-835-3027; casablancabedandbreakfast.com), a couple of blocks from the Owl Cafe. Rates range from $90 to $110, double occupancy. Pets are negotiable. The inn is closed Apr through Sept.

FAVORITE ATTRACTIONS/EVENTS IN SOUTHWESTERN NEW MEXICO

Bosque del Apache National Wildlife Refuge
Socorro County
(575) 835-1828
fws.gov/refuge/bosque_del_apache

Catwalk National Recreation Trail
near Glenwood
(575) 539-2481 (Glenwood Ranger District office)
fs.usda.gov

Gila Cliff Dwellings National Monument
north of Silver City
(575) 536-9461
nps.gov/gicl

Very Large Array
Socorro County
(575) 835-7000
vla.nrao.edu

EVENTS
Great American Duck Race
August, Deming
(575) 544-0469
demingduckrace.com

Hatch Chile Festival
Labor Day weekend, Hatch
(575) 267-1095
hatchchilefest.com

Pie Festival
September, Pie Town, west of Very Large Array on US 60
(575) 772-2711
pietownfestival.com

Festival of the Cranes
November, Bosque del Apache National Wildlife Refuge
(575) 835-1828
friendsofthebosque.org/crane

One of the least accessible and most eerie places in New Mexico is open to the public only twice a year. ***Trinity Site***, ground zero to the world's first nuclear explosion, is located in a remote part of the usually off-limits White Sands Missile Range, deep in southeastern Socorro County. Following more than two years of research and development in Los Alamos (see the Los Alamos County entry in the North-Central New Mexico chapter), the Manhattan Project, which brought together some of the world's most important scientists to develop a nuclear weapon, culminated in the detonation of the bomb at 5:29.45 a.m. on July 16, 1945. The blast was visible for 160 miles, including in Albuquerque and Santa Fe, and windows were shattered in Silver City, 120 miles from the site.

Most signs of the blast have been removed—even the 1,200-foot-diameter, 8-foot-deep crater resulting from the blast has been filled in. However, part of the blast area at ground zero has been left intact for display purposes. A fence encloses much of the ground-zero area. Small pieces of Trinitite, the fused silica rock formed by the extreme heat of the blast, still litter the site, and folks say it's radioactive enough to fog photographic film. A black lava monument erected in 1965 and a National Historic Landmark plaque dedicated by the National Park Service in 1975 are about all that remain.

Open-house tours of Trinity Site by reservation are held on the first Saturday of April and October from 11 a.m. to 4 p.m. For information and reservations, call the White Sands Missile Range public affairs office (575-678-1134). Further information is at wsmr.army.mil/PAO/Trinity/Pages/Home.aspx.

Catron County

In the nation's most lightning-struck region sits **The Lightning Field**, an art installation by American sculptor Walter De Maria. You can't just drop by for the show, though: All visits are overnight affairs and require reservations. The Lightning Field is large-scale environmental art created by De Maria and completed in 1977. The work, which was commissioned and is maintained by the New York–based ***Dia Center for the Arts***, is composed of 400 steel poles measuring 15 to 20 feet long that have been placed in a grid measuring 1 mile by 3,330 feet. The tips of the poles form an exact even plane, like a bed of nails for some evil giant. During thunderstorms the poles act as lightning rods, creating a dazzling light show.

The adventure starts in the town of ***Quemado***, on US 60, where, after meeting with the caretaker early in the afternoon, you're taken for a 45-minute ride on dirt roads to a visitor cabin. You, along with any other visitors, are then left there until late the next morning. During the day, take the two-hour hike to the field to get a closer look at the rods and wander among them; as long as there's no lightning, you're safe. Otherwise, you can safely view the lightning strikes as long as you stay outside the perimeter of the field.

Because late summer is prime time for thunderstorms, a visit in July or August gives you the best chance for a spectacular show. The field is also attractive during other times of the year, however, because the shiny rods provide shows of another sort with the help of sunshine or, on a clear night, moonlight.

Visiting season is May 1 through October 31, and reservations are taken from March on. For more information and to check available dates, call (505) 898-3335 in Corrales. For comprehensive information and to make reservations online, visit Dia Center's website at diaart.org/visit/visit/walter-de-maria-the-lightning-field. A one-night stay costs $150 per person (students/children are $100 per person), which includes meals and transportation to and from Quemado. (**Note:** During July and August, rates go up to $250, which still does not cover the center's actual cost of operations; therefore, additional contributions are appreciated.) Despite the high adventure of viewing the lightning field, keep in mind that it is fine art on a grand scale; no photographs are permitted.

Just east of Quemado, and about 30 minutes from the Very Large Array, you'll find **Pie Town**, a blink-and-you'll-miss-it hamlet at mile marker 56 on US 60, astride the Continental Divide, which for decades has been famous for—you guessed it—homemade pie. Pie Town was built up during the Dust Bowl years by poor farming families fleeing adverse conditions. By as early as the 1920s, a general store owner had already begun baking pies to sell to miners in the area, and the name Pie Town stuck. It was such a model of hardscrabble ingenuity and enterprise that it attracted the attention of a photographer from Texas, Russell Lee, who, like Dorothea Lange and others, was documenting conditions in rural areas during FDR's New Deal era. It was largely those 600 or so extraordinary black-and-white photos, now housed in the Library of Congress, that brought wider public attention to Pie Town. That, and the chance of some delicious homemade pie in the back of beyond. Today, residents of this tiny burg continue to serve up good cheer, camaraderie, and fresh pie to grateful and very hungry travelers.

There are several cafes in town dedicated to pie, and each has its fans. The **Pie-O-Neer Cafe**, on the north side of the highway in a historic wooden building with a scenic front porch, has a particularly strong following, as much for its upbeat and energetic Pie Lady, Kathy Knapp, as for her delicate and outrageously tasty pies. Kathy is a skilled baker from a family of bakers and has been regularly featured in media and even a documentary and cookbook. When the cafe is open, Kathy and her partner, Stan, are always there to personally greet you and make time for a sit-down and a photo. This is a haven for travelers of all kinds, including bicyclists on the Divide Trail who are looking for good company and food. A Pie Bar showcases the many daily choices, of which I can highly recommend the strawberry-rhubarb, peach-green chile, or chocolate chess with red chile. If you call ahead (a good idea when you are coming this far), Kathy will make your favorite pie and save you a slice or the whole thing to eat in or take home. Pie-O-Neer is only open Mar 14 to Nov 25, Thurs through Sat from 11:30 a.m. to 4 p.m., or until the pies are all gone; (575) 772-2711; pieoneer.com.

Note: If the Pie-O-Neer is closed when you drive through, you can usually still find pie at **The Gatherin' Place** next to the post office (575-772-2909; gatherinplace.wordpress.com), **The Pie Source** (575-772-1021; piesource .com), or **The Top of the World General Store**, which are all open daily year-round for longer hours. If possible, try to visit during the famed Pie Town Festival in September, an annual weekend event for the whole family, when all things pie are celebrated with great enthusiasm.

As New Mexico's most sparsely populated but geographically largest county, Catron County contains the bulk of the 3-million-acre Gila National Forest. In this region you'll find the atmospheric semi–ghost town of **Mogollon** (muggy-on), set in a narrow valley flanked by canyon walls along Silver Creek. For about 60 years after the great gold strike of 1878, Mogollon earned a reputation for lawlessness, as the Mogollon Mountains continued to give up millions of dollars' worth of gold, silver, and copper. Perhaps because of its inaccessibility, neither territorial troops nor the Apache warriors Victorio and Geronimo could tame this onetime headquarters of Butch Cassidy and his crew.

Today, Mogollon has a population of 15 souls, and the old buildings are only slightly marred by the presence of facades built for the 1973 Western *My Name Is Nobody*, starring Henry Fonda. Mogollon is, however, still one of New Mexico's best-preserved ghost towns. During the summer, several residents run shops, a restaurant, a dusty museum, and a bed-and-breakfast open nightly May through Oct, to serve the trickle of visitors who venture into these parts.

Mogollon is located about 9 miles east of US 180 (about 37 miles south of Reserve) on Highway 159—a very narrow, cliff-hugging road with many hairpin turns. (It's paved, but be sure to keep your eyes on the road.) If you're feeling adventurous and you have the time, keep going past the town and into the Gila National Forest and Mogollon Mountains, where you will find exquisite backcountry hiking and camping. Roads and trails are generally well marked, but take a US Forest Service map, available at the general store back in Glenwood or the Glenwood Ranger Station, for more precise exploring expeditions.

The best place to stay in Catron County is in Mogollon—the **Silver Creek Inn**. This historic bed-and-breakfast may be the quietest place you've ever slept. The building was constructed in 1885 as a hotel and general store and is one of the few examples in New Mexico of a two-story adobe structure. The owners, Stan King and Kathy Knapp of the Pie-O-Neer Cafe in Pie Town, have renovated it with contemporary southwestern flair, including a terra-cotta tile roof and Santa Fe Territorial–style redbrick trim. You'll want to arrive early enough to drive safely into Mogollon on the mountain road (check-in is 4 p.m.; the inn door is locked at 10 p.m., so call if you are going to be late) and to spend some time relaxing on the enclosed patio with its waterfall and sweeping, curved exterior staircase.

There are four rooms, and advance reservations are required. Room rates are $110–$135 per night for two adults with continental breakfast, and $150–$175 per night for two adults with full breakfast. Guests may bring food to cook other meals in the kitchen, and the staff will do the cleanup for a $10 fee. The inn does not have TV or Wi-Fi, only accepts adults age 21 and older, and has a no-pets policy—the owners explain that the ghosts scare them. Open May through Oct. Contact: (866) 276-4882; silvercreekinn.com.

Dining options are limited in Mogollon, another reason to get here early and be prepared. The Purple Onion Cafe is located in the old 1900 post office and offers food May through October on Sat and Sun from 9 a.m. to 5 p.m. It is known for its hearty breakfasts, excellent green chile cheeseburgers, and barbecue. (**Note:** Highway 159 is undergoing a yearlong road construction in 2016–2017. Call ahead to check on conditions before making the drive.)

About 3½ miles farther south of the turnoff for Mogollon, on US 180, you'll come across the tiny village of **Glenwood**. Here you can explore one of the truly awesome sights in New Mexico: **Catwalk National Recreation Trail**. Plan this outing in late fall or early winter, during the week if possible, to avoid seeing another soul. You can't find a better site for a picnic.

Set in beautiful Whitewater Canyon, just outside Glenwood, the Catwalk trailhead is covered with stately old sycamores and cottonwoods. The perfectly clear Whitewater Creek rushes alongside the trail, completing the pristine setting. The canyon was a favorite hideout for Apaches and desperados, including Butch Cassidy, in the 1880s.

The initial rocky trail soon turns into the Catwalk, a narrow metal walkway (with a sturdy rail) that hugs the sheer rock wall of the gorge as it winds along the creek up the canyon for about 1 mile past the gorge. Though the gorge is 100 feet deep (and the canyon walls rise 1,400 feet), the Catwalk stays about 20 feet above the river. The point is that a walk on the Catwalk is exciting and visually stimulating, but it's not scary. The Catwalk is well maintained for safety.

The Catwalk got its start in 1893, when pipelines were laid through the canyon to provide water for a mill that serviced nearby gold and silver claims. Because the lines needed continual maintenance, the workers who had to walk along the suspended pipes referred to them as the catwalk. Today, despite a major recent refurbishment, you can still see parts of the old pipelines.

The Catwalk trailhead is located about 5 miles from US 180 in Glenwood (40 miles south of Reserve), at the end of Highway 174 (well marked with signs), also known as Catwalk Road. For more information, call Glenwood Ranger Station in Glenwood (575-539-2481; fs.usda.gov/gila; Mon through Fri from 8 a.m. to 4:30 p.m.); admission is $3 per vehicle.

Grant County

Silver City is the largest community in Grant County and home of Western New Mexico University. As its name implies, mining played a key role in the town's history. Billy the Kid also figures into Silver City's past—he spent part of his childhood here before moving on to establish his notoriously lawless career.

Unlike most of New Mexico's old mining towns, Silver City survived the boom-bust pattern of the industry to become Grant County's trade center and county seat. At the turn of the 20th century, the town capitalized on its dry climate to become a haven for people with tuberculosis. This delightful climate, with its four distinct seasons, continues to attract new residents, particularly retirees.

Take a stroll down Bullard Street (around Broadway) near the city's center to check out its historic downtown district. You'll find an eclectic mix of shops and cafes, including the famous Buffalo Bar, housed in architecturally significant late-1800s buildings. Like Las Vegas, New Mexico, up north (see the San Miguel County entry in the chapter on Northeastern New Mexico), Silver City's core is enhanced by a choice selection of Victorian homes. During the past few years, Silver City has become something of an artists' colony, and now has about two dozen contemporary art galleries and a couple of coffeehouses with Wi-Fi.

One of the city's finest examples of Victorian architecture is now the home of the **Silver City Museum**. This unusual brick structure was originally the home of mining magnate Harry Ailman, who had it built in 1881. Later it served as the city hall and as a fire station before becoming a museum in 1967. This is the place to start investigating Silver City's rich history, from the prehistoric Mogollon Indians who inhabited the area, through the mining days, to the present. The museum sponsors special, long-running exhibits such as

More Than Civilizers: Women of Silver City, 1870–1910. Visitors can even climb to the top in the museum's cupola, built for ventilation, and get a 360-degree view of the town.

Silver City Museum is located at 312 W. Broadway; (575) 538-5921; silver citymuseum.org. It's open Tues through Fri from 9 a.m. to 4:30 p.m. and weekends from 10 a.m. to 4 p.m. A suggested donation of $3 per person is requested.

Another local museum worth a visit is the **Western New Mexico University Museum**, which houses the country's largest permanent exhibit of pottery made by a branch of the Ancestral Pueblo people, the Mimbres, living in the Mogollon region of southwest New Mexico. In addition to this spectacular pottery collection, the museum features other pottery, ancient tools, jewelry, and historic artifacts from the archaeologically significant Casas Grandes (Paquime) site in the state of Chihuahua, just south of the border in Mexico. Paquime was a famous trading center, which traded extensively with Ancestral Pueblo people of the Mogollon highlands, as well as Chacoans in northwestern New Mexico. Images on Mimbres pots show some of these trading items, including parrots, which were raised at Paquime and prized for their feathers by people in the Southwest.

The museum is located in Fleming Hall, 1000 W. College Ave., on the WNMU campus in Silver City; (575) 538-6386; wnmumuseum.org. It's open Mon through Fri from 9 a.m. to 4:30 p.m. and Sat and Sun from 10 a.m. to 4 p.m.; closed school holidays and Christmas break; free admission.

The most distinctive lodging in the Silver City area can be found at the extensively renovated **Bear Mountain Lodge**, a luxury bed-and-breakfast located on 178 acres bordering the Gila National Forest. The lodge was originally constructed in 1928 as the Rocky Mountain School (reputedly a place for delinquent boys), with later incarnations as a country club and a dude ranch before being purchased by Myra McCormick, legendary birder and avid conservationist, who ran the lodge for 41 years. Before her death in 1999, McCormick bequeathed her lodge and her land in trust to The Nature Conservancy, with the stipulation they continue to run it as a lodge for 10 years. After spending a significant sum transforming the rustic lodge into a chic establishment emphasizing local and sustainably sourced furnishings, toiletries, and cuisine, the Conservancy used the lodge as a base for tours of the Conservancy's nearby Gila River preserves and also banded hummingbirds on-site. The Conservancy sold the lodge to the owners of the Blue Dome Gallery in Silver City in 2009. The new owners have kept up the lodge's reputation as a relaxing, upscale destination B&B with excellent birding and delicious, substantial breakfasts, while also expanding its focus on local arts and cafe offerings to include dinner, by advance request, and packed and restaurant lunches; weekend brunches and holiday meals are also open to local residents.

The lodge offers 11 luxuriously appointed rooms, each with a private bath and locally handcrafted Mission-style furnishings. Despite the extensive renovations, the lodge retains its historical charm and integrity, as evidenced by the hand-hewn beams, striking pine staircase, stone fireplaces, and hardwood floors throughout.

To get to Bear Mountain Lodge from Silver City, head north on US 180 (it takes a right turn at Mr. Ed's Do-It Center and becomes 14th Street in town); turn right (north) on Alabama Street, which becomes Cottage San Road; head north about 2¾ miles; and the road to Bear Mountain Lodge is marked to your left. Nightly room rates range from $160 to $180 in the Main Lodge and Myra's Retreat; $185 for the Wren's Nest, which has a queen and full bed but no Wi-Fi; and $265 for the Coop, which has two rooms with king and twin beds. Rates include a full breakfast; surcharge and two-night minimum on major holidays; (575) 538-2538; bearmountainlodge.com. There is Wi-Fi at the lodge, but no TV. The lodge is pet friendly—you can even bring your horse, as long as you feed it; children under 10 are discouraged.

newmexicotrivia

The grave of Billy the Kid's mother, Catherine Antrim, is located in Silver City.

An economical as well as historical lodging option can be found downtown at the **Palace Hotel**. Established in a former bank building built in 1882, the hotel originally opened in 1900 as a modern showplace. Restored to its former elegance in 1990, the hotel offers 17 guest rooms and suites and a complimentary continental breakfast served in the skylit garden room upstairs.

You'll find the Palace Hotel at 106 W. Broadway; (575) 388-1811; silvercitypalacehotel.com. Rates range from $58 to $94 per room per night.

Silver City may be remote, but it is a university town, and that means a vibrant student population alongside a burgeoning number of retirees and artists, lots of cultural offerings, outdoor activities in the surrounding mountains, and a growing number of really good historic inns and bed-and-breakfasts and eclectic restaurants begun by young and enthusiastic chefs that offer excellent food at a reasonable price point.

Silver City restaurants include everything from authentic Mexican and modern American food to globally inspired cuisine, a chef-owned pop-up weekend restaurant, a microbrewery in downtown, hip coffeehouses, and bistros serving fresh takes on continental and Italian cuisine. Plan on eating very well in this great little mountain town.

Just north of Silver City, on the edge of the Gila National Forest, the village of Pinos Altos ("Tall Pines") is a prime spot for any off-the-beaten-pather. Though Pinos Altos's mining history dates from 1803, it was a later gold discovery by three forty-niners from California in 1860 that led to the establishment of Pinos Altos as a mining camp. Roy Bean operated a general store here with his brother before moving to Texas to become "the law west of the Pecos." During the past few years, several of the town's old stores have been replaced by modern shops.

Pinos Altos's points of interest include *Hearst Church*, *Buckhorn Saloon*, *Pinos Altos Opera House*, and *Pinos Altos Museum*. The small though architecturally interesting Hearst Church was built in 1898 with money donated by Phoebe Hearst, mother of newspaper tycoon William Randolph Hearst, whose late husband, George, had left her mining interests in Pinos Altos. The adobe, stone, and wooden-shingle church, originally called the Gold Avenue Methodist–Episcopal Church, now houses Pinos Altos Gallery, run by the Grant County Art Guild. It also contains the hearse that carried the body of Pat Garrett (killer of Billy the Kid), along with other horse-drawn vehicles. The building is open mid-May through mid-Oct, Fri through Sun and holidays from 10 a.m. to 5 p.m.; gcag.org.

With its faded whitewashed facade, *Buckhorn Saloon* on Main Street in Pinos Altos is one of the West's finest and most atmospheric old bars, distinguished by 18-inch-thick adobe walls, rustic timbers, and a hidey-hole said to have been used by Billy the Kid. Following a year-long renovation, this famous hostelry reopened under the new ownership of executive chef and California native Thomas Bock in 2010 (575-538-9911; buckhorn saloonandoperahouse.com). Bock has kept the popular steaks and burgers (don't miss the juicy buffalo burger) that have always made this a wonderful destination dining spot and expanded the menu to include homemade ice cream. You can eat in 3 dining areas, including the bar, from late afternoon on. The adjoining *Opera House*, which was used to stage popular melodramas in the summer for many years, now is used for concerts by some of the Southwest's best musicians, including Round Mountain and the Bill Hearne trio. There is live music 4 nights a week, as well as an open-mic night.

Pinos Altos Museum, just across the road from the Buckhorn, is located in the rear of the Log Cabin Curio Shop. The tin-roofed log cabin was the county's first private schoolhouse, built around 1866. The museum's holdings include an extensive collection of Indian arrowheads and equipment and furnishings from the area's mining heyday. The shop and museum are open daily from 10 a.m. to 5 p.m.; (575) 388-1882; pinosaltos.org.

Pinos Altos is located about 6 miles north of Silver City, just off Highway 15. Most of the roads in and around Pinos Altos are dirt, but this should present few difficulties; they remain in good condition unless there's been a lot of rain.

If you continue for 40 more miles beyond Pinos Altos on Highway 15—a very narrow and twisting mountain road that requires slow driving—you will come to road's end in the Gila National Forest at *Gila Cliff Dwellings National Monument* (575-536-9461; nps.gov/gicl).

Gila Cliff Dwellings is a wonderful little park, the top visitor attraction in the area. It is the only unit of the National Park System that specifically interprets the ancient Pueblo people who lived in the Mogollon region of southwest New Mexico. They were long known as the Mogollon culture, but archaeologists now call them Ancestral Puebloan, in recognition of the cultural florescence that started in southwestern New Mexico and spread north. Several branches of the culture inhabited the region. The best known were the Mimbres, who lived in the adjoining Mimbres River drainage—talented artisans who developed the magnificent black-on-white Mimbres pottery that continues to wow us today. Another branch of the Mogollon lived north of Alamogordo, at what is now the Three Rivers Petroglyph Site.

In the early Christian era, the Mogollon enjoyed a remote existence in these resource-rich mountains, where they were expert hunter-gatherers who lived in extended family units in scattered pit-house villages. Contact with travelers from Mesoamerica around 2,000 years ago led them to develop pottery very early on, beginning with a lovely basic reddish ware and ending up with the refined Mimbres ceramics. These were recognizably related to Pueblo pottery manufactured in Chaco and Mesa Verde and became the hottest trade items in the prehistoric Southwest. The village in the cliff here was built in AD 1280, in five caves that had been used for centuries by early hunters and later Mogollon people.

To visit Gila Cliff Dwellings, you will need to hike a mile on a steep trail that ascends some 200 feet up the canyon walls to the site. The dwellings themselves are tucked into caves in the cliff and are made of adobe and timber. Most visitors are extremely quiet when walking among the rooms of the dwellings, partly because the caves' acoustics amplify voices but also because they're showing respect for the people who lived here so long ago. On the edge of the Gila National Wilderness, and along the Gila River, the monument is a peaceful and beautiful place for a hike; there is a campground nearby.

The trail to the cliff dwellings is open daily from 9 a.m. to 4 p.m.; all visitors must be off the trail by 5 p.m. The visitor center, 2 miles from the trailhead, is open 8 a.m. to 4:30 p.m. There are extended opening hours in summer; check with the visitor center before making the drive. Admission is

$5 per person for anyone age 16 or older; passholders and those under 16 are free. (**Note:** The park is actually in Catron County but is accessible only through Grant County.) The signs along Highway 15 near Pinos Altos claiming the drive to the monument will take two hours seem greatly exaggerated—at least in good weather—but you should allow a full day for a visit to the park.

There are several places to camp near Gila Cliff Dwellings, including the park's pleasant little campground. One of the more unusual and reasonably priced private facilities is **Wildwood Retreat and Hot Springs**, which offers developed hot springs pools of different temperatures along the river, tent and car camping sites, and two cabins. Day use of the hot springs costs $10. Shady campsites are along the river and located not far from bathrooms with hot showers and flush toilets and a basic kitchen. Overnight camping costs $12 per night. Two cabins are available for those who don't wish to rough it. Willow Cabin has a queen-size bed and rents for $50 per night single, $60 double. The 25-square-foot circular Strawbale Hogan is a unique adobe cabin that has a double futon bed; it rents for $70 per night single, $80 double. Well-behaved and restrained dogs are permitted in the campground; neither dogs nor children are permitted in the Strawbale Hogan. Multiday lodging discounts are available (575-536-3600; wildwoodhotspringsretreat.com).

While in the Gila region, check out beautiful **Lake Roberts** along Highway 35, about 3 miles east of its intersection with Highway 15. It's quite pleasant by New Mexico lake standards, meaning the shoreline is somewhat wooded and meandering—very nice for canoeing!

About 15 miles east of Silver City along Highway 152, you'll come across the impossible-to-miss **Santa Rita Copper Mine**. Regardless of how you feel about the environmental impact of such an open-pit operation, its size and scope are hard to ignore. Currently run by a subsidiary of the mega-mining concern Phelps Dodge Corporation, the mine is 1½ miles long by 1 mile wide by 1,800 feet deep, and it produces 300 million pounds of copper annually. As one of the oldest operating mines in North America, the site was originally mined by American Indians and later by colonial Spaniards before the modern era of mechanized mining began; it's been an open-pit operation since 1910.

Visitors are allowed to view the mine only through a chain-link fence from above; no one is allowed in the pit itself. The stair-step design through the multicolored bedrock—required for trucks to remove the ore—looks somewhat like an inverted version of the ancient Aztec and Mayan ruins in southern Mexico and Central America. The parking and viewing areas are clearly marked; no phone; no fee.

Heading southeast of Silver City on US 180, toward Deming, you'll find **City of Rocks State Park** in Faywood. This relatively flat park is filled with vertical rock formations, some as high as 50 feet, resembling the monoliths at Britain's Stonehenge. The rocks are the result of erosion on the remains of volcanic eruptions that occurred millions of years ago. Because you can climb on the rocks, as well as hide behind them, this park is a natural playground for kids of all ages. Picnic and camping facilities are available. The park is located 31 miles southeast of Silver City via US 180 and Highway 61; (575) 536-2800; emnrd.state.nm.us/spd/cityofrocksstatepark.html. It's open daily from 7 a.m. to 9 p.m. Admission is $5 per vehicle. Camping is available for $8 per night for a primitive campsite (no water), $10 per night for a developed campsite (with water), $14 per night for a developed campsite with electric hookup or sewage hookup, and $18 per night for developed campsites with electricity and sewage hookups.

Hidalgo County

Texas and Oklahoma may have their "panhandles," but New Mexico's got its "boot heel"—and Hidalgo County is it. Closer to Tucson, Arizona, than to Albuquerque, New Mexico, most of this area is desolate, although cattle ranching and, more recently, vineyards have made their imprint on the land.

The largest town is Lordsburg, but perhaps the most unusual place is *Shakespeare*, a ghost town 2½ miles southwest of Lordsburg.

Originally settled in the 1850s as Mexican Springs, a stage stop on the Butterfield Overland Trail, Shakespeare was named in 1879 by mine promoters to honor the bard and perhaps improve the town's fortunes. The town was the site of a couple of mining hoaxes, including the Diamond Swindle of 1870—when the area was seeded with diamonds to attract investors—before a real silver boom hit in 1879, only to fizzle some 15 years later. Shakespeare's last hurrah came with a second silver strike in 1907. The silver played out in the 1930s.

Because the town has been privately owned since 1935, it has been protected from weekend ghost-town looters, and the admission charge goes toward further preservation and restoration. It's accessible to the public only through guided tours that include the interiors of several buildings. One of these structures, the Stratford Hotel, is said to have briefly employed Billy the Kid as a dishwasher.

newmexicotrivia

Hidalgo County was named for the town of Guadalupe Hidalgo in Mexico, where the Treaty of Guadalupe Hidalgo was signed in 1848, bringing the New Mexico Territory into the US. pbs.org/kera/usmexicanwar/war/wars_end_guadalupe.html

To get to Shakespeare, take the Main Street exit off I-10 in Lordsburg, turn south, and follow the signs. Tours are offered only at 10 a.m. and 2 p.m. on the second Saturday and Sunday of each month. Reservations are not required; just turn up at the gate and join either the morning or afternoon tour groups. On the third or fourth weekend of April, June, August, and October, historical reenactments are staged. The ghost town is not open at any other times. Call (575) 542-9034 to verify the current year's dates. The admission charge is $4 for adults and $3 for children ages 6 to 12 ($1 higher for reenactments). Visit shakespeareghostown.com.

Luna County

Luna County's primary community is **Deming**, known for its pure air and fast ducks. Yes, ducks. Deming is home of the world-famous **Great American Duck Race** (demingduckrace.com), held annually on the fourth weekend in August. Thought up just over 20 years ago in a bar as a way to create more interest in the area, the duck races have captured international media coverage for Deming. More than just a duck race, the "fowl event" includes a parade, a golf tournament, a chile cook-off, a hot-air balloon rally, several sporting tournaments, and even a "Duck Queen" contest. It has also become one of New Mexico's most well-attended events.

Deming is more than ducks, though. The city is also home to the impressive **Deming Luna Mimbres Museum**. Located in the three-story, 1916 red-brick National Guard Armory building, the museum has about 25,000 square feet of exhibition space. There's a bit of everything here, as evidenced by the many "theme rooms," including the Military Room, the Quilt Room, the Doll Room, and the Tack Room. The museum also depicts life in the Southwest, focusing on ranching, railroading, and mining. The Mimbres Room showcases examples of centuries-old Mimbres Indian pottery (see Silver City). The pottery's distinctive black-on-white geometric designs are known for the way they mismatch animal body parts.

The museum is located at 301 S. Silver in Deming; (575) 546-2382; luna countyhistoricalsociety.com. It's open Mon through Sat from 9 a.m. to 4 p.m. Admission is by donation. Across the street the museum has renovated an old customs house into another space that showcases the area's border-town past.

Most parks make a big deal about leaving everything as you found it and strictly forbid visitors from taking anything with them when they leave. But at **Rockhound State Park**, located on the west side of the Little Florida Mountains, "taking a little of the park" is encouraged. That's right—visitors may each take up to 15 pounds of rocks with them per visit. You'll find all kinds and colors here, including varieties of quartz crystals, agates, and opals. Even after years of rock hounds carrying away mementos of their visit, old-timers say it's hard to tell that the place is any different than it was years ago. Plan to spend a lot of time staring at the ground here, and while you're on the lookout for your personal gems, watch out as well for loose rock and inconspicuous drop-offs.

Rockhound State Park is off Palomas Road via Highway 11, southeast of Deming; (575) 546-6182; emnrd.state.nm.us/spd/rockhoundstatepark.html. It's open Wed through Sun from 7 a.m. until sunset. There's a $5-per-vehicle admission charge. Camping is available: $8 per night for a primitive campsite (no water), $14 per night for a developed campsite (with water and/or electric or sewage hookup), and $18 per night for campsites with water and electricity and water hookups.

If you drive 32 miles south of Deming on Highway 11, you'll reach the Mexican border at the little town of **Columbus**. Although it's so far off the beaten path that most of its 1,634 inhabitants (2014 estimate) are Border Patrol officers and their families, its solitude has, in fact, attracted a number of former Santa Feans. The occasional visitor is surprised to find that the community has a good restaurant (the Patio), a large art gallery, and an attractive modern hotel (Martha's Place).

The town's website (columbusnewmexico.com), which serves as a sort of hometown newspaper and visitor information virtual meeting place, is quite a revelation and makes for great reading. The activities of better-known town residents get column inches in the ColumBUZZ section, and there are also Amazon links to books by Robert Ransom Odom (*Autobiography of a Redneck Hindu*) and cowboy Mexican bride matchmaker Ivan Thompson (*Cowboy Cupid, Cowboy del Amor*), information on border crossings, and even an ad for the adjoining intentional community of City of the Sun ("Does living off the grid in an Earth-ship home flip your lid? Turn On—Tune In—Drop Out at City of the Sun"). It may be postage stamp–sized, but this tiny town is, yes, just a little different.

newmexico**trivia**

The state of New Mexico shares 175 miles of border with the country of Mexico in Hidalgo, Luna, and Doña Ana Counties.

Martha's Place Hotel (204 W. Lima; 575-531-2467; marthasplacehotel .com) is right in the downtown historic district and functions as a welcoming and super-helpful base for visitors to Columbus, some of whom use it as a base while driving over the border to Mexico for medical and dental treatment, doing trainings in the area, or hiking/bicycling the Divide Trail. The owners, Philip and Diana Skinner, can assist with travel planning and offer secure equipment storage, laundry facilities, transportation, business services, and UPS/FedEx/US postal delivery and shipping for those that might need to send supplies and equipment to and from Columbus. They are also willing to arrange pickup and drop-off at the local airport.

Starting out as a purpose-built bed-and-breakfast inn in 1991, the Skinners have recently opted to keep their prices down by no longer including their popular full breakfast in the nightly rates. There are five large upstairs rooms and one large room downstairs for those with mobility issues. Prices range from $45 per night single to $59 per night double occupancy; weekly rates are $300 single and $370 double occupancy. All include free coffee, satellite TV, and Wi-Fi.

Note: The Skinners have recently remodeled and are in the process of changing the name of the hotel to Los Milagros (you will see the name Martha's Place still in use on the website and social media). In addition to the main hotel, they also now offer a two-bed private room with its own bathroom and kitchen facilities, accommodating up to four guests on AirBnB. Rate is $67 per night, a good option if you wish to share a room and save a bit of money. Martha's also now offers RV spots for $20 per night, $100 weekly.

Columbus is best known for having been invaded during the 1916 Mexican Revolution by insurgent leader Pancho Villa and 1,000 of his men in a ferocious battle that left 160 Americans and Mexicans dead. The incident is recounted in the **Columbus Historical Museum**, located in a former railroad depot in the center of town. The free museum is open daily from 10 a.m. to 4 p.m. Sept through Apr and 10 a.m. to 1 p.m. the rest of the year; (575) 531-2620; columbus historicalsociety.org.

Also worth visiting is the large cactus garden in **Pancho Villa State Park**, featuring 30 varieties of desert succulents. The 60-acre park has old army vehicles that were used by General John Pershing in the US retaliation for Villa's raid. The park, which also has picnic facilities and an RV campground, is always open. Admission is $5 per vehicle; camping costs $18 per night for sites with full hookups; (575) 531-2711; emnrd.state.nm.us/spd/panchovil-lastatepark.html.

Mariachis from the neighboring Mexican town of Palomas play on the town plaza most weekends.

Sierra County

Sierra County is home to New Mexico's largest body of water, **Elephant Butte Lake**. It's named for a huge gray rock formation, or butte, that rises from the water and resembles an elephant. Near the lake you'll come across the city of

Truth or Consequences. The city changed its name from Hot Springs to Truth or Consequences in 1951, following an open challenge over the airwaves from the popular radio show of the same name to honor its 10th anniversary. As a reward for the name change, the show pledged the city an annual festival during which the show would be broadcast. The show, along with its later television incarnation, has long since ended, but the annual Truth or Consequences Fiesta is still going strong. Ralph Edwards, former host of the show, had not missed the event for almost a half century when he retired from his annual appearance in 1999.

Truth or Consequences (usually known as "T or C," for short) is popular for its many therapeutic hot springs (from which the community got its first name). In fact, there's a contingent of folks who'd like to change the town's name back to Hot Springs (some old-timers and newcomers alike use "T or C–Hotsprings" as part of their return address), but after several ballot defeats through the years, the name Truth or Consequences seems destined to endure for this scruffy little community, which continues to attract retirees and "snowbirds"—those seniors who like to winter where it's warm. Since the late 1990s, however, the town's relative isolation, eclectic residents, and funky desert aesthetic have become part of its appeal for younger "regulars" from Albuquerque and Santa Fe, as well as for visitors from around the globe.

The prehistoric Mimbres people of southern New Mexico, ancestors of modern-day Pueblo people, likely sought out the area's natural hot springs more than 1,000 years ago for the water's sacred healing powers. Later, the springs were used by Geronimo and other Chiricahua Apaches as soaking places and neutral ground for intertribal meetings. Much has changed through the centuries, but the healing waters remain, along with scientific mineral analysis of their healing properties. There are currently 10 bathhouses in Truth or Consequences offering half-hour soaks for as little as $6, which is quite a bargain when compared to the pricier hot springs options in northern New Mexico. One such bathhouse is the historic and evolving ***La Paloma Hot Springs & Spa***. Originally established in the late 1920s as ***Marshall Hot Springs***, the spa was rescued in 1998 after years of deferred maintenance and lack of vision, and renovations began to transform "the Marshall," as it was known locally, into a first-rate healing center and spa.

Boasting 5 natural flowing pools, as opposed to "pump and drain" tubs used by several of the local hot springs establishments, La Paloma exudes unpretentious New Age New Mexico at its laid-back best. A private soak in one of the tubs is quite a treat, especially with the knotted rope dangling above the center of the square cement pool, playfully perfect for stretching tired muscles.

A dimmer switch and peaceful Native American flute music playing low in the background complete the truly sensory experience.

After several years' hard work, the old on-site motel (which was once cabins used by workers during the construction of nearby Elephant Butte Dam, ca. 1912) now has 13 unique guest rooms with private baths, all with kitchenettes or full kitchens, and a cottage. In addition, a large studio space has been created, which is used for classes such as belly dancing, qi gong, and yoga, as well as for various retreats; and the bathhouse, which also has been expanded, contains a very nice gift shop featuring handcrafted jewelry among other exquisite and sensory items.

newmexicotrivia

Sierra County, home to Elephant Butte and Caballo Lakes, boasts more water than any other county in New Mexico.

Lodging rates range from $65 to $140 per night; soak rates are $10 per person per hour, or $6 for a half-hour soak; free soak on your birthday. You'll find La Paloma Hot Springs, along with the other free-flowing hot springs near downtown T or C, at 311 Marr St. (at Pershing Street); (575) 894-3148; lapalomahotspringsandspa.com.

Another unique choice nearby is **Riverbend Hot Springs**, the only outdoor soaking option in T or C. On the banks of the Rio Grande, Riverbend offers a variety of lodging accommodations—private suites and the budget Artist rooms and dormitory-style, two-person semiprivate rooms. The communal tubs, which are filled twice per day, morning and evening, for Riverbend guests, have a nice view of Turtleback Mountain. A few years ago Riverbend completely renovated its tubs and constructed two new beautiful ones separate from the original soaking area. The new tubs are more private and have great views of the river and the mountains, especially during sunset, when, if you're lucky, you'll see ravens playfully soaring in the updrafts off Turtleback Mountain. The resort is aimed at singles and couples, and groups and children are limited. If you're not staying at Riverbend, you may still book a private day-soak there. Communal tubs cost $10 per hour per person; private tubs cost $15 per hour per adult.

Riverbend Hot Springs is at 100 Austin St. near the city park; (575) 894-7625; riverbendhotsprings.com. Lodging rates are $78.75 for the budget Artist rooms (each room has a TV and shower and is sponsored by a local artist whose work hangs there) and $115 to $168 for the other rooms and suites (most with full baths, private entrances, and kitchenettes). A cottage rents for $147 per night.

At 501 McAdoo St. is the plush *Sierra Grande Lodge and Spa*. As T or C's answer to Santa Fe chic, the beautifully and meticulously renovated 1920s apartment building seems somewhat out of place amid the otherwise dusty, rough-and-tumble, anything-goes nature of downtown T or C. But its elegance may be just what the doctor ordered for some—and a relief if you're not into the tumbledown charm of T or C's typical fare.

Media mogul and philanthropist Ted Turner, who owns two nearby ranches, bought Sierra Grande from its French owners in 2013. In 2015 the hotel was added to Ted Turner Expeditions tours as a luxury base for those wishing to do day and overnight tours and recreational activities on Turner's Ladder and Armenderis Ranches.

This is a lovely place, make no mistake. The luxury guest suites are beautiful but practical. All have original hardwood floors, warm Southwest furnishings, and flat-screen TVs, DVD players, Wi-Fi, and mini-fridges. The spa offers top-notch therapeutic massage, skin-conditioning body wraps, antiaging facials, and other holistic treatments, in addition to soaks in the hot springs in a private room. Guests have free use of the hotel's fitness facility. Ground-floor rooms accept pets with a fee.

The Restaurant at Sierra Grande, the hotel's gourmet restaurant, has now been remodeled in a light, bright, and welcoming way and reopened in a totally new form. Led by award-winning restaurateur Tatsu Miyazaki, the restaurant offers seasonal New American cuisine with Southwest and global

STATE PARKS IN SOUTHWESTERN NEW MEXICO

Online at emnrd.state.nm.us/spd

Caballo Lake/Percha Dam State Park
18 miles south of Truth or Consequences
(575) 743-3942

City of Rocks State Park
28 miles northwest of Deming
(575) 536-2800

Elephant Butte Lake State Park
7 miles north of Truth or Consequences
(575) 744-5421

Leasburg Dam State Park
15 miles north of Las Cruces
(575) 524-4068

Pancho Villa State Park
in Columbus
(575) 531-2711

Rockhound State Park
14 miles southeast of Deming
(575) 546-6182

influences. Breakfast, lunch, and dinner are served; breakfast is included in the room rate for hotel guests.

Lodging rates range from $195 to $240, a lot for T or C but still great value if you are looking for an upscale romantic getaway. For reservations, call (877) 288-76317; sierragrandelodge.com.

Near the town's center, you'll find **Geronimo Springs Museum**, named after a spring frequented by Geronimo. The spring itself has been incorporated into a very playful and colorful ceramic tile sculpture by noted New Mexican artist Shel Neymark of Embudo. The warm springwater meanders through the sculpture, which is accented by landscaping and seasonal plantings.

The museum is a typical hometown affair, consisting largely of a broad assortment of artifacts from the area donated by residents. The exhibits can be found in a series of rooms with names such as Apache Culture, Hispanic Culture, Homestead, Pottery and Tools, Ranching, Ralph Edwards, Sierra Grande, Wilson, and Heritage. This last room really takes visitors by surprise, with its floor-to-ceiling murals of famous locals painted by noted local cowboy artist Delmas Howe, who was born in Truth or Consequences. The room also contains four bronze statues of other famous New Mexicans, each sculpted by Hivana Leyendecker, an accomplished native New Mexican artist.

The museum is located at 211 Main St., across from the post office; (575) 894-6600; geronimospringsmuseum.com. It's open Mon through Sat from 9 a.m. to 5 p.m. and Sun from noon to 4 p.m.; closed major holidays. Admission charges are $6 for adults, $3 for children ages 6 to 18, and $15 for a family; children age 6 and under get in free.

A Sierra County visitors' attraction that has recently opened for tours, and that you won't want to miss, is located in a remote area 30 miles east of Truth or Consequences on the desolate Jornado del Muerto Plain. Here, the state of New Mexico has constructed **Spaceport America**, the first US commercial spaceport, in partnership with several aerospace companies and Virgin Airlines founder Sir Richard Branson's Virgin Galactic, which plans to offer suborbital passenger tours into space at $200,000 a person. Temporary launchpads at the site have been used to launch prototype spacecraft and Spaceloft XL rockets since 2006, with 24 launches to date. A change in governors in New Mexico created a few political headaches for the Spaceport and led to delays while liability issues were hammered out. In April 2013, state lawmakers unanimously signed legislation expanding liability protections currently in place for spaceflight operators to also include spaceflight manufacturers and suppliers, thereby removing the remaining hurdles in getting the Spaceport up and running.

The facility is open to the public for tours by advance reservation. Tours start at the Spaceport America Visitor Center on Foch Street in Truth or

Consequences, which offers exhibits before boarding a shuttle to the Spaceport. On arrival, visitors walk up the Astronaut Walk into the Gateway Gallery, featuring hands-on multimedia exhibits as well as the G-Shock Simulator, which allows you to experience the same type of acceleration as astronauts do on launch into space. Spaceport personnel are available to discuss their work in the Spaceport Operations Center. The entire tour lasts four hours. For more information and to make reservations, call or visit the Spaceport online (844-7-2SPACE or 844-727-7223; spaceportamerica.com).

Southwest of Truth or Consequences, the village of **Hillsboro** is the quintessential one-horse town. Established in 1877 as the result of a gold discovery in the hills surrounding Percha Creek, Hillsboro is perfect for just pulling off the main street and strolling around town.

You'll find several shops, a small winery tasting room, a cafe, an old saloon, and the **Black Range Museum**. This small historical museum is in a former hotel and brothel across from a public picnic area on the east side of the village. Hours vary, but it's generally open long weekends and by appointment; (575) 895-5233. Admission is by donation. Hillsboro is the kind of place where all the townspeople and merchants know one another and where a few well-cared-for "community" dogs take naps in the middle of Main Street. Steeped in mining history, the town is an enchanting, slow-paced marvel that has lured more than its share of artists and writers to become residents.

Speaking of enchanting, the **Enchanted Villa Bed & Breakfast** (575-895-5686, newmexico.org/listing/?lid=21445) has a home along Hillsboro's main street. Run by innkeeper Maree Westland, this large whitewashed home was designed by Maree's great-aunt in 1941 as a romantic retreat for a member of Burmese royalty called Sir Victor Sassoon, a multinational entrepreneur. From the outside it seems a little dated now, but inside, the inn's 2 large, attractive guest rooms have well-positioned windows for maximum light and feature king-size beds and en suite bathrooms. Rates are $55 single, $84 double per night, which includes full breakfast. The inn has a large library and also offers Wi-Fi.

Hillsboro General Store Cafe is the only place to eat in town, so plan accordingly. Continuously open since 1879, the store has survived boom and bust while variously serving as a post office, stage stop, telegraph office, soda fountain, and phone company. The place phased out its "general store" function in the late 1990s and now concentrates on serving up hearty breakfasts and lunches daily (and dinners on Saturday only), featuring soups, sandwiches, burgers, and a few New Mexican selections. Though the store no longer stocks the necessities of a rural household, it has adopted a gift-shop function, and the ambience of the old general store remains in the period decor and glass display

cases. The cafe is located at 100 Main St.; (575) 895-5306; hillsborogeneralstore
.com. Hours are Fri through Tues from 8 a.m. to 3 p.m., Sat until 7 p.m.

New Mexico wines have grown quite a following in recent years, so it's
a delightful surprise to come upon the tasting room for *Black Range Vine-*
yards, in an attractive 1890s adobe building in this semi–ghost town. Founded
in 2007 by Nicki and Brian O'Dell, this small winery grows pinot noir and
cabernet sauvignon grapes in a nearby canyon in the foothills of the Black
Range and specializes in dry red vintage wines. Their tasting room and patio is
open by appointment and also serves other local wines and tapas. Call for an
appointment at (575) 895-3334; blackrangevineyards.com.

Hillsboro is 30 miles southwest of Truth or Consequences: 12 miles south
on I-25 and then 18 miles west on Highway 152.

Nine miles farther west on Highway 152, you'll enter the Black Range of
the Mimbres Mountains in *Kingston*, a blink-and-you'll-miss-it community—so
check your odometer and don't blink. Kingston, population 32, is pretty much
a ghost town now, although a tiny museum is housed in the old Percha Valley
Bank building and the original schoolhouse is used as the meeting place for
the Spit and Whittle Club. Kingston's history mirrors that of its neighbor Hillsboro—it saw more prosperous days during the silver boom of the 1880s, when
the population soared to 7,000.

Ivy-covered *Black Range Lodge* stands as testimony to those earlier days.
Run by Hollywood escapee and filmmaker/innkeeper Catherine Wanek and

The Mystery of Victorio Peak

Though inaccessible to the public for more than 40 years, Victorio Peak remains the
subject of legend. Thousands of gold bars are rumored to be stashed in a crevice
of the domed mountain, located on the federal government's White Sands Missile
Range in Doña Ana County.

Milton "Doc" Noss, a foot doctor and well-known treasure hunter, was killed in 1949,
allegedly by a disgruntled business partner, over ownership issues regarding the
gold, said variously to be the hoard of colonial Spanish officials, the Emperor Maximil-
ian, or perhaps the Apache chief Victorio. Noss's widow, Ova "Babe" Noss, along
with a crew of treasure hunters, tried unsuccessfully for years to locate the gold—
even after she was forced to leave the site when the military boundary was extended
in the 1950s. After she died in 1979, her grandson Terry Delonas inherited the family's gold fever. It literally took an act of Congress in 1990 to allow Delonas prolonged
access to the range to explore. After years without success, the latest expedition
was evicted in the mid-1990s by the military over a dispute regarding fees paid for
access. And so the legend, and the lure of Victorio Peak's fabled gold, lives on.

her husband, Pete Fust, the lodge is now a bed-and-breakfast with the feel of an Old West boardinghouse. It's one of the few bed-and-breakfasts that welcome pets—a great relief when the kennel fills up at the last minute and Rover needs a weekend getaway just as much as you do. It is also group- and family-friendly, with separate buildings that can sleep multiple guests.

The innkeepers' background in the entertainment business is evident in the large common area of the lodge's second floor. Those who may need more stimulation will find a piano, a CD player, a satellite-television-and-DVD system complete with DVD library, and video games. There is Wi-Fi, too, of course, as well as a computer with Internet access for guests. A boccie ball court was recently installed. For those who appreciate the tranquility of the lodge's natural setting, however, hunting for crystals along the rocky trails near the inn is a relaxing pastime—sort of like hunting for seashells on the beach.

The owners' passion for alternative and sustainable housing shows in their popular luxury straw-bale guesthouse, with fully equipped kitchen, Jacuzzi, and satellite dish. The guesthouse is uphill from the lodge and thus has breathtaking views of the mountains of the Black Range. It sleeps four. There is also a studio apartment, which sleeps two adults and two children, and the family-oriented Percha Creek House, which sleeps 14. The lodge offers workshops and retreats, in addition to overnight lodging. Check their website for details.

If you find Kingston, you'll find Black Range Lodge—trust me. But just in case: the address is 119 Main St.; (575) 895-5652 or (800) 676-5622; blackrange lodge.com. Rates for the 7 lodge rooms range from $79 to $105 for double occupancy, with an extra $15 charge for each additional person in a suite. A studio apartment with kitchenette costs $110 per night; the straw-bale guesthouse is $149 per night; and a 5-bedroom house with a large deck rents for $210 per night with a two-night minimum. Included in the rate is a full breakfast featuring organic coffee and local free-range eggs. Guests may keep food in the guest fridge at the lodge and use the kitchen to prepare their meals at other times. That's good, because there is no place to eat in Kingston; Hillsboro has the closest cafe, but it has limited hours.

If you have time, try to stop and walk around the historic Kingston Cemetery. Gravestones date to the 1880s and tell many tales of this former mining town. There is a good view of the Black Range from here.

Doña Ana County

Doña Ana County is home to New Mexico's second-largest city, **_Las Cruces_** ("The Crosses"), which in turn is home to New Mexico's second-largest college, New Mexico State University. Located in the fertile Mesilla Valley, between the

Organ Mountains and the Rio Grande, Las Cruces is now New Mexico's fastest-growing city.

Fine art and hospitality meet at the **Lundeen Inn of the Arts**, which has long been the most popular bed-and-breakfast in the Las Cruces area, conveniently located only five minutes from Old Mesilla (see listing below). Run by Linda and Jerry Lundeen, this bed-and-breakfast adjoins Linda's gallery and Jerry's architectural office, but it's hard to tell where one begins and the other ends. Works by southwestern artists are everywhere, including the guest rooms. And because most of the 300-plus pieces are for sale, if you enjoy your stay in a particular room, you can arrange to take a piece of it home.

The inn consists of 2 historic adobe homes joined by a Southwest-style great room with a soaring cathedral ceiling. In addition to being the place where breakfast is served, this naturally lighted common area is the focal point for much of the inn's art. Each of the 7 oversize guest rooms is unique in both configuration and decor and is named after an American artist, such as Georgia O'Keeffe and Navajo artist R. C. Gorman. All rooms have queen-size beds and private baths, and some even have fireplaces and kitchenettes.

newmexicotrivia

Noted astronomer and professor Dr. Clyde Tombaugh, who codiscovered the dwarf planet Pluto in 1930, helped found the astronomy department at New Mexico State University in Las Cruces, where he died in 1997, two weeks and four days before his 91st birthday.

The Lundeens are energetic and engaged hosts who love to share information with guests, and this is a full-on, classic B&B experience with a lot of personal interaction. The inn even offers weeklong architecture and arts classes, including silversmithing and pottery making; Jerry is a lay minister who performs wedding ceremonies at the inn. It's located at 618 S. Alameda; (575) 526-3326 or (888) 526-3326; innofthearts .com. Rates range from $79 for a single room to $155 for a suite; weekly and monthly rates are available. Pets are welcome with fee.

Sprawling Las Cruces has a fair number of chain hotels. If you want to stay in a hotel but want something with personality, look no farther than Spanish Colonial–style **Hotel El Encanto de Las Cruces** in downtown Las Cruces, a former Hilton hotel with a lot of charm. This is certainly not a hotel that is off the beaten path, but it's very comfortable and luxurious and a good value for the money, with all you'll want for a night's stay, from soothing dark-wood furnishings to Wi-Fi and an on-site bar/restaurant serving some delicious meals. It's managed by Heritage Hotels and Resorts, which also runs the distinctive Chimayo de Santa Fe and Lodge at Santa Fe hotels in Santa Fe, two good bets in the "City Different." El Encanto is located at 705 S. Telshor Blvd.; (575) 522-4300; hotelencanto.com. Rooms start at $84 and go up to $137 per night; ask about the bed-and-breakfast-for-two option. The hotel has been designated a Doña Ana County Virgin Galactic Preferred Hotel for astronauts and their families taking part in the Spaceport America commercial flights and has been performing upgrades in anticipation of the beginning of spaceflights.

If you're an urban dweller with kids, a visit to the **New Mexico Farm and Ranch Heritage Museum** in Las Cruces can be especially enjoyable. Located between the lush, irrigated farmlands of the lower Rio Grande Valley and the cattle ranches on the slopes of the dramatic Organ Mountains, the 47-acre museum complex stands as a monument to a way of life that is increasingly remote to most Americans. In addition to historical exhibits—such as a pit house from the ancient Mogollon culture of southwestern New Mexico and a replicated grain storage room from Chaco Canyon, as well as horse-drawn plows and early mechanized farm equipment—the center also showcases the computerized, laser-leveling implements of the modern, scientific agricultural era. Outdoor exhibits include an adobe blacksmith shop, a relocated log cabin, and a windmill. Regular demonstrations include blacksmithing, weaving, quilting, and butter churning; however, the milking demonstration in the dairy barn has proved to be the most popular among old and young alike. The museum also sponsors such classes as adobe making, gardening, roping and other cowboy skills, photography, and wool spinning. Besides dairy cows, other animals on the grounds include Belgian draft horses, longhorn cattle, Jerusalem donkeys, and churro sheep and goats. The museum hosts La Fiesta de San Ysidro (the patron saint of agriculture) each May; call ahead for details.

The museum is at 4100 Dripping Springs Rd. (1½ miles east of the NMSU Golf Course; **Note:** University Boulevard becomes Dripping Springs Road); (575) 522-4100; nmfarmandranchmuseum.org. It's open Mon through Sat from 9 a.m. to 5 p.m. and Sun from noon to 5 p.m. Admission fees are $5 for adults, $4 for seniors, $2 for military and veterans, $3 for young people ages 5 to 17, and free for kids under 5, museum members, and military veterans.

Although it's a separate community, **Mesilla** (alternately La Mesilla or Old Mesilla) connects to the southwest side of Las Cruces. This rural suburb of Las Cruces played an important role in the history of New Mexico. The Gadsden Purchase—which annexed Mesilla to the US from Mexico and established the current international borders of New Mexico and Arizona—was signed here in 1854. Mesilla is also the place where Billy the Kid was convicted of murder, sentenced to hang, and jailed for a short time in 1881. The village was even briefly declared the Confederate capital of a territory extending all the way

Famous New Mexican Entertainers & Artists

Kathy Baker, actress	**Val Kilmer,** actor
Carol Burnett, comedienne	**Ottmar Liebert,** musician
Bill Daily, actor	**Ali MacGraw,** actress
Jane Fonda, actress	**Shirley MacLaine,** actress
Greer Garson, actress	**Roger Miller,** musician
R. C. Gorman, Navajo artist	**Demi Moore,** actress
Gene Hackman, actor	**Georgia O'Keeffe,** artist
William Hanna, cartoonist	**Eliot Porter,** nature photographer
Peter Hurd, artist	**Sam Shepard,** actor, writer
Burl Ives, musician	**Vivian Vance,** actress

to California. The tree-lined Old Mesilla Plaza is anchored by the San Albino Church and is surrounded by uncluttered shops and restaurants; it's a great place to visit on an autumn Saturday afternoon. Just across Highway 28 from Old Mesilla Plaza at 1875 Boutz Rd., you'll find the privately owned **Gadsden Museum**, which displays Indian, Civil War, and Old West artifacts. It's open Wed through Sat by appointment only. Call (575) 526-6293; gadsdenmuseum mesilla.com.

If you've got a few hours and would like to savor the flavors of the countryside, consider heading south from Mesilla on the scenic **Oñate Trail** (Highway 28). Named for Spanish explorer Don Juan de Oñate, often cited as the founder of New Mexico, the roadway traces part of the route that Oñate took into New Mexico more than 400 years ago. Roughly parallel to both the Rio Grande and I-25, this more leisurely route connects the many rural communities southwest of Las Cruces, which are home to several interesting places to stop and shop.

Six miles south of Mesilla, near the village of San Miguel, you'll pass **Stahmann Farms**. Originally started in 1932 as an innovative move to supplant the one-time cotton farm with the then-foreign pecan crop, Stahmann's now boasts 168,000 pecan trees on 3,200 acres, making it one of the world's largest pecan groves. These beautiful trees produce up to 8 to 9 million pounds of pecans annually. Stahmann's runs a major wholesale business from here, but sadly, due to the impact of the recession, it has now closed its on-site country store—which was filled with pecan confections, specialty foods, gift baskets, and samples of their delectable pecans—as well as the second store in Mesilla. The farm is located at 22505 Hwy. 28 S., La Mesa; (575) 526-2453; stahmann pecan.com.

About 17 miles farther south, at 4201 S. Hwy. 28, is **La Viña Winery** (575-882-7632; lavinawinery.com), New Mexico's oldest winery, in operation since 1977. La Viña has a tasting room, which features its cabernets, zinfandels, and chardonnays, as well as a wine and gift shop. The winery also hosts a Harvest Festival in October, a Fourth of July Picnic, and a Spring Festival at the end of April; all feature wine tasting, food, and live music. The winery is open Thurs through Tues from noon to 5 p.m., with tours given daily by appointment at 11:30 a.m. Note that there is a small fee for both tastings and tours.

newmexicotrivia

Anthony, New Mexico, is a twin city with Anthony, Texas, between Las Cruces, New Mexico, and El Paso, Texas.

Heading north on I-25 out of Las Cruces, you'll find **Fort Selden State Monument**. The now-abandoned adobe military fort that contributed to the growth of Las Cruces was one of many forts built in the mid-1800s to protect settlers and travelers from Apache attacks. It was the boyhood home of General Douglas MacArthur from 1884 to 1886, when his father was the post commander; moreover, the acclaimed Buffalo Soldiers, a regiment of black soldiers honored for their success in subduing the Plains Indians, were also stationed here.

A visitor center explains the history of the fort and displays articles of interest found here. Outside, you can walk along the trails that wind around the adobe ruins. Interspersed along the trails are interpretive signs whose replicas of old photos show the fort as it was in the 1800s.

The monument is located 15 miles north of Las Cruces off I-25, at 1280 Fort Selden Rd. Take the Radium Springs exit and head west a couple of miles; (575) 526-8911; nmmonuments.org/fort-selden. It's open Wed through Mon from 8:30 a.m. to 5 p.m. The admission charge is $5, but young people age 16 and younger are admitted free. New Mexico residents get in free on Sunday.

In northwestern Doña Ana County is the community of **Hatch**, the self-proclaimed "Chile Capital of the World." Its reputation is well earned for producing some of the highest quality, as well as largest quantities, of New Mexico's lucrative chile pepper crop. During Labor Day weekend, the community hosts the **Hatch Chile Festival** (575-267-1095; hatchchilefest.com), which includes a chile cook-off and *ristra* (strings of red chiles) arrangement competition, among other events. You'll find Hatch on Highway 26, 2 miles southwest of I-25 (exit 41).

More time in the area will also allow you to check out 496,330-acre ***Organ Mountains–Desert Peaks National Monument*** surrounding Las Cruces, set aside by President Obama in May 2014 to protect significant historic, prehistoric, geologic, and biologic resources of scientific interest. The monument is divided into three main sections: the spectacular 9,000-foot-high Organ Mountains, east of Las Cruces; the Desert Peaks, which comprise the Robledo Mountains, Sierra de las Uvas, and the Doña Ana Mountains, northwest of Las Cruces; and the remote Potrillo Mountains, southwest of Las Cruces, which contain volcanic features, including Kilbourne Hole Volcanic Crater National Historic Landmark, an 80,000-year-old volcanic maar crater used by Apollo space program astronauts to train for lunar landings.

This is a huge, largely undeveloped national monument that attracts nature and history lovers. ***Dripping Springs Natural Area***, the most developed section of the monument, located in the Organ Mountains off US 70, 10 miles east of Las Cruces, is your best bet for a quick look. Here you'll find a visitor center with rangers, information, exhibits, restrooms, water, and trailheads for desert hikes, mountain biking, and horseback riding at Aguirre Spring, Soledad Canyon, Sierra Vista, and Tortugas Mountain. Camping and picnicking are available in the popular ***Aguirre Campground***, which has 57 developed family campsites and 12 picnic sites; primitive camping is available throughout the monument at no charge.

One of the trails at Dripping Springs takes you past ***La Cueva Rock Shelter***, whose use dates back to 5,000 BC and which was later occupied by Apaches, then later by an eccentric recluse named Giovanni Maria Agotino, known to locals as "the Hermit." In the mid-1970s, approximately 100,000 artifacts were recovered here by the University of Texas at El Paso. Another trail leads past the ruins of the 1870s ***Dripping Springs Resort***, built by Colonel Eugene Patten and, in 1917, converted to a sanitorium that continued in use for decades.

Dripping Springs Visitor Center (575-522-1219) is open daily from 8 a.m. to 5 p.m.; the entrance gate is open from 8 a.m. to 7 p.m. May through Oct and 8 a.m. to 5 p.m. the rest of the year. Entrance fee is $5 per vehicle. Camping is $7 per site.

Northwest of Las Cruces, off I-10 and I-25, you'll find 15 miles of trails for hiking, mountain biking, and horseback riding at ***Picacho Peak Recreation Area*** adjoining 4,959-foot-high Picacho Peak in the Desert Peaks section of the monument. It has a few shaded picnic sites and trails but no water or restrooms.

Next to Picacho Peak is the 5,280-acre ***Prehistoric Trackways National Monument***, set aside by President Obama early in his presidency, in 2009, to protect the numerous fossilized footprints of amphibians, reptiles, insects, and plants and petrified wood from the Paleozoic era, 280 million years ago, a time predating the dinosaurs when this part of the Southwest was a shallow, warm inland sea. It is one of the most significant Early Permian period track sites in the world.

Unfortunately, although hiking and horseback riding are possible in a few places here, this is an undeveloped area kept pristine for scientific research, and there are no opportunities to view fossilized trackways on-site. If you are interested, check out the 30-foot and 15-foot tracks from the site on display at the ***Las Cruces Museum of Nature and Science***. Other fossilized trackways are on display as part of the Jerry MacDonald Paleozoic Trackways Collection at the New Mexico Museum of Natural History and Science in Albuquerque.

Note: In both national monuments, come well prepared for an exposed, low-elevation desert environment that is scorching hot in summer and largely shadeless. Wear a broad-brimmed hat, clothing with roll-down sleeves and legs, high SPF factor sunscreen, and sturdy shoes, and consume plenty of salty, nutritious snacks and a gallon of water per person per day if you plan any outdoor activities here.

For more information on both Organ Mountains–Desert Peaks National Monument and Prehistoric Trackways National Monument, contact the Las Cruces office of the BLM at 1800 Marquess St., Las Cruces; (575) 522-1219; blm .gov. It is open Mon through Fri from 8 a.m. to 4 p.m.

Monuments to Main Street, an annual monthlong celebration of the many attractions in Doña Ana County, takes place every September and features special themed tours, helicopter rides over Kilbourne Crater, health and fitness classes in the Organ Mountains, the Hatch Chile Festival, and other activities. For more information, contact Las Cruces Convention and Visitors Bureau at (575) 541-2444 or visit monuments2mainstreet.com.

Where to Stay in Southwestern New Mexico

SOCORRO COUNTY

Casa Blanca Bed and Breakfast Guesthouse
13 Montoya St.
San Antonio
(575) 835-3027
casablancabedand
breakfast.com
Moderate

Holiday Inn Express
1040 N. California St.
Socorro
(575) 838-4600
(888) 526-4567
ihg.com/holidayinnexpress/
hotels/US/en/socorro/
socnm
Moderate

San Miguel Inn
916 California St. NE
Socorro
(575) 835-0211
(800) 548-7938
Inexpensive

CATRON COUNTY

Silver Creek Inn
HC 61, Box 306
Mogollon
(866) 276-4882
reservations@silvercreekinn
.com
silvercreekinn.com
Expensive

Whitewater Motel
Highway 180
Glenwood
(575) 539-2581
whitewatermotel.com
Inexpensive

GRANT COUNTY

Bear Creek Cabins
88 Main St.
Pinos Altos
(575) 388-4501
(888) 388-4515
bearcreekcabins.com
Moderate

Bear Mountain Lodge
60 Bear Mountain
Ranch Rd.
Silver City
(575) 538-2538
bearmountainlodge.com
Expensive

Palace Hotel
106 W. Broadway
Silver City
(575) 388-1811
silvercitypalacehotel.com
Inexpensive

Wildwood Retreat and Hot Springs
111 W. Fork Rd.
Gila Hot Springs
(575) 536-3600
wildwoodhotspringsretreat
.com
Moderate

HIDALGO COUNTY

Days Inn and Suites
1426 W. Motel Dr.
Lordsburg
(575) 542-3600
wyndhamhotels.com/days
-inn
Inexpensive

Motel 6 (formerly Best Western Western Skies Inn)
1303 S. Main
Lordsburg
(575) 542-8807
Inexpensive

LUNA COUNTY

Best Western Mimbres Valley Inn
1500 W. Pine
Deming
(575) 546-4544
bestwestern.com
Moderate

Grand Motor Inn
1721 E. Pine St.
Deming
(575) 546-2632
grandmotorinndeming.com
Inexpensive

Holiday Inn Express and Suites Deming
3801 E. Cedar St.
Deming
(575) 545-6500
ihg.com/holidayinnexpress
Moderate

SIERRA COUNTY

Black Range Lodge
119 Main St.
Kingston
(575) 895-5652
blackrangelodge.com
Moderate

Blackstone Hot Springs
410 Austin St.
Truth or Consequences
(575) 894-0894
blackstonehotsprings.com
Moderate

Charles Motel and Hot Springs
601 Broadway
Truth or Consequences
(575) 894-7154
(800) 317-4518
charlesspa.com
Inexpensive

Elephant Butte Inn and Spa
401 Hwy. 195
Elephant Butte
(575) 744-5431
elephantbutteinn.com
Moderate

Enchanted Villa Bed & Breakfast
Main Street
Hillsboro
(575) 895-5686
newmexico.org
Moderate

La Paloma Hot Springs & Spa
311 Marr St. (at Pershing Street)
Truth or Consequences
(575) 894-3148
lapalomahotspringsandspa.com
Moderate

Riverbend Hot Springs Resort
100 Austin St.
Truth or Consequences
(575) 894-7625
riverbendhotsprings.com
Moderate

Sierra Grande Lodge & Spa
501 McAdoo St.
Truth or Consequences
(877) 288-7637
sierragrandelodge.com
Expensive

DOÑA ANA COUNTY

Hotel El Encanto de Las Cruces
705 S. Telshor Blvd.
Las Cruces
(575) 522-4300
hotelencanto.com
Moderate

Josefina's Old Gate Inn
2261 Calle de Guadalupe
Mesilla
(575) 613-4820
josefinasgate.com
Expensive

Lundeen Inn of the Arts
618 S. Alameda
Las Cruces
(575) 526-3326
(888) 526-3326
innofthearts.com
Moderate

Where to Eat in Southwestern New Mexico

SOCORRO COUNTY

Bear Mountain Coffee House and Gallery
902 W. 1st St.
Magdalena
(575) 854-3310
bearmountaincoffeehouse.com
Inexpensive
Homemade quiche, pies, pastries, coffee

Buckhorn Tavern
68 US-380
San Antonio
(575) 835-4423
buckhornburgers.com
Inexpensive to moderate
Famous for its green chile cheeseburger and New Mexican food

Frank & Lupe's El Sombrero
210 Mesquite
Socorro
(575) 835-3945
Inexpensive
New Mexican

Magdalena Cafe & Steakhouse
109 S. Main St.
Magdalena
(575) 854-2696
Inexpensive
Southwestern cuisine, burgers, and steaks

The Owl Bar & Cafe
US 380
10 miles south of Socorro
San Antonio
(575) 835-9946
Inexpensive to moderate
Famous green chile cheeseburgers and New Mexican food

Sofia's Kitchen & Burrito Tyme
105 Bullock Ave.
Socorro
(575) 835-0022
Inexpensive
New Mexican

SELECTED CHAMBERS OF COMMERCE/VISITOR BUREAUS IN SOUTHWESTERN NEW MEXICO

Catron County Chamber of Commerce
97 Main St.
Reserve, NM 87830
(575) 533-6116
catroncounty.org

Deming–Luna County Chamber of Commerce
800 E. Pine
Deming, NM 88031
(575) 546-2674
demingchamber.net

Hatch Valley Chamber of Commerce
201 W. Hall St.
Hatch, NM 87937
(575) 519-4723
villageofhatch.org

Las Cruces Convention and Visitors Bureau
211 N. Water St.
Las Cruces, NM 88001
(575) 541-2444
lascrucescvb.org

Lordsburg–Hidalgo Chamber of Commerce
206 Main St.
Lordsburg, NM 88045
(575) 542-9864
lordsburghidalgocountry.net

Magdalena Chamber of Commerce
400 1st St.
Magdalena, NM 87825
(575) 854-3560
magdalena-nm.com

Silver City/Grant County Chamber of Commerce
500 E. 18th St.
Silver City, NM 88061
(575) 538-3785
silvercity.org

Socorro County Chamber of Commerce
101 Plaza St.
Socorro, NM 87801
(575) 835-0424
socorrochamber.com

Truth or Consequences & Sierra County Chamber of Commerce
207 S. Foch St.
Truth or Consequences, NM 87901
(575) 894-3536
torcchamber.com

CATRON COUNTY

Buckhorn Saloon and Opera House
Main Street
Pinos Altos
(575) 538-9911
buckhornsaloonand
operahouse.com
Moderate
Steak, burgers, pasta

Diane's Restaurant and Bakery
510 N. Bullard St.
Silver City
(575) 538-8722
dianesrestaurant.com
Moderate
Globally influenced bistro food, sandwiches, breads, and baked goods

Jalisco Cafe
100 S. Bullard St.
Silver City
(575) 388-2060
Inexpensive to moderate
Traditional Mexican and eclectic southwestern

Little Toad Creek Downtown
200 N. Bullard St.
Silver City
(575) 956-6144
littletoadcreek.com
Inexpensive to moderate
Microbrewery with elegant pub grub

1zero6
106 N. Texas St.
Silver City
1zero6-jake.blogspot.com
Moderate to expensive
Order-ahead Asian, Italian, Oaxacan, fusion, and international gourmet cuisine by advance reservation, weekends only

Pie-O-Neer Cafe
US 60 at mile marker 56
Pie Town
(575) 772-2711
pieoneer.com
Inexpensive
Nationally known as the premier spot for its many fresh-made pies; limited hours

HIDALGO COUNTY

El Charro
209 Southern Pacific Blvd.
Lordsburg
(575) 542-3400
Inexpensive to moderate
Mexican and American

Kranberry's Family Restaurant
1405 S. Main
Lordsburg
(575) 542-9400
Inexpensive to moderate
American

Ramona's Cafe
904 E. Motel Dr.
Lordsburg
(575) 542-3030
Inexpensive to moderate
American

LUNA COUNTY

Adobe Deli
3970 Lewis Flats Rd. SE
Deming
(575) 546-0361
adobedeli.com
Moderate to expensive
Western-style steak house known for its huge juicy steaks and French onion soup; also has a saloon, cigar and oxygen bars, and a deli serving Boar's Head meats

El Camino Real
900 W. Pine
Deming
(575) 546-7421
Inexpensive to moderate
Mexican

SIERRA COUNTY

Bellaluca Cafe Italiano
303 Jones St.
Truth or Consequences
(575) 894-9866
cafebellaluca.com
Moderate to very expensive
Chef-owned eatery serving locavore Italian food

Latitude 33
304 S. Pershing St.
Truth or Consequences
(575) 740-7804
latitude33.com
Moderate
Asian fusion

Pacific Grill
800 N. Date St.
Truth or Consequences
(575) 894-7687
Moderate to expensive
Top-rated fresh seafood, Italian, and Pacific Rim fare

Passion Pie Cafe
406 Main St.
Truth or Consequences
(575) 894-0008
deepwaterfarm.com
Inexpensive
Healthy vegetarian breakfast and lunch cafe food

The Restaurant at Sierra Grande
Sierra Grande Lodge
501 McAdoo St.
Truth or Consequences
(877) 288-7637
sierragrandelodge.com
Moderate to very expensive
Upscale contemporary American and Southwest cuisine with global influences from renowned chef Tatsu Miyazaki

DOÑA ANA COUNTY

Andele Restaurant
2184 Avenida de Mesilla
Mesilla
(575) 526-9631
andelerestaurant.com
Moderate
A local favorite for Mexican food in a casual atmosphere

Chilitos
3850 Foothills Rd.
Las Cruces
(575) 532-0141
chilitos.net
Moderate
Mexican and American
(Second location at 2405
S. Valley Dr., Las Cruces;
(575) 526-4184)

Double Eagle on the Plaza
2355 Calle de Guadalupe
Old Mesilla
(575) 523-6700
double-eagle-mesilla.com
Moderate to very expensive
Eclectic high-end
restaurant famed for steaks
and New Mexican food

La Posta de Mesilla
2410 Calle de San Albino
On the Plaza
Old Mesilla
(575) 524-3524
laposta-de-mesilla.com
Inexpensive to moderate
New Mexican

Sparky's
115 Franklin St.
Hatch
(575) 267-4222
sparkysburgers.com
Inexpensive
Big, juicy green chile
cheeseburgers and
barbecue served up in
a fun fair-like vintage
atmosphere in Hatch, the
center of the known world
for green chile

Northwestern New Mexico

Northwestern New Mexico proudly bears the name Indian Country on account of its large American Indian population. Part of the Navajo Nation—the largest Indian reservation in the US—is located in this region, as are the Zuni, Acoma, Ramah Navajo, and Laguna Indian reservations. The vast juniper-dotted mesas and multihued rock formations will leave you in awe, especially if you're an urban dweller. It's a great place to just wander for a few hours or even a few days.

The three counties composing this sparsely populated region are huge, so notable attractions are often widely scattered. Look closely at the mileage scale on your trusty map, and come along to discover some of the special spots in northwestern New Mexico.

McKinley County

Named after David L. Gallup, a paymaster for the Atlantic and Pacific Railroad, the city of *Gallup* was founded in 1881. Situated near the Arizona border, along old Route 66, Gallup thrives in the heart of Indian Country. The Navajo and Zuni

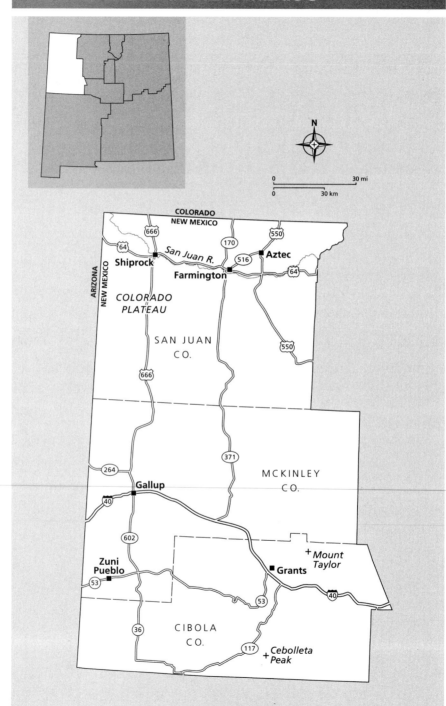

Indians swell this small town's population to more than 100,000 on weekends, when they come to town to trade.

Almost everything in Gallup is located along its main street (alternately Highway 118 and East or West Historic Route 66), a healthy stretch of old **Route 66**, "America's Mother Road," which was stripped of its legendary identity when I-40 homogenized its path in the 1960s but is now gradually coming back. For an overview of Gallup's past with an emphasis on 19th-century coal mining, check out **Gallup Historical Society's Rex Museum** (505-863-1363; gallupnm.gov/index.aspx?NID=208) at 300 W. Historic Route 66. It is open Mon through Fri from 8 a.m. to 3:30 pm. Admission is free.

Gallup's downtown main strip is lined with its own brand of distinctive pawnshops. Whereas in most cities pawnshops are seen as seedy places of last resort for desperate borrowers, in Gallup this image couldn't be farther from reality. In addition to providing ready markets for Indian wares, Gallup's pawnshops act as financial institutions for many Indian people. An advanced system of barter and credit has evolved over the years.

The pawnshops are veritable museums of Indian jewelry and other artifacts. Display cases and vaults gleam with turquoise and silver. If you want a good deal on authentic Indian arts and crafts, including jewelry, here's the place to buy. Retailers come from all over to Gallup to buy Indian wares, which they then sell elsewhere—at a sizable markup. A favorite of Navajos since 1918, **Richardson's Trading Company and Cash Pawn**, a historic trading post in Gallup, is perhaps the best place to view the trade, as well as to get a fair price from a reputable dealer with a wide selection, including exquisite "old pawn" items such as squash blossom necklaces. Located at 222 W. Historic Route 66; (505) 722-4762; richardsontrading.com. Richardson's is open Mon through Sat from 9 a.m. to 6 p.m.

East of downtown, the notable **El Rancho Hotel** commands attention from passing motorists. In 1987 the well-known Indian trader Armand Ortega bought the historic property, as it was threatened with demolition. After extensive renovations, the hotel reopened in May 1988.

Originally built in 1937 by the brother of movie mogul D. W. Griffith, El Rancho became known as a Hollywood hideaway in the 1940s and 1950s. Scores of actors were drawn to Gallup by the many films (mostly Westerns) made in the area. Spencer Tracy, Katharine Hepburn, Humphrey Bogart, Rita Hayworth, and Ronald Reagan all stayed at the hotel. Restored to its former rustic glamour, the hotel's two-story lobby is lined with autographed photos of Hollywood's brightest stars of the era who stayed at El Rancho.

El Rancho is located at 1000 E. Historic Route 66; (505) 722-2285; route-66hotels.org. Room rates range from $98 for a double to $120 for a room with two queen beds; suites, such as the Ronald Reagan, go for $166 per night.

FAVORITE ATTRACTIONS/EVENTS IN NORTHWESTERN NEW MEXICO

Chaco Culture National Historical Park
San Juan County
(505) 786-7014
nps.gov/chcu

El Morro National Monument
Just east of Ramah
(505) 783-4226
nps.gov/elmo

El Rancho Hotel
Gallup
(505) 863-9311
route66hotels.org

Four Corners Monument
New Mexico, Arizona, Colorado, Utah
(928) 871-6647
navajonationparks.org

La Ventana Natural Arch
El Malpais National Monument
Just east of El Morro
(505) 287-7911
nps.gov/elma

Shiprock
San Juan County

Sky City Cultural Center and Haaku Museum
Acoma Pueblo
Cibola County
(800) 747-0181
acomaskycity.org

Zuni-Acoma Trail
Cibola and McKinley Counties

Zuni Pueblo
(505) 782-7238
zunitourism.com

EVENTS

Crownpoint Rug Auction
Third Friday of the month, Crownpoint
(505) 786-7386
crownpointrugauction.com

Gallup Inter-Tribal Ceremonial
August, Gallup
(505) 863-3896
gallupceremonial.com

Red Rock Park, minutes from the center of town, is a wonderful place to explore. *Red Rock Museum*, located in the park, showcases area artifacts from the Ice Age to the present, and rare Indian arts and crafts are also on display. The museum's garden areas identify the plants native to the high mesa region. The park itself, with its exquisite crimson cliffs, is one of New Mexico's top nonforest spots for camping. If you want solitude, however, visit during the week. For good weather without the crowds, plan your stay during early spring or late fall.

Red Rock Park is off Highway 566, via Highway 118 or I-40, about 10 miles east of Gallup; (505) 722-3839; gallupnm.gov. The museum is open daily from 8 a.m. to 6 p.m. Memorial Day through Labor Day, and Mon through Sat from 8 a.m. to 4:30 p.m. the remainder of the year. Suggested donations are $1.75 for adults and $1 for children.

The park hosts the annual *Gallup Inter-Tribal Ceremonial (ITC)*, held each year since 1922. The ITC includes an all-Indian rodeo, an arts and crafts show, and the ceremonial dances of 30 tribes throughout the West, from Canada to Mexico. The ITC begins the second Wednesday in August and is known as the largest Indian gathering of its kind in the world, with over 50,000 spectators over its five days. The ITC Association can be reached at (505) 863-3896 or (888) 685-2564, or theceremonial.com.

For those interested in authentic, hand-loomed Navajo rugs, plan your visit to the area to coincide with an internationally acclaimed local event—the monthly *Crownpoint Rug Auction*, held the third Friday of every month in the Navajo Nation community of Crownpoint, 25 miles north of Thoreau via Highway 371. Attracting Navajo weavers from around the region and individual and commercial buyers internationally, the auction is more than just a market event; it's like a small town fair with arts and crafts and Navajo food vendors. Because you're purchasing direct from the source during the auction, most of the rugs sell for less than comparable ones found in local trading posts. Depending on quality and size, rugs may go for as little as $50 or as much as several thousand dollars. Auctions are held in the local elementary school cafeteria; preview starts at 3 p.m., with the auction beginning at 7 p.m. For more information, contact Crownpoint Rug Weavers Association, PO Box 1630, Crownpoint, NM 87313; (505) 786-7386; crownpointrugauction.com.

About 38 miles south of Gallup you'll enter *Zuni Pueblo*, New Mexico's largest Indian pueblo, with a population of about 9,000. Zuni's isolation from New Mexico's other 18 Rio Grande–situated pueblos makes its history, culture, and language unique.

The Zuni people have occupied this area for more than 1,700 years. Their ancestors played an important role in the early recorded history of the Southwest. In search of the Seven Cities of Cibola—the fabled cities of gold—Spanish explorers first discovered Zuni in 1539. Encouraged by persistent rumors

STATE PARKS IN NORTHWESTERN NEW MEXICO

Online at emnrd.state.nm.us/spd

Bluewater Lake State Park
28 miles west of Grants
(505) 876-2391

Navajo Lake State Park
25 miles east of Bloomfield
(505) 632-2278

(as well as Indian fabrications to persuade the Spaniards to go elsewhere in search of the gold), more explorers, including Coronado, followed but failed to find riches.

The pueblo has several shops where you can purchase Zuni-made arts including stone- and shell-carved fetishes (birds and other animals used since prehistoric times for luck in hunting and fertility in crops) and the turquoise petit point and needlepoint jewelry for which the pueblo is famous. Zuni is located on Highway 53, via Highway 602, about 38 miles south of Gallup; (505) 782-4481.

The first place to stop during a visit to Zuni is ***A:shiwi A:wan Museum and Heritage Center***, located in the historic Hebadina Building, south of Highway 53 at the intersection of Pia Mesa Road and Ojo Caliente Road. The center's unusual name comes from the name for the Zuni people in their native language. ***Note:*** Early Spanish explorers in the New Mexico territory gave Spanish names to all of New Mexico's Pueblo Indians, which are the common names used today; however, each pueblo has its own unique name in its own language.

Be sure to tour the center's permanent exhibit, *The Hawikku: Echoes from Our Past*, which offers a historical perspective on the Zuni that spans more than five centuries. The exhibit includes hand-painted migration story murals, which portray the emergence of the Zuni people from the Fourth World described in their creation story. The murals record the perilous journey of the people as they searched for the Middle Place, their spiritual homeland. The museum is located at 2 E. Ojo Caliente Rd., Zuni; (505) 782-4403; ashiwi-museum.org. It is open Mon through Fri from 9 a.m. to 6 p.m. and is free. The director of the museum, Tom Kennedy, also runs the delightful ***Cimarron Rose Bed and Breakfast***, east of Zuni off Highway 53.

If you are interested in buying some of the beautiful pottery, carved stone fetishes, or famed channel-inlay jewelry for which Zuni artisans are famous, be sure to visit one of the trading posts in Zuni selling arts and crafts. Regrettably, the Pueblo of Zuni Arts and Crafts Gallery is now closed, but try ***Pueblo Trading Post***, 1192 Hwy. 53, in the heart of Zuni; (505) 782-2296; pueblotradingzuni.com. It is open Mon through Sat from 10 a.m. to 6 p.m. and Sun from 10 a.m. to 5 p.m.

In 1629 the Spanish established ***Mission Church of Nuestra Señora de Guadalupe*** (also known as Our Lady of Guadalupe and the Old Mission) at Zuni. The church was restored in 1970, and internationally known Zuni artist and muralist Alex Seowtewa began painting his colorful murals on the interior of the church walls. There are now 24 murals depicting Zuni kachinas. Seowtewa's work has drawn some famous admirers to Zuni, among them

Talking Turkey about Turquoise

Sue Carlson of Richardson's Trading Company in Gallup, one of the area's oldest and most reputable pawnbrokers, and American Indian artisan Jo Ann Valencia of Santa Fe have provided information that helps demystify that most classic of southwestern jewelry gemstones, turquoise. After a sprinkling of media reports on the proliferation of domestic and Asian-imported knockoffs, some buyers have become more aware of the differing quality, and in some cases, the authenticity, of southwestern jewelry. There are various types of "turquoise," from the real deal—gem-quality stone—right on down to the most insidious fake: plastic. It's important to work with a reputable dealer, Carlson notes, because some of the fake stuff is pretty difficult to recognize.

Because turquoise is porous, it absorbs body oils and fumes from the air and can change color, usually becoming greener, with years of wearing. Gem-quality turquoise, which ranges in color from pale blue to bright blue, is less porous and therefore less subject to changes in color. Here's the breakdown:*

Natural turquoise: not treated in any way.

Stabilized turquoise: chemically hardened with a polymer of liquid resin or plastic, but its color has not been changed.** Stabilized turquoise is frequently used in southwestern jewelry because it resists chipping or breaking while it's being worked.

Treated turquoise: altered to produce a change in color of the natural stone, usually detectable by a shiny, unnatural color.

Reconstituted or composite turquoise: turquoise particles and dust that have been combined with plastic resins and solidly compressed to resemble natural turquoise.

As for the brown or black webbing seen on most turquoise, it's referred to as the "matrix" of a stone and is formed by mineral deposits. Its presence does not necessarily increase or diminish the quality of the stone.

*Information source: *Turquoise: Gem of the Centuries* by O. T. Branson

**As defined by the federal Indian Arts and Crafts Sales Act of 1978

Jackie Onassis and Mother Teresa. In fact, Mrs. Onassis had never visited the American Southwest until the mid-1980s, but she was reported to have been affected deeply by its beauty. She was given a personal tour by former secretary of the interior and author Stewart Udall, who was raised in the area, and noted photographer Jerry Jacka. The two were collaborating on a book called *Majestic Journey: Coronado's Inland Empire*, the latest edition of which is dedicated, in memory, to Mrs. Onassis.

Seowtewa continues work on the murals with the assistance of his son Kenneth and a grant from the National Endowment for the Arts. Sadly, due to instability in the adobe walls of the church from moisture, the pueblo has closed the church for tours. Stop in at the Zuni Visitor Center, 1239 Hwy. 53, or call (505) 782-7238 for more information.

The *Inn at Halona* offers guests a rare bed-and-breakfast experience, as it's located in the heart of Zuni Pueblo on the south side of the Zuni River at the prehistoric pueblo site of Halona. Operating under special license by the Zuni tribe, the Inn at Halona is the only such establishment in the pueblo, and possibly in any Indian pueblo. Run by innkeepers Roger Thomas, a native of Chambéry, France, and his wife, Elaine Dodson Thomas, the pueblo-style inn was completely remodeled in 1998. Elaine is the granddaughter of Andrew and Effa Vander Wagen, Dutch immigrants and missionaries who first arrived in Zuni in 1897 and later opened a trading post near Halona Plaza, which is currently also run by the Thomases.

The inn boasts 8 unique guest rooms on 3 levels, some with private baths, which are decorated with Zuni and other southwestern art. Each room contains an ongoing "room diary," and guests are encouraged to record their thoughts and impressions during their stay. Several comfortable common areas are available for lounging, including a private flagstone patio, which is lit by lampposts in the evening. Guests may select their breakfast from a diverse menu, which includes a European-style continental offering, a traditional, full American breakfast, and such chef specialties as huevos rancheros or breakfast burritos.

The Inn at Halona is located 3 blocks south of Highway 53, at 23 Pia Mesa Rd.; (505) 782-4547; halona.com. Rates start at $75 per person per night, and may vary depending on the season and length of stay. Group and government rates are also available.

Though there have been controversial reintroduction efforts of the endangered Mexican wolf, or lobo—limited numbers of which live only in captivity— into the wilderness areas of southeastern Arizona and southwestern New Mexico, most of the animals have not survived. The efforts are applauded by environmentalists as loudly as they're cursed by area ranchers. Politics notwithstanding, the best way to begin to experience the untamed majesty of wolves is with a visit to *Wild Spirit Wolf Sanctuary*, formerly known as the Candy Kitchen Rescue Ranch, south of Ramah.

newmexicotrivia

Of the 20 American Pueblo Indian tribes in the US, all but one—the Hopi of Arizona—are located in New Mexico.

Founded in 1991 by artist Jacque Evans, Wild Spirit Wolf Sanctuary is a nonprofit organization providing sanctuary to abused and abandoned

Tips for Visiting New Mexico's Indian Lands

While visiting New Mexico's pueblo or nonpueblo Indian reservations, keep in mind that they're all sovereign, self-governing nations with their own laws. While almost all pueblos welcome visitors, visitors are expected to observe local rules and etiquette. Here are a few commonsense tips.

If there's a pueblo visitor center, stop there first and register. Many such centers screen films or have museums, which are great ways to orient yourself before visiting pueblo sites. Some pueblos, such as Acoma and Zuni, offer guided tours for a fee.

Photography should always respect people and place. Most pueblos allow photography only by permit, for which a fee must usually be paid. Never photograph dances or ceremonies. These events are traditional, and often religious, ceremonies rather than entertainment. Applause is not appropriate. Never photograph a person or group without asking first. If permission is given, you may be asked to pay a small fee for the privilege.

Sketching, painting, and note taking on the pueblos may also be restricted. Check with the pueblo governor's office or visitor center.

Observe quiet and orderly conduct when watching pueblo dances and ceremonies, and avoid chatting, asking questions about what is going on, and generally being noisy. It's good form to stand toward the back of the crowd, so as not to block the ceremony from pueblo residents or participants. Dress conservatively at dances; women in particular should cover up, and both sexes should avoid wearing shorts and flip-flops or exhibiting bare skin, as a mark of respect.

Never enter a pueblo home, kiva, or building without being invited to do so, but if you are invited to join a family for a meal, very common on feast day, it is good manners to accept, eat what is offered, and then leave so that others may be seated; no payment is expected—this is a long-standing tradition of hospitality. Most pueblo churches are open to visitors without special request; exceptions include Zuni and Acoma, where you must take a tour of the old pueblo with a guide.

Never take alcohol onto Indian lands.

Do not hike, bike, or four-wheel across open Indian lands without permission. Contact local authorities for permits and information. (See appendix for pueblo listings.)

captive-bred wolves and wolf dogs. Its original name came from the fact that the refuge is located at the old headquarters for the Candy Kitchen Ranch, where piñon nut candy was made during the 1920s and 1930s. During Prohibition, it's rumored that liquor was distilled here, with the piñon candy serving as a front for the large amounts of sugar used to make the illegal moonshine. The refuge changed its name in 2004 to better reflect its mission.

Visitors are not permitted to walk around the sanctuary unaccompanied, so you must take one of the several daily tours offered to see the animals. Standard tours are an hour long and do not require reservations; all other special tours must be reserved ahead of time. The wolves are by necessity kept in large pens; however, to the extent possible, the animals are kept in compatible pairs or small groups. With a focus on education, ecology, and the responsible ownership of wolf dogs, the ranch currently cares for 65 wolves, wolf dogs, and coyotes, with the hope that rescue organizations will someday no longer be needed.

The sanctuary is a unique place to spend the night. Accommodations include tent and RV campsites; an off-grid simple two-bedroom log cabin for $125 per night; Wolf Den Lodge, a modern three-bedroom cabin with Wi-Fi for $150 per night, and the Retreat Center, a larger more luxurious four-bedroom cabin with all modern conveniences for $200 per night. For reservations, call (505) 775-3032.

To get to Wild Spirit, turn south onto Highway 125 off Highway 53 (2½ miles west of El Morro National Monument or about 8 miles east of Ramah). Go 8 miles (about halfway, you'll pass through Mountain View), then turn west onto Highway 120 and go 4 miles; 378 Candy Kitchen Rd.; (505) 775-3032; wildspiritwolfsanctuary.org. The ranch is open to the public Tues through Sun from 10:30 a.m. to 5 p.m.; tours are offered at 11 a.m., 12:30 p.m., 2 p.m., and 3:30 p.m. Donations are greatly appreciated.

Back in the small community of Ramah, check out the **Ramah Historical Museum**, located downtown just off Highway 53. Housed in the Joseph A. B. Bond House, ca. 1905, the museum focuses on pioneer Americana and the history of the village, from its earliest days as a Mormon settlement. The museum is open by appointment only. Call (505) 783-4150 and a caretaker will take you around. Admission is free.

The best place to eat in the immediate area is **Ancient Way Cafe**, a backcountry diner in a small log cabin that serves hot, filling home-cooked food, such as house-smoked brisket and homemade bread and desserts that

newmexicotrivia

Ancestral Pueblo people, the prehistoric farming peoples found throughout the Four Corners region, were initially known by the Navajo word *Anasazi*, meaning "enemies of our ancestors." Their modern Pueblo descendants in New Mexico and Arizona have long been uncomfortable with this one-sided description, though; the preferred term in use throughout the Southwest now is Ancestral Pueblo, or better yet, to use the culture name of each tribe—for example, Chaco, Mesa Verde, Kayenta, and so on. The Hopi refer to their Ancestral Pueblo ancestors as Hisatsinom.

Zuni Pueblo's Shalako Ceremonial

All of New Mexico's Indian pueblos conduct annual ceremonials and feast days—some open to the public and some not—to honor or celebrate certain events or deities. One of the more dramatic is the **Shalako Ceremonial** at Zuni Pueblo, which is held in late November or early December. As one of the most important events in the Zuni religious calendar, Shalako celebrates the end of the current year and the beginning of the new.

During the ceremony six Zuni men channel the spirit of the Shalakos, or divine beings, by wearing wood-framed, 10-foot-tall costumes covered with colorfully designed fabrics and topped with masks. The ceremony, which begins with the ritual crossing of the Zuni River, winds through the pueblo's streets as the Shalako performers dance throughout the night and bless the houses that were built during the year. A ritual footrace is conducted the next day, during which participants plant offering sticks in the ground to bring health and fertility to the pueblo.

Because of past instances of disrespect shown by outsiders during Shalako, the event is now closed to the public. Call (505) 782-4481 or (505) 782-4403 for current information. For a dramatic, fictionalized Shalako scene, read Tony Hillerman's *Dance Hall of the Dead*, a murder mystery set on and around the Zuni Reservation.

locals as well as visitors rave about. Located just east of nearby El Morro National Monument, the cafe is not much to look at, but inside it is cozy and friendly. They also rent out RV campsites and tiny log cabins, a boon if you get caught in a snowstorm here, as I have done in the past; cabin rental with dinner for two is offered on weekends for $105 per night. The cafe is open for hearty breakfasts and lunches and serves espresso and homemade baked goods, such as pie, cookies, scones, and dessert specials. A prix fixe dinner menu is served on weekends only and is popular. It includes "very good pie." Hours are Sun through Tues and Thurs from 9 a.m. to 5 p.m., and Fri and Sat from 9 a.m. to 8 p.m. Call (505) 783-4612 or visit elmorro-nm.com/ancient-way-cafe for more information.

Cibola County

Acoma Pueblo, or "Sky City," as it's sometimes called, is the oldest continuously inhabited community in the US; archaeologists have traced the pueblo's occupation to 1150. But it wasn't until 1540 that the Spanish explorer Coronado became the first non-Indian to enter Acoma, and outsiders have been fascinated with Sky City ever since.

The old pueblo is located on a 367-foot-high mesa on the Acoma Indian Reservation outside Grants. The tribe operates the beautiful new *Sky City Cultural Center and Haaku Museum* at the base of the mesa, which includes a museum and gift shops as well as an excellent cafe serving native foods and Starbucks coffee. Guided tours of Acoma—the only way outsiders can view the pueblo—are offered hourly starting from the center, with the exception of private ceremonial periods. Small buses provide transportation to the top of the mesa, and from there an Acoma guide will point out the various elements of the pueblo while filling you in on Acoma's long and colorful history. The mesa-top pueblo provides stunning views of the surrounding area, including spectacular 400-foot-high *Enchanted Mesa*, said to be the home of the ancestral Acomas.

The singularly most impressive structure in the old mesa-top pueblo is *Mission San Esteban Del Rey*, a church completed in 1640 after 11 years of intense labor by Acoma residents. The massive roof beams were carried from the forests of Mount Taylor, 40 miles away—without ever touching the logs to the ground, according to Acoma legend. The church, whose adobe walls are 7 to 9 feet thick, has no windows, because it was used as a fortress.

Most Acoma residents live in communities nearby, but some 12 families live in the old mesa-top pueblo, even though it has no electricity or running water. Some old pueblo residents sell their world-famous, intricately designed pottery during tours, and often you can purchase bread baked in the beehive-shaped *hornos*, or adobe ovens, that dot the pueblo. The tour guide will also point out and explain the use of kivas, or sacred semi-subterranean ceremonial chambers. *Note:* Entrance to kivas is strictly prohibited for visitors.

To get to the cultural center from Grants, head east on I-40, take exit 96 (across from the Acoma casino resort), and follow the signs to the cultural center; (800) 747-0181; acomaskycity.org. From Albuquerque, head west on I-40 (about 55 miles), take exit 108, and do the same. Tours are offered daily Mar through Oct from 9:30 a.m. to 2:30 p.m.; Nov through Feb, the cultural center and museum are open only on weekends and for tours. Cultural center and museum hours are 9 a.m. to 5 p.m.; the cafe closes at 4 p.m.

Each year tours cease during Easter weekend (it varies; call ahead), June 24 and 29, July 10–13, July 25, either the first or second weekend in October (it varies), and the first Saturday in December. *Note:* The pueblo may be closed to the public during other times of the year without much advance notice, so call before you venture out.

Tour admission is $23 for adults, $20 for military personnel and senior citizens, and $15 for children age 6 and older. Children age 5 and younger are free. Camera and sketching fees apply, and there are photographic restrictions, including a ban on camcorders and digital cameras. There's no admission fee for the cultural center and Haaku Museum, however.

The *Shrine of Los Portales* lies in a hidden grotto near the old Spanish land-grant village of *Syboyeta* (sometimes spelled Seboyeta or *Cebolleta* on maps), north of Laguna Pueblo and east of the city of Grants. A statue of St. Bernadette of Lourdes is the focal point of the beautiful, mysterious shrine.

Brought from Spain, the original statue for the shrine, Our Lady of Sorrows, is now protected in the mission church of the same name in Syboyeta. The legend goes that during one of the last Navajo raids in the 1800s, the women and children took refuge in the natural fortress while the men were away. The women vowed that if their husbands and sons returned safely, the women would build a shrine to the Virgin Mary at which to hold an annual Mass.

The shallow cave or overhang of the rounded cliff that forms the large semicircular enclave is perfect for meditation or prayer, as evidenced by the many melted candles that can be seen at the shrine. Weatherworn wooden pews face the shrine at an angle. Springwater, considered holy, seeps from the cliff and collects in several small pools. Because of the abundance of moisture, this protected area is unusually green and forms a small oasis that contrasts with the barren land of the surrounding region.

Syboyeta is on Highway 279, off Highway 124, which connects to I-40 near Laguna Pueblo. To get to the shrine, proceed on the main road to Our Lady of Sorrows church at the center of town. Continue winding around the church as the paved road turns to dirt. After 1/10 mile, turn left and continue for 1 mile until you see a very large tree with exposed roots around its base; the approximately 100-yard-long trail to the shrine begins here. *Note:* If there's been a lot of rain, do not attempt this trek unless you have a four-wheel-drive vehicle.

Heading west on I-40 you'll soon be in *Grants*, the largest town and county seat of Cibola County. Grants's past as a classic Route 66 town is preserved with 1950s-era motels, shops, and cafes along the main strip, now called Santa Fe Avenue. Just off Santa Fe Avenue you'll find the *New Mexico Mining Museum* at 100 N. Iron St. (505-287-4802 or 800-748-2142; grants.org/museums-galleries.aspx)—although it was uranium, not iron, that put Grants on the map. The first floor of the museum traces the history of uranium mining in the area from 1950, the year Paddy Martinez, an Indian laborer and occasional prospector, discovered a mother lode of the dusty yellow rock.

The best part of the museum is the underground portion called Section 26, an eerily accurate reproduction of a working uranium mine. You start by taking an elevator down the mine "shaft." Although you don't travel very far, it feels as though you're hundreds of feet below the earth's surface. The tour uses handheld listening devices that explain the exhibits at scheduled stops. Adding to the realism are artifacts from working mines that fill the space—right down to the tool company "girlie calendar" in the miners' lunchroom.

The museum is open Mon through Sat from 9 a.m. to 4 p.m. Admission is $3 for adults, $2 for seniors over 60 and young people ages 7 to 18, and free for children age 6 and younger.

Highway 53, which connects Grants with Zuni Pueblo (see the McKinley County entry at the beginning of this chapter), is the most scenic drive

Ah, Wilderness!

New Mexico has 26 federally designated wildernesses—roadless, undeveloped areas that have been selected by Congress as providing outstanding opportunities for solitude and nonmotorized recreation. Most of them also contain ecological, geological, or other features of scientific, educational, scenic, or historical value.

A wilderness designation protects an area in several ways. First, and most important for visitors, it limits human travel to hiking, horseback riding, and llama trekking. All motor vehicles are prohibited. So are mountain bikes, although this has been a source of controversy for many years. In addition, only preexisting land uses are allowed—hunting, sometimes cattle grazing, occasionally mining. All road development is banned. All natural ecological processes, including forest fires, are allowed to operate freely without human intervention.

New Mexico has the largest wilderness area in the Lower 48—the *Gila Wilderness* in the remote southwestern part of the state. Together with the adjoining, more mountainous *Aldo Leopold Wilderness*, it covers 760,000 acres, or nearly 1,200 square miles. It is so vast that it was selected as the safest place to reintroduce near-extinct Mexican gray wolves into the wild.

Wilderness areas can be managed by various federal agencies. *Bandelier Wilderness*, part of Bandelier National Monument, is managed by the National Park Service. The otherworldly rock formations of the *Bisti–De Na Zin Wilderness* fall under the jurisdiction of the Bureau of Land Management. The high, marshy, little-known landscape of *San Pedro Parks* is part of a national forest.

The most visited of all New Mexico wilderness areas, *Pecos Wilderness*, encompasses most of the high peaks of the Sangre de Cristo range and spans so much territory that you can trek across it for two weeks without crossing a road. It has 4 major gateway trailheads—Santa Fe Ski Basin on the west, Pecos River Canyon on the south, El Porvenir (near Las Vegas) on the east, and Rio Santa Barbara (near Peñasco) on the north.

Wilderness does not have to be hard to get to. *Sandia Mountain Wilderness* includes most of Sandia Crest above Albuquerque. Hikers can drive to the mountain's summit or ride the Sandia Tramway to the top, then hike into the wilderness for miles along the ridgeline without ever losing sight of the city sprawled nearly a mile below.

in northwestern New Mexico—and you'll find a few interesting stops along the way.

El Malpais National Monument and Conservation Area, jointly managed by the National Park Service and the Bureau of Land Management, protects more than 590 square miles of lava flows, lava tubes, ice caves, cinder cones, geological windows, and other volcanic features that resulted when Mount Taylor erupted 2 to 4 million years ago, as well as sandstone canyons, natural arches, forests, and pueblo remains, all located between Highway 53 and Highway 117, south of Grants. Although some of the sites are accessible to passenger cars traveling along the two highways, El Malpais ("The Badlands" in Spanish) is heaven for hikers and backpackers.

After several years with only minimal development, both the monument and conservation area now have two remote sites where visitors can get information and maps. Malpais Information Center (nps.gov/elma), run by the National Park Service, has information and exhibits about 23 miles south of Grants on Highway 53 in the national monument area managed by the National Park Service. It is open daily from 9 a.m. to 6 p.m. in summer, 10 a.m. to 5 p.m. in spring and fall, and is closed in winter. Malpais Ranger Station (505-280-2918; blm.gov), run by the Bureau of Land Management, on Highway 117 in the national conservation area, is closer to Grants, at 9 miles south of I-40. **Note:** This ranger station is closed indefinitely, but you might like to stop to hike the 1.5-mile nature trail behind the station.

If you are coming from the freeway, by far the best place to get information is at the attractive and informative multiagency *El Malpais Visitor Center* (505-876-2783; nps.gov/archive/elma/mac.htm), just off I-40 at exit 85. The visitor center is staffed by rangers and offers comprehensive information on the region, as well as stunning views of the badlands through its huge picture windows. The center is open daily from 8 a.m. to 5 p.m. year-round.

Among the sites accessible along Highway 117 are the *Sandstone Bluffs Overlook* (10 miles from I-40), *La Ventana Natural Arch* (17 miles south of I-40), and the *Narrows* (1 mile farther south), where the highway passes through a narrow corridor created when lava flowed near the base of huge sandstone cliffs. You'll see intriguing lava formations in this area. If you were farsighted enough to pack a picnic, you'll find great spots for lunch at the south end of the Narrows, as well as underneath La Ventana.

One of the more accessible hiking adventures in El Malpais can be had in *Junction Cave* in the *El Calderón Area* of the national monument, 20 miles south of Grants on Highway 53. A well-marked trail from the parking area leads to the cave entrance. Not really a cave but, rather, a 3,000-foot-long lava tube, Junction Cave provides hikers with a relatively safe and easy spelunking experience. Plan on wearing sturdy walking shoes with nonslip soles and long pants to protect your legs against the sharp lava if you stumble, and bring more than one quality flashlight. At times, you may notice bats clinging to the cave's wall; don't disturb them, as they're harmless. Another trail from El Calderón parking lot leads you past interesting sinkholes to Bat Cave, which is closed off to humans; however, it's a great area from which to enjoy a dramatic New Mexico sunset and watch the bats emerge at dusk.

Negotiating with private property owners for the sale of parts of El Malpais has been quite a process, and some agreements have yet to be finalized. As a result, two of the more interesting and accessible features of El Malpais are still privately owned but popular roadside attractions that you won't want to miss.

Candelaria Ice Cave and ***Bandera Crater*** are located in a parklike setting covered with ponderosa pine, spruce, and piñon trees. You start your trek at the trading post on the property, which was once a summer resort complete with cabins. After paying the fee, you hike ½ mile alongside lava flows until you reach a wooden stairway. The steps lead to Candelaria Ice Cave (named for the present owners of the property), located in part of a collapsed lava tube where the temperature never rises above 31 degrees. Though walking into the cave is prohibited, due to liability, you can still get a good view of the greenish ice from the viewing platform.

To see Bandera Crater, brace yourself for a longer and steeper hike—about 1½ miles. The 1,000-foot-deep crater was formed during a volcanic eruption 5,000 years ago. Nature has since transformed the crater into a beautiful spot flecked with hardy ponderosa pines. The breezy coolness of the 8,000-foot altitude makes the ridge of the crater a nice place to relax on a hot summer day.

The entrance to Candelaria Ice Cave and Bandera Crater is located a little less than 26 miles south of Grants on Highway 53 on Ice Caves Road; (888) 423-2283; icecaves.com. Hours are daily from 9 a.m. to 5 p.m., closed Nov 1 through Mar 1; admission is $11 for adults and teenagers, with 10 percent discount for seniors and military; $5 for children ages 5 to 12; children under 5 are admitted free.

Former National Park Service ranger Sheri McWethy and her partner, Tom Kennedy, director of the A:shiwi A:wan Museum and Heritage Center (see page 44), the main Zuni cultural center, run the charming country eco-inn ***Cimarron Rose***, right off Highway 53 in the forested Zuni Mountains. The 3 guest rooms are all suites, with knotty-pine walls, wood and tile floors, beamed ceilings, Mexican tile, and kitchens. The Cimarron and Zuni Mountain suites have romantic wood-burning stoves; the Bandera is large enough for a group and has a lovely private patio.

Gourmet breakfast is brought to each suite daily and can include quiche lorraine, salmon cakes, or salmon or vegetarian entrees, such as quiche Florentine, pecan french toast, free-range eggs for omelets, or New Mexican specialties such as tamales, burritos, or rellenos; you can even get gluten-free items. There's a nice garden room with library and art gallery. Discounts are available for stays of three to five days.

Obviously the biggest plus for anyone visiting this area of immense scenic beauty and cultural richness is that both owners are deeply tied to the landscape and people here, with a huge fount of knowledge they can share with you, if you wish.

El Morro National Monument is the third-oldest national monument in the US. It was protected within months of the passage of the 1906 Antiquities Act, which empowers the US president to unilaterally set aside for preservation places of scientific, historic, or cultural significance without congressional approval. Also known as Inscription Rock, El Morro is an oasis in the middle of nowhere; nevertheless, travelers have been stopping here for centuries to drink from the pool of water at the base of the cliff—and to leave behind a little historic graffiti. A sporadic account of southwestern history from 1605 through the 19th century is recorded on what Spanish conquistadores named El Morro, meaning "The Promontory."

The inscriptions etched into the vertical sandstone surface provide a permanent record of the different cultures that influenced the area over the past 400 years. Fifteen years before the Pilgrims landed at Plymouth Rock, the first Spanish inscription was made by explorer Don Juan de Oñate on April 16, 1605, extolling his discovery of the "Sea of the South," now known as the Gulf of California or Sea of Cortez.

The easy, flat, mile-long Inscription Trail around the base of El Morro offers a chance to view the inscriptions. Touching them or defacing any surface is strictly forbidden. For those who just can't resist the urge to write in stone after viewing El Morro, however, the visitor center provides a rock near the parking area on which travelers may etch a word or two.

Much earlier visitors to El Morro left their own graffiti in the form of petroglyphs, or ancient rock carvings. You'll find the unrestored ruins of ancient Atsinna Pueblo atop Inscription Rock, which may be visited via a steep but scenic trail. Dating from the 13th century, these have been traced to Ancestral Pueblo ancestors of the Zuni Indians.

If you wish, you can camp for free at the monument's attractive 9-site primitive campground. Campsites have graveled tent pads, picnic tables, ground grills, and water. Sites are available year-round on a first-come, first-served basis. ***Morro RV Park and Cabins*** is just east of El Morro National Monument and has excellent food and comfortable lodgings.

El Morro is located just off Highway 53, 43 miles from Grants; (505) 783-4226; nps.gov/elmo. Admission is free. Daily hours in winter are 9 a.m. to 5 p.m. for the visitor center; trails close 1 hour earlier. The visitor center and trails stay open 1 hour later in spring and fall, and 2 hours later in summer.

For a combination of traditional and contemporary culture after your visit to ancient El Morro, head east on Highway 53, 1 mile from the monument turnoff, to the ***Old School Gallery***, housed in the historic El Morro School building across from Ancient City Cafe. The gallery is the home of the El Morro Area Arts Council (EMAAC) and contains exceptional work by some of this area's many talented artists. It also hosts a Saturday morning farmers' market and seed exchange, receptions, dances, and various art classes and ongoing workshops, such as drumming, qi gong, yoga, and tai chi. Gallery hours are Thurs through Mon from 11 a.m. to 5 p.m.; extended hours in summer; (505) 783-4710; theoldschoolgallery.org.

San Juan County

Similar to Gallup's role in McKinley County, ***Farmington*** serves as the major trading center in San Juan County for the Navajo Nation just west of the city. Though Farmington is near the center of the vast, dry Four Corners region (more about this later), the city is a virtual oasis and a fisherman's paradise with its three rivers flowing around town—the San Juan, the Animas, and the La Plata. San Juan County is also a great place to get in touch with New Mexico's past by visiting its three significant Ancestral Pueblo ruin sites.

Chaco Culture National Historical Park (known colloquially as Chaco Canyon) contains the finest examples of Ancestral Pueblo ruins in New Mexico—or arguably, in any state. Located on the Navajo Nation, deep in the vast, oil-rich San Juan Basin, Chaco Canyon may be the remotest tourist attraction in the state, yet people from all over the world find it every year.

Chaco Canyon emerged as the first major center of Ancestral Pueblo civilization in the early 10th century. Known as the Chaco Phenomenon, it dominated a vast area of the Southwest and beyond for 200 years. The park's cultural importance (and renaming in 1987 to reflect that fact) grew out of the long-running archaeological Chaco Project, which led to the discovery in 1980 of a network of radiating "roads" connecting Chaco Canyon with far-flung Ancestral Pueblo communities, or outliers. This, along with the vast scale of the preplanned public buildings (known as great houses, due to their immense size) and small but powerful elite year-round population, led to the conclusion that Chaco was the political and spiritual center of the Ancestral Pueblo world at that time. In many ways—in their architecture, community life, and social organization—the Chacoans were far more advanced than any other Ancestral Pueblo people of the region. They were players on a national stage, in fact, with trading ties all the way to the Mississippi region, the Pacific, and far into Mesoamerica.

Although Chaco Canyon has been intensely studied for more than 100 years and scholars theorize about the people who once lived here, many mysteries remain. One of the most intriguing aspects of Chacoan life is its ties with Mesoamerica, particularly Casas Grandes (Paquime) in the northern Mexican province of Chihuahua, a major trading pueblo known for raising macaws. These were traded north through Mogollon-area pueblos to Chaco Canyon, where live macaws were kept penned at Pueblo Bonito and used as a prized source of feathers in ceremonials. Macaws, native to northwestern Mexico, copper bells, and seashells were all unknown in this area. Mesoamerican cultural ties can also be seen in a number of astronomical and architectural details at Chaco, and have given archaeologists a great deal of material for theories, some quite controversial.

According to archaeological evidence, Ancestral Pueblo people from far and wide visited Chaco for seasonal planting ceremonies and to trade and socialize, but Chaco Canyon seems to have had only a small permanent population, primarily made up of powerful astronomer-priest leaders, or ritual specialists. They lived in the great houses, made daily observations of the movements of the planets, then called people from surrounding farming villages to the canyon for ceremonial observations.

newmexicotrivia

Contrary to widespread belief, the word *Anasazi*, the old word for the Ancestral Pueblo people, doesn't mean "the ancient ones"; rather it comes from the Navajo language and means "enemies of our ancestors."

But power may have concentrated in this remote canyon to too great a degree, focused on a prehistoric political system supported by farming and trade. Today, we are all too familiar with the devastating effects of climate change among human populations, but civilizations have long risen and fallen as a result of the vagaries of nature. Such may have been the case at Chaco. When the Southwest climate dried out in the early 1100s and the astronomer-priests' predictions proved unreliable, these ritual leaders may have lost their power, as harvests withered and disaster ensued for the thousands of villagers who relied on farming and trade.

Whatever occurred at Chaco—and archaeologists are still formulating a unified theory about it—the Chaco Phenomenon crashed and burned in the early 12th century, and the empire seems to have fragmented, leaving starving farmers across the San Juan Basin with failing crops, leaders they no longer had faith in, and struggling for their very survival. Beginning in 1130, they fled the arid region in search of areas with adequate rainfall for farming. Many families moved southeast to the Pajarito Plateau in the Jemez Mountains near Santa Fe, a volcanic area historically used for gathering obsidian for tools, where they built pueblos in and around Bandelier National Monument and took up farming again.

The elite astronomer-priests of Chaco seem to have moved their center of power to what is now Aztec Ruins National Monument, a major Chacoan outlier pueblo on the Animas River within the boundaries of the present-day town of Aztec in northwestern New Mexico. The pueblo clearly had been built earlier as a potential Chaco successor, with the resources required for Chaco culture to continue across the centuries, albeit an echo of its former self. Chaco and Aztec ruins were reoccupied by refugees from Mesa Verde in southwest Colorado in the 1200s.

Arriving in small family groups, Mesa Verdeans built pueblos and kivas in a looser, more practical style of architecture that never approximated the elegant architectural beauty of Chacoan engineering and aesthetics. By AD 1250, they too were gone, also to the Rio Grande of New Mexico and the Little Colorado River area of Arizona, as the Great Drought gripped the Southwest, emptying out the pueblos of the Four Corners forever.

To properly experience Chaco Culture National Historical Park, allow an entire day to get there and visit the main ruins. Even better, try to stay overnight, as this is a very remote area and there's a lot you will want to see, including backcountry pueblos on the surrounding cliffs located on Chaco's famous "roads." The backcountry pueblos seem to have served as line-of-sight signaling stations announcing the arrival of wayfarers. The 48-site primitive tent campground ($15 per night) is so popular, it is now on a reservation system (walk-ins are allowed Nov 1 to Feb 28, but be well advised, Chaco is frigid in winter, so come well equipped for the conditions and with plenty of food and water. I highly recommend making the effort to camp there. Waking up at Chaco is one of the greatest experiences, on the bucket list of anyone who loves Southwest archaeology—truly memorable.

Note: There is *no* gas, food, or lodging in this remote backcountry park; the nearest lodgings are in Bloomfield, a long way to the north. Plan your time carefully. If you only have one day, get to the park early and stop at the visitor center to view exhibits in the museum, use restrooms, fill water bottles, pay entrance fees, and get information. Then set out on the 9-mile paved auto loop and trails linking the great houses strung beneath the cliffs. To reach the backcountry pueblos farther into the canyon and up on the surrounding cliffs, you will have to hike on dirt trails that lead to these outliers. For most people, it's best to do the main canyon on the first day and the backcountry pueblos on the second, as the distances are quite great.

The largest and most impressive great house ruin in Chaco Canyon itself is Pueblo Bonito, one of the most iconic pueblos in the Southwest. For the famous aerial view, climb the steep trail to the clifftop directly above and marvel at the engineered architecture. Well-marked trails lead through Pueblo Bonito's main plaza, with its 30 ceremonial clan kivas, and blocks of multistory rooms. The elegant back wall was once strong but is now propped up by struts following a severe rockfall that almost demolished the beautifully laid, tapering dry walls.

The visitor center is the only place in the park where you can fill up your water jugs. It's a good idea when you are traveling anywhere in New Mexico, but particularly here, to carry a 5-gallon container in the back of the car and use it to fill up your water bottle, or buy liter bottles of water to carry on hikes. You can also buy prefilled 3-gallon water bottles with spigots from supermarkets. The common advice to carry and drink a gallon of water per person per day when hiking in the Southwest is advice you should heed. Chaco Canyon is an extremely barren, arid, exposed landscape, especially in the summer, when temperatures soar. Whatever you do, be sure to eat adequate high-energy food before you set out on any hike, and both snack and keep hydrated by sipping water regularly. It's easy when you are this far from restaurants and cafes to be sloppy about eating and drinking, but it's essential that you be well prepared for outdoor exertion—you're a long way from a hospital or medical assistance. As noted, winter is extreme here, too, so think twice before hiking and camping in subzero temperatures; there is no shelter in the San Juan Basin.

newmexicotrivia

Farmington's San Juan County Fair is the oldest continuously operated fair in New Mexico—even older than the New Mexico State Fair, held annually in Albuquerque.

The best approach to Chaco Canyon is to turn off US 550 at mile 112.5 (3 miles south of Nageezi) and follow the signs on San Juan County Roads 7900 and 7950 to the park via the Navajo Nation. These are 26 miles of pretty excruciating, washboard-type dirt and gravel roads and are not recommended for large motor homes or trailers. Though passenger cars are usually adequate, the roads can be impassable during or after substantial rainfall; accordingly, call ahead to check road conditions. Once you get to the federally maintained park, however, the roads are perfectly paved; (505) 786-7014; nps.gov/chcu. Admission is $20 per vehicle, or $10 per individual if arriving in a group. The visitor center is open daily from 8 a.m. to 5 p.m.

For those who are intrigued by Ancestral Pueblo ruins but aren't up for a trek to Chaco Canyon, two Chacoan outlier pueblos lie close to Farmington: Aztec Ruins National Monument and Salmon Ruins. Both are easily accessible on paved roads.

The first thing you'll notice about **Aztec Ruins National Monument**, especially if you visited Chaco Canyon first, is the abundance of trees and a nearby river—and also the distinctive Chacoan appearance of Aztec Ruins. Despite the name, these ruins had nothing to do with the Aztec Indians of central Mexico. In fact, the Aztecs lived hundreds of years after this large pueblo was abandoned, first by Chacoans and later by Mesa Verdean refugees. Early Anglo settlers named the site Aztec because they mistakenly believed the Aztecs built the pueblos.

Aztec was expanded and now protects an amazing number of ruins in a small area; however, only one pueblo is open for visitation. The main reason to visit Aztec is to view the country's only fully restored great kiva, a sacred ceremonial chamber used by the whole community (Casa Rinconada in Chaco Canyon is also a great kiva, though unrestored). A quiet walk through the very atmospheric kiva is definitely the highlight of the visit.

The visitor center for Aztec Ruins is northwest of the city of Aztec (northeast of Farmington), near the junction of US 550 and Highway 516; (505) 334-6174; nps.gov/azru. The monument is open daily from 8 a.m. to 6 p.m. Memorial Day through Labor Day and 8 a.m. to 5 p.m. the rest of the year. Admission is $5 per person, with those age 15 and younger admitted free; Interagency Annual Passes and Golden Age and Golden Access Passes for seniors are accepted.

Salmon Ruins, on the northern bank of the San Juan River, preserves the remnants of an important Chacoan great house once connected to Chaco Canyon by a prehistoric road; it is the other major Chacoan outlier in San Juan County. The Chacoans who lived here were apparently specialists who raised a particularly hardy form of corn that was traded at Chaco by way of a road that came through Kutz Canyon to the site on the San Juan River. Salmon, named for the settler who once lived here, not the fish, is an interesting site, owned by the county. It offers many public archaeology programs aimed at local kids, including rare tours of "pueblitos" (little pueblos) in the nearby Dinetah (the Navajo ancestral homeland), on what is now the Jicarilla Apache Reservation, a region where early Navajo and Pueblo people lived together during the volatile times following the 1680 Pueblo Revolt. Salmon is also home to the San Juan

Archaeological Research Center and Library, an excellent place to do a little research. Children will enjoy using the computers in the main visitor center to "virtually visit" all of Chaco's outliers via a software program. This is a great place to keep kids happy.

Salmon Ruins is on US 64, 2 miles west of the community of Bloomfield; (505) 632-2013; salmonruins.com. Hours are Mon through Fri from 8 a.m. to 5 p.m. and Sun from 9 a.m. to 5 p.m. (winter hours: Nov through Apr Sun noon to 5 p.m.), and admission is $4 for adults, $1 for children ages 6 to 16, $3 for seniors, and free for children age 5 and younger.

Back to civilization, a leisurely walking tour of the Aztec Historic District in downtown Aztec offers a great change of pace. Centering on the ***Aztec Museum and Pioneer Village***, more than 75 business and residential buildings, including shops and restaurants, are listed on the National Register of Historic Places. The museum houses a fine collection of early pioneer Americana, plus an old wooden oil drilling rig—a tribute to the lucrative oil-and-gas industry in San Juan County. The museum is at 125 N. Main Ave.; (505) 334-9829; aztecmuseum.org. Open June through Sept only, Tues through Sat from 9 a.m. to 4 p.m. Admission is $5 for adults, $3 for young people ages 12 to 17, and free for children age 11 and younger.

An important landmark in the mostly featureless landscape of the San Juan Basin for people traveling the Chaco road system was ***Angel Peak Recreation Area***, 12 miles south of Aztec off US 550, within the sight line of Salmon Ruins. The peak itself is easy to spot from a distance. The rock spire on top of the steep-sided butte resembles a winged angel (if you have a good imagination). The sign marking the road that turns off to the east into the recreation area is not so obvious. Following this wide gravel road for ½ mile will bring you to a scenic vista overlooking Kutz Canyon, a surprise spectacle of red-and-white-painted desert. Continue for 2 more miles and you'll come to a small picnic area and campground from which a trail follows the canyon rim. There is no admission fee, and no phone. This is a very exposed spot, so take that into account before setting off.

The city of Farmington, farther west on US 64, is an oil-and-gas town that serves as the main shopping center for the surrounding area, as well as home to San Juan College. Every year, it hosts a theatrical production at the ***Lions Wilderness Park Amphitheater***. Performances usually run from mid-June through July. Tickets can be purchased at the Farmington Civic Center box office at 200 W. Arrington in Farmington; online at fmtn.org/civiccenter; and over the phone at (505) 599-1148 or (877) 599-3331.

For an otherworldly experience in northwestern New Mexico, plan a visit to the ***Bisti–De Na Zin Wilderness***, commonly known as the Bisti Badlands, south of Farmington. The 45,000-acre wilderness is a barren landscape of steeply eroded badlands topography on the Navajo Nation, featuring unusual rock spires called hoodoos. The area's desolate present belies its ancient past as a lush swampland roamed by dinosaurs and other life-forms millions of years ago. Time and the natural elements have etched out a fantasy-world moonscape of strange rock formations and fossils, creating an ever-changing environment.

An easy way to experience the Bisti is to take a leisurely day hike by following the Gateway Wash from the undeveloped parking lot into the heart of the badlands. Because there are no developed trails or signs inhibiting your wilderness experience, take extra care to avoid getting lost. This is a primitive wilderness area, and there are no services, so plan accordingly and, as mentioned before, be sure to bring lots of drinking water and nutritious food, as this area can get quite hot during summer. The Bisti is a great place not only for hiking but also for photography and primitive camping, especially on full-moon nights.

Besides the natural landscape, you may also find the fossilized remains (isolated teeth and bones) of the various creatures that once lived here: fish, turtles, lizards, mammals, and dinosaurs. However, federal law prohibits the collection of vertebrate fossils and petrified wood. Any collection interferes with scientific research and eliminates the opportunity for others to view and to photograph these unusual wilderness features. Also, climbing on rock formations is dangerous and prohibited, as it accelerates erosion and destroys the scenic value of the area.

To get to the Bisti–De Na Zin Wilderness from Farmington, head south on Highway 371 for about 30 miles and then exit left and travel 6 miles on a gravel road that will take you past the old Bisti Trading Post to an undeveloped parking area and access to the wilderness. The area can also be approached from Crownpoint, by traveling north on Highway 371 for about 46 miles and following the same gravel road just described. Travel on the gravel road is good during dry conditions, but the road can get slippery and rutted during the rainy season, normally in spring and late summer. There's no phone, but for more information, you can contact the Farmington Convention and Visitors Bureau at (505) 326-7602 or (800) 448-1240; farmingtonnm.org. Or contact the Bureau of Land Management, which oversees this wilderness, about visiting the site: blm .gov/nm/st/en/prog/wilderness/bisti.html.

If you've been inspired by the ancient pueblo cliff dwellings at nearby Mesa Verde National Park in southwestern Colorado, are in excellent physical condition, and are looking for adventure, then look no farther than **Kokopelli's Cave Bed & Breakfast**, north of Farmington—the only such establishment I know of that requires guests to sign a waiver of liability for potential accidents.

The brainchild of Farmington geologist Bruce Black, Kokopelli's Cave was blasted out of a 65-million-year-old sandstone formation, 280 feet above the La Plata River, but unlike the ancient cliff dwellings of the Southwest, this cave is actually 70 feet below the surface; the entrance on the cliff face is accessible only by taking a series of trails, paths, and steps. If you're willing and able to make the climb, you'll be rewarded by views of four states and several mountain ranges. And despite its remoteness and accessibility challenges, Kokopelli's is pure luxury once you actually make it down into the cave, boasting all the comforts of home, plus a cascading "waterfall" shower and a flagstone hot tub.

Traditional Food of New Mexico

Green Chile Stew

Green chile stew is New Mexico's wintertime equivalent to chicken soup for the rest of the country—good for what ails you. Flavorful and satisfying, this dish is made in most homes and available in most restaurants serving New Mexican food. As an alternative, prepare it without meat and add fresh corn—*muy sabroso!*

2 pounds chicken, pork, beef, or bison, cubed

¼ cup flour

2 tablespoons shortening or corn oil

2 medium onions, chopped

3 cloves garlic, minced

1 small can tomatoes

3 medium potatoes, peeled and cubed

6 cups water

2 cups chopped fresh or frozen green chiles (more or less, according to taste)

2 teaspoons salt

1 teaspoon ground cumin

1. Dredge the meat in flour. Place the shortening in a heavy skillet and brown meat at medium heat. Place meat in a large stewing pot.

2. Saute the onions and garlic in the remaining shortening and add to stewing pot.

3. Add all remaining ingredients to stewing pot and simmer at low heat for 1 hour. Serve hot with plenty of warm flour or corn tortillas. Makes 6–8 servings.

In lieu of being served breakfast, you'll find the refrigerator and cabinets well stocked with breakfast fixings, including fresh fruit. And remember, pack light, because there are no elevators! Because even getting to the cave's trailhead is complicated, guests are asked to meet their hosts at their home in Farmington to be escorted out to the site. This way you won't get lost, and you'll also get a personal rundown on the systems in the cave so you'll know how to work them; (505) 325-7855; kokoscave.com. Rates are $260 per night for 1 or 2 people; $300 per night for 3 or 4 people, with an additional $50 per individual over 4 persons; two-night minimum. It's closed Dec through Feb due to cold-weather conditions.

Hogback Trading Post, on the edge of the Navajo Nation, is the place to purchase authentic Navajo arts and crafts in San Juan County. Established in 1871, the Hogback is the oldest trading post—on or off the reservation—serving the Navajos. (The better-known Hubbell Trading Post in Ganado, Arizona, wasn't established until 1876.) The Hogback is now run by Tom Wheeler, the great-grandson of the trading post's founder, Joseph Wheeler. The trading post contains almost 10,000 square feet of display space on 2 levels and specializes in fine Navajo-woven rugs. It's located 15 miles west of Farmington on US 64 in the community of Waterflow. The Hogback is at 3221 Hwy. 64; (505) 598-5154; and is open Mon through Sat from 8 a.m. to 5 p.m.

Another interesting trading post is *Big Rock Trading Post*, in neighboring Fruitland, 12 miles west of Farmington on US 64. You'll likely first notice Big Rock by seeing its sign on a large, white propane tank out front. Run by father and son Chuck and Charlie Dickens, Big Rock serves not only as a general store, trading post, and pawnshop (filled with authentic American Indian jewelry for sale) but also as something of an Old West cowboy and Indian museum—complete with a saddle collection along with other southwestern artifacts. Big Rock is open Mon through Fri from 8:30 a.m. to 5:30 p.m. and Sat from 9 a.m. to 5 p.m.; (505) 598-5184; bigrocktradingpost.com.

One of the most memorable places to visit, purely for its I-stood-on-the-spot value, is the *Four Corners Monument*, a Navajo tribal park, northwest of Farmington. The absolute barrenness of the area is remarkable. But you can stand on the spot—the only such spot in the US—where you will truly be in four states at once: New Mexico, Arizona, Utah, and Colorado. It's amazing how far people will travel out of their way to visit a spot that would otherwise hold no appeal whatsoever. Still, it is a kick.

To get to Four Corners Monument, take US 64 west of Farmington until it meets US 160 at Teec Nos Pos, site of another excellent trading post. (You're now in Arizona.) Then take US 160 north until it meets Highway 597. (You're back in New Mexico.) Go left on Highway 597 to the monument. Open daily from 8 a.m. to 7 p.m. October 1 through April 30 and from 8 a.m. to 5 p.m. May 1 through September 30. Admission is $3 per person; (928) 206-2540; navajonationparks.org.

On the way to Four Corners Monument from Farmington—along US 64, west of the largest Navajo Nation town of *Shiprock*—you'll pass within viewing distance of one of the most majestic and mysterious rock formations in New Mexico: Ship Rock (*Note:* The landmark is spelled Ship Rock, and the town is Shiprock). The 1,700-foot peak gets its name from its shape, which at a distance resembles a two-masted ship sailing on a sea of desert. Though Ship Rock changes its appearance throughout the day, it's said that it looks most like a ship during a midsummer sunset, occasionally appearing to shimmer and drift on an imaginary ocean. Navajos refer to the immense formation as *Tse Bi dahi*, which means "The Rock with Wings," and several of their folk myths contain references to it. (Some say that Ship Rock switches positions across the horizon as you drive by it.)

Where to Stay in Northwestern New Mexico

MCKINLEY COUNTY

El Rancho Hotel
1000 E. Hwy. 66
Gallup
(505) 863-9311
route66hotels.com
Moderate

The Inn at Halona
23B Pia Mesa Rd.
Zuni Pueblo
(505) 782-4547
(800) 752-3278
halona.com
Moderate

CIBOLA COUNTY

Cimarron Rose, a Zuni Mountain Bed and Breakfast
689 Oso Ridge Rte. (off Highway 53)
Grants
(800) 856-5776
cimarronrose.com
Moderate to expensive

Holiday Inn Express
1496 E. Santa Fe Ave.
Grants
(505) 287-9252
(800) 315-2621
ihg.com/holidayinnexpress/
hotels/us/en/grants/grtnm/
hoteldetail
Moderate

SAN JUAN COUNTY

Courtyard Farmington by Marriott
560 Scott Ave.
Farmington
(505) 325-5111
marriott.com/hotels/travel/
fmncy-courtyard-farmington
Moderate

Holiday Inn Express and Suites
2110 Bloomfield Blvd.
Farmington
(505) 325-2545
ihg.com/holidayinnexpress
Moderate

Silver River Adobe Inn Bed & Breakfast
3151 W. Main St.
Farmington
(505) 325-8219
(800) 382-9251
silveradobe.com
Moderate

Step Back Inn
103 W. Aztec Blvd.
Aztec
(505) 334-1200
(800) 334-1255
stepbackinn.com
Moderate

Where to Eat in Northwestern New Mexico

MCKINLEY COUNTY

Badlands Grill
2201 W. Hwy. 66
Gallup
(505) 722-5157
badlandsgrill.com
Moderate to very expensive
Fine dining; steaks, including game meats, and seafood

Earl's Family Restaurant
1400 Historic Route 66
Gallup
(505) 863-4201
Inexpensive to moderate
New Mexican and American

El Metate Tamale Factory
610 W. Mesa Ave.
Gallup
(505) 722-7000
Inexpensive
Mexican

El Rancho Hotel Restaurant
1003 E. Hwy. 66
Gallup
(505) 863-9311
route66hotels.com
Inexpensive to moderate
Traditional New Mexican

Gallup Coffee Company
203 W. Coal Ave.
Gallup
(505) 410-2505
Inexpensive
Espresso, tea, quiche, and pastries

SELECTED CHAMBERS OF COMMERCE/VISITOR BUREAUS IN NORTHWESTERN NEW MEXICO

Aztec Chamber of Commerce
110 N. Ash
Aztec, NM 87410
(505) 334-9551
new.aztecchamber.com

Farmington Convention and Visitors Bureau
3041 E. Main St.
Farmington, NM 87401
(505) 326-7602
(800) 448-1240
farmingtonnm.org

Gallup–McKinley County Chamber of Commerce
106 W. Hwy. 66
Gallup, NM 87301
(505) 722-2228
(800) 380-4989
thegallupchamber.com

Grants/Cibola County Chamber of Commerce
100 N. Iron Ave.
Grants, NM 87020
(505) 287-4802
(800) 748-2142
grants.org

CIBOLA COUNTY

Ancient Way Cafe
4018 Hwy. 53 (just east of El Morro)
Ramah
(505) 783-4612
www.elmorro-nm.com/ancient-way-cafe
Inexpensive to moderate
Home-smoked meats, barbecue, steaks, burgers, sandwiches; New Mexican

Coco Bean Café
333 Nimitz
Grants
(505) 285-4143
Inexpensive
Espresso, smoothies, and pastries

La Ventana Steaks and Spirits
110½ Geis St.
Grants
(505) 287-9393
laventanagrants.com
Moderate to expensive
Classic American and New Mexican

SAN JUAN COUNTY

Los Hermanitos Restaurant
3501 E. Main St.
Farmington
(505) 326-5664
loshermanitos.com
Inexpensive to moderate
New Mexican

Si Señor
4015 E. 30th St.
Farmington
(505) 324-9050
sisenorfarmington.com
Inexpensive to moderate
Mexican

Spare Rib BBQ Company
1700 E. Main St.
Farmington
(505) 325-4800
spareribbbq.com
Inexpensive to moderate
Barbecue

Three Rivers Brewery Block
101 E. Main St.
Farmington
(505) 324-2187
threeriversbrewery.com
Moderate
Classic pub grub in a brewpub with historical atmosphere; pizzeria

North-Central New Mexico

North-central New Mexico is a land of Indian pueblos, forested mountains, hidden hot springs, and magnificent rock formations. The region's beauty so inspired artist Georgia O'Keeffe that she made her home here. In contrast, this region also was home to the production of the world's first atom bomb.

You'll detect a strong tradition of Hispanic culture and pride in north-central New Mexico. The first Spanish colony in the territory was established here, and some of the state's oldest Hispanic communities continue to thrive in this region. The Hispanic influence lives on in the old Catholic churches, the centuries-old adobe homes, and the high regard for family and quiet respect for cultural traditions.

As you set out to explore the intrigue of north-central New Mexico, keep in mind that once the sun goes down—even during the summer—it's very cool.

Rio Arriba County

Although situated in one of the most economically depressed areas of the state, Rio Arriba County offers the intrepid traveler a host of adventures. As a bridge between the often stark

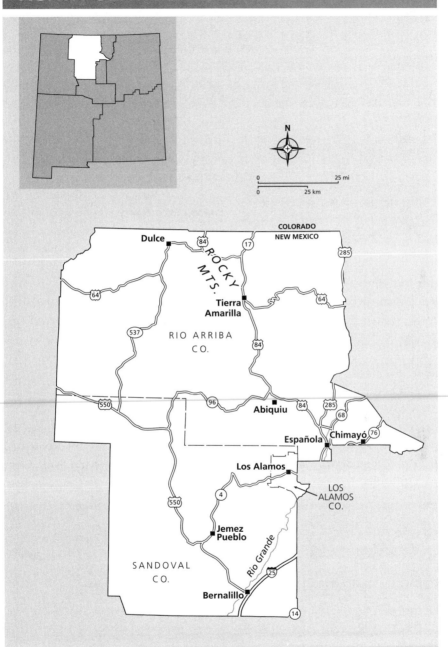

landscape of the Four Corners region to its west and the forested, mountainous region to its east, Rio Arriba County is certainly a blending of the two.

In southern Rio Arriba County you'll find the city of **Española** (partly located in Santa Fe County). Lying near the site of the first Spanish settlement in New Mexico, designated San Juan de los Caballeros in 1598 by Spanish explorer Don Juan de Oñate, Española is a bit of a rough diamond. However, it's a good place to get gas (Santa Clara Pueblo's in-town gas station is particularly low priced), grab an inexpensive bite to eat, and start exploring the county.

newmexicotrivia

The first Spanish colony in what is now New Mexico was established near San Juan Pueblo, north of present-day Española, in 1598.

Just southwest of Española lies **Santa Clara Pueblo** proper. The pueblo itself, like most of New Mexico's Rio Grande–area pueblos, is similar to a small rural town and centered on a mission church and plaza. Santa Clara is famous for its polished red and solid-black pottery, prized by collectors. The neatly maintained pueblo is home to many potters and several small galleries. **Merrock Galeria** (505-753-2083) in Española features the work of contemporary Pueblo artists, such as bronze sculptor Paul Speckled Rock and famed ceramic artist Roxanne Swentzell.

From Española take Highway 30 south (on the west side of the Rio Grande) 1¼ miles. The well-marked pueblo entrance is on the left; (505) 753-7326.

Also on the Santa Clara Indian Reservation, 10 miles west of the pueblo, you'll find **Puyé Cliff Dwellings**, a National Historic Landmark located in tribally owned **Santa Clara Canyon**. This ancestral home of the Santa Clara

FAVORITE ATTRACTIONS IN NORTH-CENTRAL NEW MEXICO

Bandelier National Monument
Northern Sandoval County
(505) 672-3861
nps.gov/band

Cumbres & Toltec Scenic Railroad
Chama
(888) CUMBRES (888-286-2737)
cumbrestoltec.com

El Santuario de Chimayó
Chimayó
(505) 351-9961
elsantuariodechimayo.us

Sandia Man Cave
Near Placitas

Spence Hot Springs
Jemez Springs

people reopened with little fanfare in spring 2009 after being closed to the public for nine years. In 2000, a huge forest fire, which also destroyed residential areas of Los Alamos, swept through Santa Clara Canyon. The intense heat made the ancient stone walls likely to crumble, and it took nearly a decade for tribal workers to finish stabilizing them. Now, once again, you can visit this magnificent archaeological site, occupied from the 900s to 1580. The earlier dwellings here were caves hollowed in the cliffs; later, adobe structures were built along the slopes and top of the mesa, where the people of Santa Clara Pueblo still hold ceremonies that are usually closed to the general public. The rest of the canyon, its forest still struggling to recover from the wildfire, remains closed to the public until further notice.

Four different guided tours of the mile-long ruins are offered Apr through Sept, daily on the hour, 9 a.m. to 6 p.m., until 4 p.m. the rest of the year. Basic entrance admits you to the Harvey House, a late 19th-century bed-and-breakfast built by the famous railroad entrepreneur Fred Harvey, at the foot of the cliffs; it is the only one built on an Indian reservation. It now serves as an interpretive center and museum and allows you to take photos of the cliff dwellings from below. There are separate tours of the cliff face and the mesa top, and one combined tour of all locations. Visitors on the mesa tour are driven to the top; cliff-face tours require hiking along a paved trail in the cliffs. Purchase tickets at Puyé Cliffs Welcome Center at the Valero gas station on Highway 30. Allow an additional 15 minutes after purchasing your tickets to get to the location of your tour. To reach Puyé Cliff Dwellings, take Highway 30 south from Española and turn west onto Highway 5 (Santa Clara Canyon Road). For more information, contact (505) 753-7326 (tribal headquarters) or (888) 320-5008 (tours); santaclaran.com/attractions.

While northern New Mexico claims several very good wineries, **La Chiripada Winery** is particularly worth seeking out. Situated among the apple orchards in the small community of **Dixon**, La Chiripada's tasting room is housed in a whitewashed adobe surrounded by colorful gardens and vineyards. Besides its selection of wines with their Mimbres Indian design labels, the tasting room also sells contemporary pottery. Brothers Michael and Patrick Johnson planted their 10 acres of grapes in 1977 and opened the winery on the banks of the Rio Embudo four years later. La Chiripada (meaning "The Stroke of Luck") gets half its grapes from its own vineyards and the remainder from other New Mexico growers.

La Chiripada is on Highway 75 in Dixon; (505) 579-4437 or (800) 528-7801; lachiripada.com. Tasting room hours are Mon through Sat from 10 a.m. to 6 p.m. and Sun from noon to 6 p.m. The winery also has a tasting room off the plaza in Taos, below Ogelvie's restaurant, that is open Mon through Sat from 11 a.m. to 6 p.m. and Sun from noon to 6 p.m.; (505) 579-4437 or (800) 528-7801; lachiripada.com.

Just inside Rio Arriba County, near its border with Santa Fe County, the village of **Chimayó** sits on the **High Road to Taos**, that romantic-sounding name for the scenic, though less than direct, winding mountain road connecting Santa Fe to Taos. The old Spanish community of Chimayó is the most interesting stop on the High Road and boasts several "must-sees."

The first place to stop is **El Santuario de Chimayó**, known as "Little Lourdes" because of its reputation for miraculous healing and cures similar to those of the famous site in southwestern France. Built in 1816, the charming and highly photogenic adobe chapel is widely known as the destination of an annual Holy Week pilgrimage, when thousands of pilgrims walk from all over New Mexico, neighboring states, and even Mexico, to arrive at the Santuario on Good Friday for Mass. It is not just an Easter tradition; people visit the Santuario all year long. This is one destination in northern New Mexico that you really should not miss.

The chapel's intricately carved and colorful altar spotlights a 6-foot crucifix, while scores of votive candles maintain a glow nearby. According to legend, the cross appeared in a strange, glowing light on this spot around 1810. Local Penitentes twice carried it to the church in nearby Santa Cruz, but each time it vanished from the church and reappeared at the site where it was found, so finally a church was built on the spot.

newmexicotrivia

The community of Española is known as the "low-rider capital of New Mexico" because of its preponderance of the specially equipped cars.

Two side rooms are attached to the chapel. The larger space is devoted to holding the various offerings made over the years, such as small statues, paintings, personal messages of thanks, and photographs. The walls of this room are lined with the crutches of those who have been cured at Chimayó. The smaller chamber at the Santuario houses the hole in the floor (El Pozo) that contains the sacred, healing dirt. Visitors are welcome to take small amounts with them—the dirt is continuously replenished and blessed by the local priest.

Inside the side room in the Santuario, you'll also find a small shrine to Santo Niño de Atocha, a Christ child–like figure popular with Hispanics, who wears a cape and carries a gourd and staff. In New Mexico, Santo Niño, as he is known, is said to wear out his shoes nightly walking the hills to bring food and comfort to the poor. Pilgrims to the Santuario leave shoes for him at this small shrine, and also in the adjoining chapel west of the Santuario dedicated to this saint.

Traditional Food of New Mexico

Simply Salsa

Why pay for expensive salsas when you can whip up a batch of your own in mere minutes at a fraction of the cost? The following recipe is easy to make and popular in New Mexico as well as throughout Mexico, where it is called *salsa casera* (home-style salsa).

1 large can tomatoes (or 1 pound fresh tomatoes*)

½ onion, quartered

5 fresh serrano chiles (or 3 jalapeños), chopped

2 cloves garlic, quartered

1 tablespoon white vinegar

½–1 teaspoon salt (to taste)

1 tablespoon fresh cilantro (optional)

Put all ingredients in a blender and pulse until desired consistency, but not too smooth. Serve with tostadas or corn tortilla chips. Makes about 2–3 cups salsa.

*Roasting or grilling the fresh tomatoes first adds a nice smoky flavor.

Chimayó is accessible from US 285, north of Santa Fe, via Highway 503 and then Highway 520. The road to the Santuario is located on the right, just as you enter the village of Chimayó on Highway 520; (505) 351-9961; elsantuario dechimayo.us (a most delightful and artistic website, complete with traditional northern New Mexico music and beautiful photography). Services are still held in El Santuario de Chimayó, with an 11 a.m. Mass on weekdays, 10:30 a.m. and noon on Sun, and it's open to the public daily from 9 a.m. to 4 p.m. Oct through Apr, until 5 p.m. May through Sept.

Less than ½ mile farther on Highway 520, you'll see the **Restaurante Rancho de Chimayó** on your right and the Hacienda Rancho de Chimayó (a bed-and-breakfast inn) on your left. If you want a romantic hideaway, stay at the hacienda. If you're hungry, visit the restaurant—and even if you're not hungry, go anyway to enjoy the surroundings.

The restaurant is the former home of Hermenegildo and Trinidad Jaramillo and has been open since 1965. The hundred-year-old adobe provides an intimate dining experience in several small rooms inside and a delightful openness on the terraced patios outside. During spring and summer, colorful flowers and warm temperatures make outside dining the obvious choice. Native New

Mexican foods are prepared according to traditional family recipes that stress locally grown products, including the peerless Chimayó red chile, which has a complex, almost winelike, flavor.

The restaurant has a full bar and carries many Mexican beers, but the house specialty is the potent Chimayó Cocktail. A waitress revealed the recipe as tequila, apple juice, triple sec, crème de cassis, and a dash of lime. The proportions are a secret, but the apple juice ice cubes and apple-slice garnish make it the perfect aperitif. If you would like to try some of these classic recipes at home, buy the excellent *Rancho de Chimayó* cookbook written for the restaurant by local foodies Cheryl and Bill Jamison, which contains recipes, stories, and history and was recently updated.

The restaurant is open daily from 11:30 a.m. to 9 p.m. and for breakfast on weekends from 8:30 to 10:30 a.m., with the exception of Mon during winter (Nov through Apr), when it is closed; (505) 351-4444 or (505) 984-2100; ranchodechimayo.com/restaurante.

The family home of Epifanio and Adelaida Jaramillo became **Hacienda Rancho de Chimayó** in 1984, after the traditional adobe had been renovated into 7 guest rooms filled with turn-of-the-20th-century antiques. Each room (dubbed Uno, Dos, Tres, Quatro, Cinco, Seis, and Siete in simple Spanish style) has a private bath and sitting area and opens onto an enclosed courtyard. Every morning your hosts serve a continental breakfast featuring pastries, fruit, fresh-squeezed orange juice, and coffee or tea. Room rates are very reasonable and range from a $69 single to a $105 double; (505) 351-2222 or (888) 270-2320; ranchodechimayo.com/hacienda.

Northern New Mexico, and particularly the Taos High Road, is a bastion of traditional weaving. So much so, in fact, that the **New Mexico Fiber Arts Guild** (nmfiberarts.org), together with the State of New Mexico, has created a series of different fiber arts trails for weaving enthusiasts to explore, featuring home studios, yarn emporiums, galleries, weaving cooperatives, and workshops.

At the junction of Highway 520 and Highway 76, you'll come across one of the most famous traditional weaving stores: **Ortega's Weaving Shop** (53 Plaza del Cerro; 505-351-4215, 877-351-4215; ortegasweaving.com) and **Galeria Ortega** (55 Plaza del Cerro; 505-351-2288, 800-743-5921; ortegasweaving.com). No matter what time of year you visit, these two neighboring stores are the perfect places to do your Christmas shopping. Eight generations of masterly weaving by the Ortega family are evident in the fine wool rugs, coats, and other outerwear for sale at the weaving shop. You can even watch weavers hand-loom rugs in a room just off the sales area. In addition, the shop has a great selection of Santa Clara Pueblo pottery and books on the Southwest. It's also the place to stock up on bags of Chimayó red chile powder.

Galeria Ortega markets contemporary New Mexican art forms. Wood carvings are featured, including a variety of *bultos*, or representations of saints crafted out of pine or cottonwood limbs. Made by craftspeople called *santeros*, these carvings are just some of the *santos* (representations of saints in various media, from carved to painted, that are uniquely local in appearance). There's also a fine collection of pottery, hand-painted shirts, and handcrafted Nambé ware, from bowls and platters to candleholders. Nambé ware is made from a proprietary eight-metal, aluminum-based shiny alloy that looks like silver but is so functional that platters and other items can be placed in the oven or frozen to keep their contents warm or cold, making it very versatile and popular (there is a Nambé seconds outlet in Santa Fe). It is named after Nambé Pueblo.

Ortega's Weaving Shop and Galeria Ortega are both open Mon through Sat from 9 a.m. to 5 p.m.

Chimayó Museum, housed in a classic adobe with dirt floors, was originally the home of the Ortega family, ancestors of the well-known Chimayó weavers. It is situated on Plaza de Cerro, the original fortified village plaza, whose entrances are wide enough for pedestrians and animals but too narrow for cars. Dedicated in 1995, Chimayó Museum exhibits historical photographs from the late 1800s and early 1900s as well as works by local traditional artists. It is home to Los Maestros, a program designed to pass on traditional New Mexican folk arts such as tinwork, pottery, *retablos* (paintings of saints on wood panels), concha embroidery, *bulto* carving, straw appliqué, and hide painting to area teens, who can sell their work at the annual Spanish Markets in Santa Fe. Hours are Wed through Sat from 11 a.m. to 4 p.m.; 13 Plaza del Cerro, Chimayó; (505) 351-0945; chimayomuseum.com. Admission is free.

Continuing along the High Road to Taos, you'll discover a series of pastoral villages dating from the 18th century, where time-honored traditions live on. Among them are Cordova, known for its hand-carved figures of saints, and Las Trampas, with its photogenic old mission church. ***Truchas***, with its exposed setting and spectacular views, is one of the most fascinating of the villages. It is set against the boundary of the vast, mountainous Pecos Wilderness at an elevation of 8,000 feet. Several of the vintage adobe buildings were constructed by Spanish settlers from Mexico in the 1750s and show fortifications learned from pueblos to rebuff Apache attacks. Cattle graze by the side of the road, and many residents live self-sufficiently, making their own clothes, shopping at the village's only store, chopping their own firewood for heat in the winter, and relying on local *curanderas* (healers), who pick healing herbs in the surrounding meadows and forests.

Cattle Mutilations & UFOs

Reports of mysterious cattle mutilations in northern New Mexico have cropped up every few years since the 1960s, peaking in the 1980s; the most recent report was in 2007, when a rancher in a small village near Gallup discovered the mutilated carcass of one of his bulls. As with previous slayings, the bull's heart was removed through a hole cut in its chest, and its sexual organs, intestines, and tongue also were removed. No blood was detected on the wounds, on the carcass, or on the surrounding grass—and there were no tire tracks or unusual markings around the remains.

Although there has never been conclusive evidence, or consensus, regarding the purpose or the cause of the slayings, several theories exist. The FBI says the mutilations are the result of predators and scavengers; New Mexico's livestock board says they're possibly caused by secret Satanic groups, whereas others blame organ-harvesting UFOs, and still others blame *chupacabras*, or goat-suckers, the mythological creatures of Mexican lore.

The large number of UFO-theory proponents, who say northern New Mexico ranks with Nevada's top-secret Area 51 as one of the country's UFO hot spots, believe that the cattle are taken aboard the alien crafts to be mutilated. The obvious question then becomes, "Why cattle?" UFO theorists believe the answer may lie in the bovine's blood. It's supposedly so similar to that of humans that it is regularly used in medical laboratories to create human blood plasma. It's an indication, theorists say, that the aliens may be studying the cattle to find out more about humans.

Until recently, the people of Truchas did not welcome outsiders, but that has changed with an influx of artists and craftspeople relocating from Santa Fe. A half-dozen galleries and 30 or more working studios line the road through town. One of the first art galleries to open in Truchas was **Hand Artes Gallery** (505-689-2443; handartesgallery.com) on the east side of the village, which displays paintings and sculpture by local artists in a lovely, airy, open space and a sculpture garden with the mountains as a backdrop. **High Road Art Gallery** (505-689-2686), an arts cooperative on the way into town, is a good place to stop and view the work of 75 local artists. Both galleries are open daily from 10 a.m. to 5 p.m. year-round.

Half a mile east of Truchas, beyond Hand Artes Gallery, you'll find **Rancho Arriba**, a small farm and elk hunting ranch that offers bed and breakfast in a stylish adobe residence built inside a Spanish Colonial *placita*, or fortified courtyard (to protect the inhabitants from Indian attacks in the 1700s). The interior has viga ceilings, handmade furnishings, and a kiva fireplace. The guest wing has three rooms: two share a bath while one has its own private bath.

Room rates are $70 single and $90 double for rooms with a shared bath; $120 for the queen room with private bath. Rates include a full breakfast cooked on a woodstove using fresh free-range eggs from the chickens that live on the premises. Contact PO Box 338, Truchas, NM 87578; (505) 689-2374; rancho arriba.com. **Note:** No credit cards.

Northwest of Española, on US 84 in the Chama River valley, the village of **Abiquiu** is known for its most famous resident, artist **Georgia O'Keeffe**, and for the stunning landscape that inspired her, which she referred to as the Far-away. Although O'Keeffe died in Santa Fe in 1986, at the age of 98, for years people have been coming from all over to look at the massive adobe walls that guard her home in the old village. Now, if you time your trip carefully, you can actually take a look inside, as the **Georgia O'Keeffe Home** is open to visitors, albeit on a very limited basis. Scheduled, seasonal guided tours (under the aegis of the **Georgia O'Keeffe Museum** in Santa Fe) allow visitors entry to the home. Numbers are limited, so you should reserve your space in advance, if possible.

To the extent possible, the house remains as O'Keeffe left it in 1984, when she moved to Santa Fe for her final years. After much speculation about the future of her home (some of which had it slated to become a state museum), the Georgia O'Keeffe Foundation was formed to preserve not only the artist's home but her legacy as well. As former foundation president Elizabeth Glassman says, "Few places exist in America where one can see how an artist lived and worked. To experience the space created by O'Keeffe and to see the places she so often painted allow the visitor a glimpse of the artist."

O'Keeffe purchased the property—parts of which date back to the early 18th century—from the Catholic church in 1945 after a 10-year campaign to convince the church that she was serious about buying the dilapidated adobe structure. After the death of her husband, famed photographer Alfred Stieglitz, in 1946, O'Keeffe spent the next three years rebuilding and renovating the house, with her friend Maria Chabot doing the work and O'Keeffe supervising from New York. By 1949, the property was ready, and O'Keeffe took up full-time residence in New Mexico, alternating living in the home at Ghost Ranch (Rancho de los Burros), which she had bought from owner Arthur Pack, and the Abiquiu house.

Many of her best-known works were inspired by the Abiquiu house and its views, including its patio and black door; the cottonwood trees along the Chama River; the "White Place," in the distance, where she liked to walk; and the road to Santa Fe. Once you experience the otherworldly beauty of the Abiquiu landscape, you'll see why this area enchanted O'Keeffe and others seeking artistic and spiritual awakenings.

One-hour tours of O'Keeffe's home and studio are offered by reservation only for groups of up to 12 people from the first week in Mar to the third week in Nov, Tues though Sat, beginning at 9:30 a.m. and continuing to 3:30 p.m. Cost is $35 per person, with a discount for students, seniors, and museum members. To reserve a place, call as far ahead of time as possible, to avoid disappointment, preferably in January, when tickets for the year go on sale. Reserve online at okeeffemuseum.org. All tours start at the Abiquiu Studio Tour Office (505-685-4016), next to the Abiquiu Inn, 50 miles northwest of Santa Fe, just before you get to the turnoff for the village. (**Note:** Special Thurs tours of the property with the Historic Properties director, who worked with O'Keeffe for 10 years, are offered between June and Nov. During non-tour times of year, you may be able to schedule a private tour. Call the museum or the Abiquiu office for more information.)

Just down from the O'Keeffe home, across US 84, is **Bode's Mercantile** (21196 US 84; (505) 685-4422; bodes.com), the kind of old-fashioned, family-run general store that has all but disappeared nowadays. It was in business when O'Keeffe lived in Abiquiu, and ever the practical midwesterner, she liked to pop in now and then to pick up nails and other items. Open since 1919, the store has everything from bandannas to local art to hardware to some pretty good green chile burgers, homemade pies, and deli foods in the cafe. There's a gas station on the forecourt.

There's something about the awe-inspiring landscape around Abiquiu that's downright spiritual and seems to attract a global religious presence. Not only will you find the Christ in the Desert Monastery and the Presbyterian Church–owned Ghost Ranch, but this area is also home to the hauntingly beautiful **Dar al-Islam Mosque**.

The mosque was built in the early 1980s to serve the spiritual needs of the area's large Muslim population. Since the terrorist attacks of September 11, 2001, it has expanded its mission to cultivating understanding of Islam among Americans of all faiths to establish commonalities and build stronger relationships. The complex, which includes a 17,000-square-foot school and library as well as a beautiful courtyard garden, is open to visitors. After visiting the mosque, continue your visit with a hike around Plaza Blanca, O'Keeffe's treasured "White Place," a beautiful white rock canyon on the grounds of Dar al-Islam.

To get to Dar al-Islam, turn right on Highway 155, ½ mile north of Abiquiu. Go about 2¼ miles; the entrance will be on your left. When the road makes a Y, stay left. The mosque is open to visitors on weekdays only; call ahead at (505) 685-4515 to visit; daralislam.org.

STATE PARKS IN NORTH-CENTRAL NEW MEXICO (INCLUDING SANTA FE COUNTY)

Online at emnrd.state.nm.us/spd

Coyote Creek/Morphy Lake State Park
Near Mora
(575) 387-2328

El Vado Lake State Park
14 miles southwest of Tierra Amarilla
(575) 588-7247

Fenton Lake State Park
33 miles northwest of San Ysidro (near Jemez Springs)
(575) 829-3630

Heron Lake State Park
11 miles west of Tierra Amarilla
(575) 588-7470

Hyde Memorial State Park
12 miles northeast of Santa Fe
(505) 983-7175

Abiquiu was once an important culturally mixed frontier trading center. By 1793 it had a population of 1,363, and by the mid-1800s rivaled Taos as a major business center. The area was settled in 1754 by *genízaros*, Hispanicized former Indian captives of low status who received land from the Spanish Crown in return for establishing villages on the frontier as a buffer between Spaniards and Indians. Plains Indians arrived every fall to trade deerskins for Spanish horses, corn, and slaves. The 1,200-mile Spanish Trail, blazed by Antonio Armijo to the Pacific Coast in 1829, sealed its importance as a place for traders to outfit themselves for the trip to the West Coast. During the American period, the US Army used Abiquiu as a headquarters for monitoring Navajo, Ute, and Jicarilla Apache activities. It served as a Ute Indian agency and trading post from 1852 to 1873. What is remarkable is that you would never know it now; Abiquiu feels like a village that time forgot, dozing in the sun, its storied history now just a memory.

Prior to the arrival of Spaniards, the Chama River valley had a thriving Ancestral Pueblo population, drawn by the well-irrigated lands for farming. Puebloans have lived in this valley for over 1,000 years. You can view the little-known Ancestral Pueblo ruin of ***Poshuouinge***, built by the ancestors of nearby Ohkay Ohwingeh (San Juan Pueblo), by hiking a steep, rocky ½-mile trail to a vista point overlooking the ruins and the Chama River. This prehistoric settlement was among the largest in the region, with 700 ground-floor rooms and 2 large plazas, with a ceremonial kiva in the larger one. Only stone foundations mark the spot today. The inconspicuous trailhead is on Bureau of Land

Management land, 2½ miles south of Abiquiu, on the west side of US 84. A plaque displays a beautiful painting by Albuquerque artist Mary Beath of what the pueblo may have once looked like.

North of Abiquiu off US 84, you'll find **Ghost Ranch Education and Retreat Center** (505-685-1000 or 877-804-4678; ghostranch.org), which contains 2 fine museums: the **Florence Hawley Ellis Museum of Anthropology** and the **Ruth Hall Museum of Paleontology**. The entire 21,000 acres that constitute what used to be the working Ghost Ranch, a dude ranch, were donated to the Presbyterian Church (USA) in 1955 by owner Arthur Pack, one of the country's earliest environmentalists. (The ranch got its name from the *brujas*, or witches, that were said to haunt the canyons on the ranch.) The conference center serves as a national adult study center and as a steward of the northern New Mexico environment. The anthropology museum centers on past and present peoples who lived within a 60-mile radius of the ranch over a span of 12,000 years, whereas the paleontology museum's focus is fossils, specifically the study of Coelophysis, a type of dinosaur whose mass burial site was discovered here in 1947.

Hours for both museums are Tues through Sun from 9 a.m. to 5 p.m.; winter hours are Mon through Sat from 10 a.m. to 4 p.m. and Sun from 1 to 5 p.m. Suggested donation for both museums is $2 for adults and $1 for children age 12 and younger and seniors. Visitors are welcome to explore the Ghost Ranch property, either on their own on a self-guided tour or as part of one of the excellent guided tours on Georgia O'Keeffe landscapes and ranch history. These guided tours run by docents leave from the Welcome Center's little cafe room, show films about Ghost Ranch and Georgia O'Keeffe, and share the movie posters of the many movies shot here.

Ghost Ranch charges a $5 day-use "conservation fee" to explore the property, payable at the Welcome Center, which you should make your first stop in order to plan your time there and get a free map. Camping is available in a nearby side canyon and includes RV and tent sites and a bathhouse with showers, ice, a fridge, microwave, and teakettle, and dishwashing facilities. (*Note:* Views are fabulous but there is little shade at Ghost Ranch, so plan accordingly.) Basic ranch-style meals for breakfast, lunch, and dinner are served in the cafeteria for an additional cost; the set menu changes daily and is posted on a board.

Overnight bed-and-breakfast lodgings are possible subject to availability (workshop attendees get first preference). Choices include dormitories, basic rooms with shared bathrooms in the old section of the building, and pleasant Southwest-style single- and double-occupancy rooms and suites, some of them en suite. This is a rustic, historic retreat center, so there are no TVs, radios, or phones in the rooms and facilities tend toward the basic; the library, dining hall, computer lab, and coffee shop in the Welcome Center have Wi-Fi available. Concerts are occasionally held in the attractive Agape Auditorium next to the library and have included performers such as Taos Pueblo musician Robert Mirabal. Tickets usually include dinner and a concert.

Farther north, about 8 miles from the turnoff to Abiquiu Lake on US 84, you'll see a sign for **Echo Amphitheater**. Echo Amphitheater is a natural amphitheater carved into a towering sandstone cliff by eons of wind and rain. The weathering and the dark, streaked, desert-varnished rocks have the appearance of blood pouring off the top of the cliffs, and indeed, stories tell that Echo Canyon was once the site of two massacres: a party of Anglo farmers who were set upon by Navajos in 1861, and then, three years later, a group of Navajos who were killed in retribution for the earlier massacre during the Long Walk years.

Despite this sad history, this is now a tranquil and lovely spot just off the highway, and with its elevated location, it's a great place to enjoy views all the way down to Abiquiu Lake and Pedernal, to watch the way the light plays off the majestic sandstone cliffs opposite around sunset or to camp under clear, starry skies during dark nights. A paved ½-mile trail leaves from the parking lot and goes up to the cliffs, and is very popular with locals and visitors.

The attractive adjoining US Forest Service campground has 9 primitive campsites and drive-through spots for RVs, with tables, firepits, flush toilets and sinks in a bathhouse, and group picnic facilities and central water. Sites are first-come, first-served; plan on arriving early to secure one. It's usually open year-round, but peak season is Mar through Oct, and water is typically turned off Oct 31.

The day-use fee is $5 per vehicle, and the nightly camping fee is $10. Both are payable via a self-service "iron ranger" at the entrance. Rangers drive through each morning, but there is no on-site ranger.

The first thing you'll notice after arriving at **Monastery of Christ in the Desert** is the quiet. Getting there is another story. The monastery lies in an isolated but dramatically beautiful canyon along the Chama River, about 27 miles north of Abiquiu, and is surrounded by miles of national forest wilderness. The monastery was founded in June 1964 by three monks from New York, and the green-built adobe building was designed by famed Japanese woodworker and architect George Nakashima. The present monastic community began arriving in 1974, seeking the Benedictine life of prayer, reading, studying, and manual labor. After a few lean years, the monastery is once again bursting at the seams with new monks and plans to expand.

If inspiration comes with solitude, then this is the place to get it. Because the monks believe they can best continue the tradition of offering hospitality in the desert by giving their guests an opportunity to share in their way of life, limited accommodations are offered to travelers (these are being upgraded; please check with the guestmaster at the monastery about availability).

If you're planning a stay here, remember that this is not the place to bring a spouse, the kids, or even a friend. It's a place to experience as a solo retreat in silence. For overnight guests, vegetarian meals are served, and library hours are maintained. The serenity of the Chama Canyon wilderness is perfect for escaping daily stresses, meditating, hiking, and just getting back in touch with yourself. *Note:* Wearing shorts is unacceptable, and dogs are not welcome.

The impressive, contemporary Pueblo Revival–style chapel, meditation garden, gift shop, and restrooms are open to all visitors, whereas other buildings and the remainder of the grounds are private. The gift shop is filled with books, cards, and other items of a religious nature. Members of the order are relatively young and Web savvy, and run several businesses that support the monastery. These include Abbey Beverage Company, a cooperative venture with the Monastery of Our Lady of Guadalupe, which brews Monk's Ale; Desert Packaging Company, a light manufacturing business; and, in Santa Fe, the Community Thrift Store, selling preowned items, and Monk's Corner, a gift shop selling folk art and gift items. You'll find many homemade items from other monasteries here and lots of locally made gifts.

newmexicotrivia

Some 85 percent of New Mexico is more than 4,000 feet in elevation.

The monastery is located off US 84, some 75 miles northwest of Santa Fe. To get there, turn left (north) about ½ mile past Ghost Ranch Living Museum (now closed) at FR 151. Most of the 13-mile drive is not paved but is usually passable in passenger cars; however, during winter and spring a four-wheel-drive vehicle may be needed. The road is continuously graded and maintained to keep access clear; check the website for current conditions. The chapel, meditation garden, gift shop, and restroom hours are daily from 9:15 a.m. to 5 p.m.; (801) 545-8567; christdesert.com.

If you wish to stay in one of the pleasant but basic rooms in the guesthouse, the suggested donation is $90 per night for most rooms and includes all refectory meals. For a summer or fall stay in the guesthouse, reservations two or three months in advance may be necessary. There is a two-night minimum stay. Check the monastery's excellent and very informative website for the latest updates on life at Christ in the Desert.

For those on a budget and looking for a wilderness experience, free camping is available in a nearby Forest Service campground along the Chama River, where you will find a number of large, attractive, shaded campsites, vault toilets, and water. Dispersed camping is allowed throughout the canyon, including close to the river takeout at Whirlpool. These campsites are very popular during warmer weather, so arrive early to secure a site; during spring and late fall, campsites in the campground may only be used for day-use picnicking, and you will have the campground to yourself much of the time. This is not the place to come in winter, though: It is frigid, and access is poor.

Continuing north on US 84 brings you to **Tierra Amarilla** ("Yellow Earth"), the county seat of Rio Arriba County and the place named for the peculiar dirt found in the area. The adjacent village of **Los Ojos** offers visitors a glimpse at the rich wool-raising and weaving tradition of the area in the form of the **Tierra Wools** store. The shop showcases yarn spun and dyed by hand, along with handwoven rugs, pillows, jackets, and other items. You'll usually find artisans at work in the back "loom room"—you're welcome to watch. The walls of the store are lined with thousands of multicolored skeins of yarn and rugs that set off the natural beauty of the timeworn wood-plank floors. The Tierra Wools cooperative is a program of Ganados del Valle ("Livestock Growers of the Valley"), whose goal is to ensure that weaving, wool growing, and sheepherding continue as a way of life in this remote region of New Mexico.

The Tierra Wools shop is at 91 Main St. in the tiny community of Los Ojos, just west of US 84, north of Tierra Amarilla; (575) 588-7231; handweavers.com. From May 1 through Oct 20, the shop is open Mon through Sat from 9 a.m. to 6 p.m. and Sun from 11 a.m. to 4 p.m.; the rest of the year, it's open Mon through Sat from 10 a.m. to 5 p.m.

Your trek up US 84 ends in **Chama**, less than 10 miles from the Colorado border. Chama is a popular spot for sports enthusiasts and thus affords many choices of rustic, low-cost lodging. The area offers big-game hunting, fishing in the Chama River and nearby Heron and El Vado Reservoirs, and some of the West's best and most consistent cross-country skiing in winter. The town is also a popular place for the nonsporting set because it's the New Mexican home of the **Cumbres & Toltec Scenic Railroad**, North America's longest and highest narrow-gauge steam railroad. The railroad, which connects Chama with Antonito, Colorado, is on the National Historic Register and owned by both the states of New Mexico and Colorado.

The railroad offers round-trip excursions to a midway point at a mountain pass on the New Mexico–Colorado state line and back from either Chama or Antonito, as well as one-way trips between Chama and Antonito with a return by shuttle van, from late spring through mid-fall. The train has fully enclosed and semi-enclosed cars, all of which provide for unobstructed viewing in comfort during your journey through groves of pine and aspen, striking rock formations, and other breathtaking views. Consider a late September trip so as to miss the crowds and catch the aspens at their golden best. Also note that all the trips take the better part of a day (10:30 a.m. to 4:30 p.m., 10 a.m. to 5 p.m., and so forth), and although summer is usually warm and pleasant, it's best to be prepared for cooler weather by wearing long pants and bringing a light jacket.

The 64 miles of railroad are the finest remaining example of a vast narrow-gauge rail network that once connected commercial outposts in the Rocky Mountain region. Spiked down in 1880 as the San Juan Extension of the Denver & Rio Grande Railroad, the Cumbres & Toltec was built to serve the rich mining camps in the mountains.

The Chama depot is on Terrace Street downtown; (888) 286-2737; cumbres toltec.com. Though tickets may be available for purchase at the depot, it's best to make reservations as far in advance as possible. The railroad has several ride options daily from late May through mid-October. Adult fares range from $95.75 for Coach to $145.75 for Tourist to $185.75 for Parlor, which includes lunch. Fares for children age 11 and younger are $49.75 in Coach and $79.75 in Tourist.

Heading west out of Chama on US 84 (it will meet US 64 about 15 miles west—continue on US 64; otherwise you'll end up in Pagosa Springs, Colorado), you'll drive through parts of the vast *Jicarilla Apache Reservation* and into the community of *Dulce*, the headquarters of the Indian reservation. Unlike New Mexico's Pueblo Indians, the ancestors of the Jicarilla Apache were Athabascan nomads, like the Navajo, from northwest Canada. Their lifestyle was determined by the seasons and migration of wildlife, and they traveled seasonally throughout southern Colorado, northeastern New Mexico, and the panhandles of Texas and Oklahoma. The reservation was established in 1887. The Spanish word *jicarilla* means "wicker basket," after the craft for which the Jicarillas were traditionally best known.

To learn more about the Jicarilla Apache, visit the *Jicarilla Arts and Crafts Museum* (575-759-3242, ext. 274; jicarillaapachepottery.com/museum), housed in a modest green building on US 64 (Jicarilla Boulevard) in Dulce. The museum is open Mon through Fri from 8 a.m. to 5 p.m.; there's no admission charge. Please note that the museum may be closed during feast days, so it's best to call ahead. The tribe will also issue permits for camping, hunting, and fishing. For attractive, modern lodging, try the tribally run **Wild Horse Casino and Hotel** (575-759-3663; apachenugget.com). It's located on US 64; rates range from $85 for a single to $125 for a king suite with kitchenette.

Los Alamos County

Los Alamos was once home only to a handful of ranchers and a school for boys. But world events in the 1940s made this small city on the Pajarito Plateau forever a household name.

As seat of New Mexico's smallest county of the same name, Los Alamos has a fascinating history because of the role it played in the top-secret Project Y (aka the Manhattan Project)—the development of the world's first atom bomb—during World War II. For historical reasons alone, Los Alamos is an interesting place to visit, but the community also happens to be situated in one of New Mexico's most beautiful and isolated settings—both as a military requirement and as a way of keeping the international cadre of scientists content during their top-secret ordeal.

In some ways Los Alamos has the feel of a company town, because **Los Alamos National Laboratory** (LANL), technological successor to the Manhattan Project, is by far the community's largest employer, providing thousands of jobs.

LANL is operated under contract for the US Department of Energy by a private consortium called Los Alamos National Security (LANS), which consists primarily of the University of California and Bechtel Corp. LANS is tasked with safeguarding and maintaining the nation's nuclear weapons stockpile, and nuclear research naturally brings with it national security challenges. In addition, hundreds of top-notch scientists researching space exploration, renewable energy, medicine, and climate change work at the lab, and many facilities are old and costly to operate. The lab also has to deal with scores of hazardous waste dumps and a plume of chromium threatening groundwater. It oversees thousands of employees and subcontractors. Most important: The lab's original mission has changed from designing weapons of mass destruction to maintaining existing ones and preventing an escalation of nuclear arms. More than 70 years later, LANL is still a controversial place, but well worth a visit to understand our nuclear age.

While you are restricted from entering many areas of LANL, there is one attraction you should not miss: the **Bradbury Science Museum**.

This extensive museum chronicles the dawning of the atomic age by focusing on achievements in weapons development, alternative energy sources, and biomedical research. Photographs, documents, and newspaper headlines provide a time line of significant world events covering the early 1930s to the mid-1960s. Throughout the day, the museum's theater presents a 20-minute film called *The City That Never Was*, which traces Los Alamos's history with actual period film footage and reenactments of notable events in the city's past.

The exhibits are very well presented, employing lots of interactive video screens to make things a little more accessible and comfortable to non-techies. More than 35 hands-on exhibits invite visitor participation: You can align a laser, pinch plasma, and monitor radiation.

newmexicotrivia

Beat generation author William Burroughs (*Naked Lunch*) attended the former Los Alamos Ranch School during the 1930s.

The museum is located at 15th and Central in Los Alamos, in the lab's Museum Park complex; (505) 667-4444; lanl.gov/museum. It's open Tues through Sat from 10 a.m. to 5 p.m. and Sun and Mon from 1 to 5 p.m. Admission is free.

While the Bradbury Science Museum is high-tech and scientific, **Los Alamos Historical Museum** is a little more low-key and personal. It traces the area's history beyond its military role, although the war years get big play here also. The small stone-and-log museum—the former infirmary and guesthouse of the Los Alamos Ranch School—preserves artifacts from Los Alamos's past, including a geology exhibit and household items common during the war years. It also has a well-stocked bookstore.

Los Alamos Historical Museum is at 1050 Bathtub Row; (505) 662-6272; losalamoshistory.org. Hours are Mon through Fri from 9:30 a.m. to 4:30 p.m. and Sat and Sun from 11 a.m. to 4 p.m. There is no admission charge.

Nearby Fuller Lodge provided the first housing for Manhattan Project scientists before the establishment was turned into a hotel and restaurant. Today, as **Fuller Lodge Art Center and Gallery**, it features the works of regional artists in its permanent collection, together with collections on loan from Los Alamos citizens, as well as traveling exhibits. Many items are for sale to the public. The art center also sponsors various classes, lectures, and shows throughout the year.

The art center is at 2132 Central Ave.; (505) 662-1635; fullerlodgeartcenter .com. Gallery hours are Mon through Sat from 10 a.m. to 4 p.m.

Sandoval County

Although Sandoval County has led New Mexico in population growth since the mid-1990s, its growth is due to the population explosion of one city—***Rio Rancho***, a boomtown bedroom community of Albuquerque. Rio Rancho is, however, very atypical of the rest of the county. The remainder of Sandoval County is pleasantly rural, containing rock formations, forests, mountains, and Indian pueblos.

Southern Sandoval County would normally be considered more "central" than "north-central" New Mexico, but because this book is divided by county, it'll be classified as the latter. The region, however, will be divided into northern and southern Sandoval County.

Northern Sandoval County

About 5 miles northwest of Cochiti Pueblo, you'll discover ***Kasha-Katuwe Tent Rocks National Monument***, or Tent Rocks for short, a unique back-country treasure that locals enjoy sharing with visitors. The delightfully surreal, conical rock formations that are the focus of the national monument are some-what uniform in shape, ranging in height from about 3 feet to almost 100 feet, and have been alternately described as looming giant tents (à la tepees, thus the name), mushrooms, castles, and inverted ice-cream cones. They look like they could be the setting of a fantastical Dr. Seuss story.

The story of their formation goes something like this: About 6.8 million years ago, volcanic explosions dumped a 1,000-foot layer of pumice, ash, sand, and gravel onto what is now the monument area. Over time, wind and water eroded the deposits to create the massive formations. Though the monument encompasses more than 4,000 acres, rest assured that a mere 2-mile loop trail will lead you through the heart of the magical rock formations; one segment takes you on narrow trails through the rocks, and a side trail goes over the top for panoramic views. Look out for Apache tears, tiny volcanic obsidian drops, which are scattered on the ground here. Look but don't take any away; all resources on federal land are protected.

To get to Tent Rocks, take the Cochiti Lake exit off I-25, about 28 miles north of Albuquerque. Go left on Highway 22 and follow the signs to Cochiti Pueblo; turn right at the pueblo water tower (painted like a drum) onto Tribal Route 92 (connects to FR 266) and travel 5 miles on a dirt road to the parking area. The monument is open daily from 7 a.m. to 7 p.m. Mar 11 through Oct 31, and from 8 a.m. to 5 p.m. the remainder of the year; entrance gates close an hour before the park closes. Day passes cost $5 for vehicles with fewer than

10 passengers and $25 for vehicles carrying 10 or more; (505) 331-6259 (BLM) or (505) 781-8955 (park ranger); nm.blm.gov or pueblodecochiti.org.

As a side note: Tent Rocks is part of the little-known National Landscape Conservation System, which includes 875 sites spanning some 40 million acres of undeveloped federal lands in the US containing national monuments, national conservation areas, national scenic and historic trails, wilderness study areas, and wild and scenic rivers. Access to the monument may be closed due to poor road conditions or by order of the governor of Cochiti Pueblo, so call ahead. No dogs are allowed.

The Jemez Mountains, particularly the *Jemez Springs* area, are a favorite with hiking, camping, and cross-country skiing devotees. Named for the many hot springs hidden in the area, the village of Jemez Springs provides the perfect getaway weekend for weary city folks.

Let *Jemez Mountain Inn* be your base for the weekend. The main part of the inn has been the center of activity in the area for more than a hundred years, serving as the town silver assayer's office and barbershop, among other things. The building assumed its role as the Amber Lodge in 1936 until 1989, when it was transformed into the Jemez Mountain Inn. Each of the 6 remodeled suites is different, and each has a story. There have even been claims that mobsters from the East Coast lay low here in the 1930s.

Like nearly everything else in Jemez Springs, Jemez Mountain Inn is on the main drag (Highway 4), within walking distance of other places and attractions; (575) 829-3926 or (888) 819-1075; jemezmtninn.com. Rates range from $85 to $125. Children and pets are not allowed.

Jemez Springs Bath House has also been around for more than a hundred years, having originally been built by the Jemez Indians to utilize the curative waters that bubble from the ground along the Jemez River. Now owned and operated by the town, the bathhouse is bare-bones and basic, qualities that add to its peculiar attraction.

Separate women's and men's wings each have 4 smooth concrete, individually screened, one-person tubs that are meticulously scrubbed after every use, even though they may not look like it because of the high mineral buildup over time. In addition to mineral soaks, which are said to relax muscles and heal sore joints, the bathhouse offers sweat wraps and massages. The bathhouse also has an outdoor cedar tub for those who don't like to soak alone.

The bathhouse has an exercise studio and a gift shop, which features a selection of aromatherapy products and natural health and beauty supplies. Baths run from $12 for a 25-minute bath to $18 for a 50-minute bath; massages using their own proprietary massage oils and products are $42 for a 30-minute massage, $75 for an hourlong massage, and $105 for a 90-minute massage. Herbal and blanket wraps are also available. The complete Jemez Package consisting of a 25-minute soak, one-hour massage, and herbal wrap costs $120. (*Note:* Ask for a free soak on your birthday!) Hours are Sun through Tues from 10 a.m. to 6 p.m. and Thurs through Sat from 10 a.m. to 7 p.m., closed Wed; 62 Jemez Springs Plaza; (575) 829-3303 or (866) 204-8303; jemezspringsbathhouse.com.

If you like your soaks au naturel, head to **Spence Hot Springs**. These two rustic backcountry pools are the more accessible hot springs in the mountainous area under US Forest Service jurisdiction and a well-known destination for hikers. In the 1970s, confrontations between skinny-dipping hippies and conservative locals led to a complicated arrangement under which nude bathing was allowed some days but not others. Today, the Forest Service simply cautions that nudity, although very common, is prohibited by state law. Rangers also warn, "Don't drink or snort the water up your nose, because some hot springs in the area may contain an amoeba called *Naegleri fowlerii*, which can cause a fatal brain infection called PAM—Primary Amoebic Meningoencephalitis." Though deaths are rare, keep your head above water just in case.

Spence Hot Springs is in the vicinity of mile markers 24 and 25 on Highway 4, 7 miles north of the Jemez Springs Bath House, on the right side of the road. You'll see a crude parking area and a sign that says "No parking after 10 p.m." (There used to be a Spence Hot Springs sign, but apparently every time one was put up someone stole it.) Then follow the primitive, easy path a little less than 1 mile up the hill. There are no admission charges or designated hours, but it's a good bet you won't be there after 10 p.m.

For a beer and burger after your soak, check out **Los Ojos Restaurant and Saloon** (575-829-3547; losojossaloon.com), across Highway 4 from the Jemez Mountain Inn. It's been around since 1947 and is a classic spot for a hearty meal. Los Ojos is home of "The Famous Jemez Burger—One Jelluva Jamburger," and you can even play a game of pool while you wait for your "jamburger." The restaurant also serves steaks, New Mexican food, and vegetarian dishes.

Los Ojos serves food Sun through Thurs from 11 a.m. to 9 p.m. and Fri and Sat until 9:30 p.m. During the winter, shave a half hour off the evening hours. The saloon is open until 2 a.m. daily, with the exception of Sun, when it closes at midnight.

For those of you who just must include something educational when you travel, don't miss nearby *Jemez State Monument*, 1 mile north of Jemez Springs on, what else, Highway 4; (575) 829-3530; nmstatemonuments.org/jemez. The monument preserves the ruins of both the old village of Guisewa, built approximately 600 years ago by the ancestors of nearby Jemez Pueblo residents, and the mission church of San Jose de los Jemez, built by Spanish colonists in the early 1620s. The visitor center exhibits interpret the area's history from the perspective of the Jemez people. The monument is open Wed through Sun from 8:30 a.m. to 5 p.m. Admission is $5 for adults; New Mexico senior residents are admitted free on Wed; all New Mexico residents get in free the first Sun of the month; young people age 16 and younger are always admitted free.

Nearby Soda Dam is about ½ mile farther north on Highway 4 from Jemez State Monument. The 50-foot-high natural dam on the Jemez River, created by limestone deposits, does not create a lake but rather channels the river through a short tunnel to provide a small waterfall and pool on the other side—perfect for cooling off in the summer. (**Note:** The pool's depth is unpredictable because of rocks often deposited by the river; accordingly, never attempt to dive into the small pool.) During cooler times of the year, when the summer crowds are gone, sightseers and picnickers can walk up the trail that snakes to the top of the rock formation and provides a peek at the river on the other side. The US Forest Service eventually plans to have a visitor information center at Soda Dam.

Bandelier National Monument, in northeast Sandoval County, is one of the most spectacular places to hike in New Mexico. It was designated a national monument in 1916 to protect one of the largest concentrations of archaeological sites in the Southwest. It contains more than 70 miles of trails and 23,000 acres of designated wilderness.

The 50-square-mile monument is named for Adolph Bandelier, a Swiss American scholar who extensively surveyed the prehistoric ruins in the region and studied the Pueblo Indians around Santa Fe in the 1880s. The most accessible feature of Bandelier National Monument is the ruins in Frijoles ("Refried Beans") Canyon and the cliff dwellings set in the canyon walls. Most of the ruins belong to the late pre-Spanish period, although a few date back to the 12th century.

The easiest way to experience Bandelier is first to orient yourself by stopping at the visitor center and viewing the slide program and then to walk the Main Ruins Trail, a 1-mile paved loop that takes about 45 minutes. If you can stay a little longer, continue up the canyon to the base of Alcove House (formerly Ceremonial Cave). The pueblo and kiva in this cave are accessible only by climbing four steep ladders, for a total of 140 feet! This ascent is not for wimps, but if you're unafraid of heights and have nonslip shoes, go for it. Once you're in the chamber, have a friend stand at one end while you stand at the other and then quietly talk into the stone walls—it's like a prehistoric intercom. Pretty cool.

Campsites at the pleasant, three-loop Juniper Family Campground on the mesa above the park are available on a first-come, first-served basis (the campground rarely fills, even in peak season). It is reached via a side road just after the park entrance. Backcountry hikes, including overnight trips that require a wilderness permit, are also allowed if you want to spend a significant amount of time exploring Bandelier. Because there are a lot of rules regarding the exploration of Bandelier's backcountry, always check with the visitor center first. Keep in mind that, as with many parts of New Mexico, brief afternoon thunderstorms are common in late summer.

The entrance to Bandelier National Monument is about 13 miles south of Los Alamos off Highway 4; (505) 672-3861, ext. 517; nps.gov/band. The visitor center is open daily from 8 a.m. to 6 p.m. during summer and from 9 a.m. to 5 p.m. in winter. Frijoles Canyon and other selected hiking areas are open dawn to dusk. Admission is $20 per car ($10 for solo entry, and $15 for motorcyclists) for a 7-day permit; no admission is charged for those age 62 and older or age 16 and younger. Camping fees are $12 per site per night. (***Note:*** Parking in Frijoles Canyon has long been a problem; there are just too many cars during peak season for too few spots. Between May and Nov, all visitors are now required to park and ride a shuttle bus to Frijoles Canyon from the gateway community of White Rock; you may drive in the rest of the year.)

Seven of New Mexico's 19 Indian pueblos are located in Sandoval County, thereby making Sandoval the county with the most American Indian communities in New Mexico. The pueblos in Sandoval County are ***Cochiti***, ***Jemez***, ***Sandia***, ***San Felipe***, ***Santa Ana***, ***Santo Domingo***, and ***Zia***. (Gamblers, take note: Sandia, San Felipe, and Santa Ana Pueblos have casinos along I-25 and US 550, and both Sandia and Santa Ana Pueblos have top-rated resort hotels and restaurants.)

The pueblos are each unique, with varying histories, beliefs, ceremonies, and customs. They are actually autonomous "nations" with laws of their own. Many of the pueblos are similar to small, rural towns, and most have a mission church as the most prominent architectural feature, the legacy of Spanish missionaries during the 17th and 18th centuries.

Although many pueblos welcome or even encourage tourists, it's best to remember that most have been around for centuries and do not exist for tourists. If you're interested in visiting the pueblos, it's a good idea to call ahead and request specific visitor information and policies, which vary greatly. The simplest way to get information is by calling the Indian Pueblo Cultural Center in Albuquerque (see the Bernalillo County entry in the Central New Mexico chapter) at (505) 843-7270 or (866) 855-7902. Or, if you have a specific pueblo in mind, contact it directly (see the list on pages 228–29).

Southern Sandoval County

The village of *Corrales* is an old, rural community adjoining Albuquerque's North Valley along the Rio Grande. While some descendants of the area's early Hispanic settlers still farm the area, many newer residents who commute to Albuquerque enjoy the large lots for their extensive gardens, apple orchards, and horses.

Corrales, which hosts a harvest festival each October on the grounds near the historic San Ysidro Church to celebrate its agricultural heritage, has several points of interest for the weekend traveler or urban dweller who wants a change of pace. At the center of the village along the main road, appropriately named Corrales Road, you'll find several distinctive shops, restaurants, and galleries.

Through the years the tranquil, elongated village has seen quaint bed-and-breakfast inns and wineries come and go. Among the newer winery offerings is *Corrales Winery*, a few miles north of the village center. Proprietors Keith and Barbara Johnstone, who resurrected existing area vineyards, opened the winery's tasting room to the public in the spring of 2001. While the winery produces an assortment of varietals from grapes grown at other New Mexico vineyards, its own grapes are used to make its award-winning muscat canelli dessert wine.

The winery is open Wed through Sun from noon to 5 p.m., with possible extended hours during summer; call ahead. Corrales Winery is located down a lane at 6275 Corrales Rd. (there's a sign), 5 miles north of its intersection with Highway 528 (Alameda Boulevard); (505) 898-5165; corraleswinery.com.

Like Corrales, the town of *Bernalillo* is a bedroom community of Albuquerque with a rural flavor. Bernalillo lies along I-25 north of Albuquerque and is home to one of the finest restaurants in the Albuquerque metro area—*Prairie Star Restaurant and Wine Bar* at Santa Ana Pueblo. Housed in a large 1940s adobe on the Santa Ana Golf Club, the restaurant commands the most dramatic view of the *Sandia Mountains* at sunset, when they turn their intense eponymous "watermelon" red; after dark, the view is replaced by the glittering lights of Albuquerque. Prairie Star's diverse menu, which changes seasonally, is a worthy match for the view. Featuring New American cuisine with a Southwest twist, the menu includes such popular dishes as Scallop Margarita, a starter consisting of scallops, green chile, onions, avocado, cilantro, tequila, lemon, and lime, and entrees such as cedar smoke tenderloin, smoked duck mac-n-cheese, and portobello ravioli.

Prairie Star is 2 miles west of I-25 on US 550 at 288 Prairie Star Rd.; (505) 867-3327. Dinner is served Tues through Sun from 5:30 to 9 p.m.

Also on Santa Ana Pueblo, just 2 miles away and a mile back from US 550, the tribe's spectacular *Hyatt Regency Tamaya Resort and Spa* (1300 Tuyuna Trail, Santa Ana Pueblo; 505-867-1234; tamaya-hyatt.com) features yet another superb fine dining restaurant: the Corn Maiden. The restaurant's signature rotisserie meats include such game as boar, bison, and rabbit, as well as beef, pork, fish, poultry, and vegetarian options, accompanied by creative renditions of Southwest dishes including traditional native foods, such as corn, beans, and squash and wild rice. Save room for one of the pull-out-the-stops desserts. Open for dinner Tues through Sat 5:30 to 10 p.m.

Coronado State Monument, located on the west bank of the Rio Grande south of the Tamaya Resort, is popular with Albuquerque visitors because of its proximity to the city. The monument commemorates the 1540 expedition of Francisco Vásquez de Coronado in search of the riches of the legendary Seven Cities of Cibola. Coronado and his soldiers camped near the now-deserted Kuaua Pueblo, the site of the monument. The park contains a trail through the pueblo ruins, which include a reconstructed kiva (ceremonial chamber) and murals. The visitor center contains exhibits on the history of the Rio Grande Valley. You can even try on an armored conquistador outfit complete with headgear, just like the kind Coronado wore.

The monument is located 1 mile northwest of Bernalillo on US 550; (505) 867-5351; nmhistoricsites.org/coronado. It's open Wed through Mon from 8:30 a.m. to 5 p.m. Admission is $5 for those age 17 or older; New Mexico seniors are free on Wed; all New Mexico residents are free on the first Sun of the month.

The small but growing community of *Placitas* lies east of Bernalillo, across I-25 in the foothills of the Sandia Mountains. Placitas was a popular place for communes in the late 1960s, and these have now been supplanted by pricey new homes in the rambling adobe tradition, though old adobes still exist near the community's historic village center.

An interesting site near Placitas, in the beautifully lush Las Huertas Canyon, is *Sandia Man Cave*, where bones of woolly mammoths, mastodons, and giant sloths killed by prehistoric hunters who lived in the cave 10,000 to 12,000 years ago were excavated by University of New Mexico archaeologists in the late 1930s. Although it's too dark to really see, the cave doesn't go more than about 20 feet before becoming a narrow tunnel that reaches back 300 feet. Attempting to venture far into the cave may be dangerous even with a flashlight; nevertheless, the first few feet give a good sense of what life was like for Sandia Man. A brief trip to the cave is a perfect urban escape from nearby Albuquerque, providing an awesome short hike to a fascinating spot. Older kids will love this!

The cave is about 4 miles southeast of Placitas on Highway 165 (3 of these miles are gravel through Cibola National Forest). You'll see a sign marking the parking area at the start of the ½-mile trail to the steps at the cave's entrance.

Along the Rio Grande between Albuquerque and Santa Fe, right on El Camino Real, you'll find the small rural community of *Algodones*, a pastoral favorite of those who opt out of the city but need to keep their city jobs. Here you'll discover *Hacienda Vargas*, a lovely bed-and-breakfast inn that offers guests the grace and elegance of historical New Mexico. In fact, the site itself has been variously a stagecoach stop, an Indian trading post, and a post office. There's even an adobe chapel nearby.

Each of the 7 guest rooms and suites boasts a kiva fireplace, French doors, and a private bathroom, and the entire inn is furnished with New Mexico antiques. You'll find the tranquility you seek in the inn's courtyard and garden areas, which contain barbecue facilities.

Rates range from $89 to $149. To get to Hacienda Vargas from Albuquerque, head north on I-25. About 5 miles past the town of Bernalillo, take the Algodones exit and head left to Highway 313 (El Camino Real). Turn left, and the inn is the first house on the right; (505) 867-9115 or (800) 261-0006 (out of state); haciendavargas.com.

Where to Stay in North-Central New Mexico

RIO ARRIBA COUNTY

Abiquiu Inn
US 84
Abiquiu
(505) 685-4378
(888) 735-2902
abiquiuinn.com
Moderate

Branding Iron Motel
1511 W. Main St.
Chama
(575) 756-2162
(800) 446-2650
brandingironmotel.com
Inexpensive

Chama Trails Inn
2362 Hwy. 17
Chama
(575) 756-2156
chamatrailsinn.com
Moderate

Hacienda Rancho de Chimayó
297 Juan Medina Rd.
Chimayó
(505) 351-2222
(888) 270-2320
ranchodechimayo.com
Moderate

LOS ALAMOS COUNTY

Adobe Pines Bed & Breakfast
2101 Loma Linda Dr.
Los Alamos
(505) 661-8828
adobepines.com
Moderate

Pueblo Canyon Inn and Gardens Bed & Breakfast
199 San Ildefonso Rd.
Los Alamos
(505) 695-0883
pueblocanyoninn.com
Moderate

SELECTED CHAMBERS OF COMMERCE/VISITOR BUREAUS IN NORTH-CENTRAL NEW MEXICO

Chama Chamber of Commerce
PO Box 306-RB
Chama, NM 87520
(575) 756-2306
(800) 477-0149
chamavalley.com

Los Alamos Chamber of Commerce
109 Central Park Sq.
PO Box 460
Los Alamos, NM 87544
(505) 661-4816
losalamoschamber.com

Española Valley Chamber of Commerce
710 N. Paseo de Oñate
Española, NM 87532
(505) 753-2831
espanolanmchamber.com

Sandoval County Region Tourism Association
264 Camino del Pueblo
Bernalillo, NM 87004
(505) 867-8687
(800) 252-0191
sandovalcounty.org

NORTHERN SANDOVAL COUNTY

Canyon del Rio Retreat, Spa & B&B
16445 Hwy. 4
Jemez Springs
(575) 829-4377
canyondelrio.com
Moderate

The Inn at 6300
16441 Hwy. 4
Jemez Springs
(575) 829-4367
jemezsprings.org/lodging
Moderate

Jemez Mountain Inn
Highway 4
Jemez Springs
(575) 829-3926
(888) 819-1075
jemezmtninn.com
Moderate to expensive

Wild Horse Casino and Hotel
13603 US 64
Dulce
(575) 759-3663
Moderate

SOUTHERN SANDOVAL COUNTY

Hacienda Vargas
(bed-and-breakfast)
Highway 313
Algodones
(505) 867-9115
(800) 261-0006
haciendavargas.com
Moderate

Hyatt Regency Tamaya Resort and Spa
1300 Tuyuna Trail
Santa Ana Pueblo
(505) 867-1234
tamaya.hyatt.com
Moderate to very expensive

Where to Eat in North-Central New Mexico

RIO ARRIBA COUNTY

Branding Iron Restaurant & Lounge
1511 W. Main St.
Chama
(575) 756-9195
(800) 446-2605
brandingironmotel.com
Inexpensive to moderate
New Mexican, sandwiches, steaks, seafood

El Paragua Restaurant
603 Santa Cruz Rd.
Española
(505) 753-3211
elparagua.com
Moderate
New Mexican, seafood

Restaurante Rancho de Chimayó
297 Juan Medina Rd.
Chimayó
(505) 351-4444
ranchodechimayo.com
Moderate
Traditional New Mexican

LOS ALAMOS COUNTY

Blue Window Bistro
1789 Central Ave.
Los Alamos
(505) 662-6305
labluewindowbistro.com
Expensive to very expensive
Soups, salads, burgers, fish-and-chips, enchiladas and tacos, and sandwiches for lunch, and elegant steak, seafood, and poultry dishes at dinner

Bob's Bodacious BBQ
3801-G Arkansas St.
Los Alamos
(505) 662-4227
Inexpensive
Barbecued ribs

Ruby K's Bagel Cafe
1789 Central Ave.
Los Alamos
(505) 662-9866
rubykbagel.com
Inexpensive
Bagel breakfast sandwiches, salads, soups

NORTHERN SANDOVAL COUNTY

Highway 4 Coffee
Highway 4
Jemez Springs
(575) 829-4655
highway4coffee.com
Inexpensive
Espresso, tea, and homemade pastries and sandwiches

Los Ojos Restaurant and Saloon
Highway 4
Jemez Springs
(575) 829-3547
losojossaloon.com
Inexpensive
Burgers, New Mexican

SOUTHERN SANDOVAL COUNTY

Abuelita's New Mexican Cafe
612 Camino del Pueblo
Bernalillo
(505) 867-9988
abuelitasnmkitchen.com
Inexpensive
New Mexican

The Corn Maiden
Hyatt Regency Tamaya Resort and Spa
1300 Tuyuna Trail
Santa Ana Pueblo
(505) 867-1234
tamaya.hyatt.com
Very expensive
Native American– and Southwest-inspired entrees; fire-roasted game meats

Prairie Star
2 miles west of I-25 on Highway 44
Santa Ana Pueblo
(505) 867-3327
Expensive
New American cuisine with southwestern flair

Range Cafe
925 Camino del Pueblo
Bernalillo
(505) 293-2633
rangecafe.com
Moderate
Modern homestyle cooking in a Western-themed dining room
(second location in Albuquerque)

Santa Fe & Taos Region

The counties that boast the art meccas of Santa Fe and Taos have more to offer the traveler than what's confined inside these cities' boundaries. Oh, but what those city limits enclose! When people daydream about New Mexico, they're most likely to conjure up images of the historic districts of Santa Fe and Taos: the narrow streets, the richly textured curves of adobe walls, the quaint shops, hidden cafes, and ever-present art galleries—all set against glorious forested mountains.

But in this region, beyond the city limits, you'll discover New Mexico's highest mountain and wildest river. You'll also find Indian pueblos, first-class downhill and cross-country skiing, historical museums, a revived ghost town, and a mineral springs resort. But most of all you'll encounter spectacular scenery and awesome adventures no matter what time of year you visit.

Santa Fe County

It's a city. It's a style. It's even a cologne and a cookie (by Pepperidge Farms). It's **Santa Fe**, of course, and it's New Mexico's own. Set against the breathtaking Sangre de Cristo ("Blood

SANTA FE & TAOS REGION

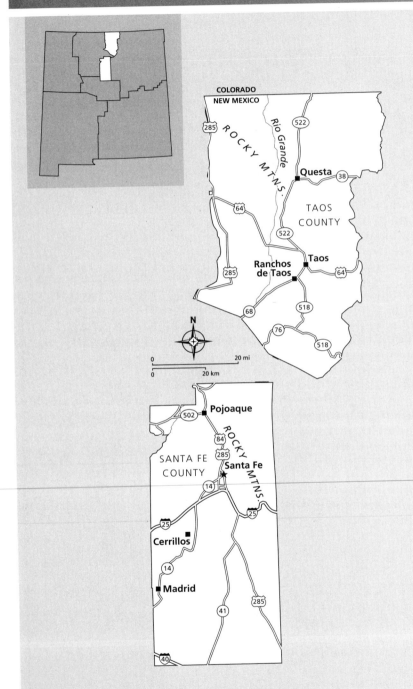

of Christ") Mountains, the city of Santa Fe, aptly located in Santa Fe County, is a city of superlatives, built around a historic plaza: It's the nation's oldest capital (founded around 1610); it's also the nation's highest capital (at 7,000 feet elevation); and it boasts the nation's oldest church (San Miguel Chapel) as well as its oldest public building (Palace of the Governors, now a museum).

Despite its fame—or rather, because of it—Santa Fe presents a major dilemma when writing a book such as this. Writing only one chapter on Santa Fe in a guidebook—albeit a selective guide—is a little like being asked to explain nuclear physics in a hundred words or less. It's a little overwhelming. Add the rest of Santa Fe County to that already challenging task, and "overwhelming" starts to be an understatement.

Santa Fe is certainly the most written-about city in New Mexico, and its labyrinthine paths have been so well beaten by visitors from all over the globe that it hardly seems anything new could be written about "The City Different"

FAVORITE ATTRACTIONS/EVENTS IN SANTA FE & TAOS REGION

D. H. Lawrence Memorial
DH Lawrence Ranch Alliance
Taos County
(575) 737-9300
dhlawrencetaos.org

El Rancho de las Golondrinas
La Cienega
(505) 471-2261
golondrinas.org

Rio Grande del Norte National Monument
(formerly Wild Rivers Recreation Area)
Questa
(575) 751-4899
blm.gov

Rio Grande Gorge Bridge
north of Taos

Shidoni Sculpture Garden and Galleries
Tesuque
(505) 988-8001
shidoni.com

Taos Pueblo
Taos County
(575) 758-1028
taospueblo.com

Ten Thousand Waves
Santa Fe
(505) 992-5025
tenthousandwaves.com

Village of Madrid
(505) 471-7605
visitmadridnm.com

EVENTS

The Burning of Zozobra
Fiesta de Santa Fe
September
(505) 471-8763
santafefiesta.org

in a travel book. Acknowledging that fact, this chapter will first offer some advice on experiencing the city's historic/shopping district, then cover a few places outside the inner core, before moving on to concentrate on those places in Santa Fe County, outside the city.

Few people remain immune to Santa Fe's charms. The city oozes quaintness, uniqueness, and all those other "nesses" that have made it New Mexico's most popular visitor destination for decades. If ever there were a New Mexico city perfect for exploring on foot, Santa Fe is it. Several museums and countless galleries, shops, cafes, and historic sites are within easy walking distance from downtown's famous plaza. Surprises lurk around every corner. To advise visitors on what to see here is pointless and would undermine what Santa Fe is really all about for the traveler: the sense of personal discovery. This is not a cop-out on the part of a lazy travel writer. Trust me.

If you must, go ahead and consult your conventional guidebook on the slickest galleries, the toniest restaurants, and the chicest shops. Then put it away and heed the following advice so that you can really "experience" downtown Santa Fe's historic core. Go by yourself—or perhaps, with a friend (a good one). But whatever you do, avoid exploring Santa Fe with a group if it's your first visit. This is a place where you tune into your senses, and you will want to be alone to do that.

Okay, here we go . . .

Take off your watch and take a deep breath. Park near the plaza, if you can find a spot. Then skip the plaza (though you'll probably want to check out the jewelry, pottery, and other crafts sold by Pueblo artisans under the Palace of the Governors portal—this is authentic and lovely stuff). Next (and this is important), head out on any one of the streets and wind around until you think you're a little lost. Relax. Drift this way and that, without agenda, entering whichever places appeal to you. Do not under any circumstances put yourself on a punishing schedule and try to see everything—you'll never have time, even if you stay here for days. Duck into a cafe for a cup of coffee or a glass of wine and rest your feet awhile. Check out the museums and historic churches, if you're so inclined. Time seems to stop when you're in Santa Fe, so above all, don't hurry. Just enjoy the sensory pleasures of the city: the smell of burning piñon wafting from the chimneys, the rich textures and curves of adobe and wood, the muted colors of the city set against that intense azure sky. You'll see much more, have more fun, and be less stressed than if you felt you had to see certain places within a specified time frame. Okay, did you do this? Good. Now you're almost ready to venture out a bit . . .

The ***Palace of the Governors***, on the north side of the plaza, served as the capitol of the New Mexico territory for over 300 years under Spanish

Colonial, Mexican, and US territorial rule. When a new capitol building was constructed at the beginning of the 20th century, the federal government planned to demolish the old adobe palace, never mind that it was the oldest public building in the US, and transform the city into someplace more American in appearance. But the building was saved at the last minute by the School of American Archaeology (now the **School for Advanced Research**, 660

Secrets of the Cathedral

One of Santa Fe's most recognizable landmarks is the *Cathedral Basilica of St. Francis*, the European Gothic-style cathedral with oddly truncated towers that stands at the eastern end of San Francisco Street, just down from the plaza. It's worth going inside this beautiful cathedral, because it has some unique attractions that are easy to miss. For example, the Chapel of La Conquistadora, to the right of the main cathedral entry, is part of an older church that stood on the site during Spanish Colonial times. The 18-inch-tall figure of the Virgin Mary in the chapel (La Conquistadora) was carried to Santa Fe by Don Diego de Vargas, New Mexico's second governor following the Pueblo Revolt of 1680–1692, and other Spanish settlers returning from 12 years in exile in the El Paso area, an event celebrated in New Mexico as the Reconquest. Every year during Fiesta in Santa Fe, La Conquistadora is carried through the streets in a reenactment of the triumphant Reconquest of New Mexico by de Vargas and returning Spanish settlers. Local Catholics continue to revere her today, as attested to by the many candles burning on the altar below her. La Conquistadora has a whole wardrobe of her own and is dressed and cared for by a *cofradía* of women.

Note, too, the keystone over the arched front doorway of the cathedral. On it are carved the Hebrew letters for YHWH (for Yahweh, an early word for God). While Archbishop Lamy, the city's first non-Hispanic Catholic clergyman, was building the cathedral, he went far over budget and ran out of money before the roof was finished. After much deliberation, the local Jewish community decided to fund the completion of the cathedral roof. In return, they asked that the inscription be carved over the church door as a lasting reminder of the unusual bond between Santa Fe's Catholics and Jews.

The roof was completed, but the Gothic spires Lamy envisioned were not. Recently, downtown real estate developers have offered to finish the spires at their own expense. Far from philanthropic, the move would exploit the Latin American tradition that no building in a town can be taller than the cathedral. Fortunately, the offer has always been rejected.

To learn more about the church and its secrets, including its private collection of classical paintings, check out the *Archdiocese of Santa Fe Museum and Archives*, hidden away at 223 Cathedral Place; (505) 982-5619; cbsfa.org. Open Mon through Fri from 8:30 a.m. to 4:30 p.m., it's the least-known of Santa Fe's many museums; even most locals have never visited it.

Garcia St.; 505-954-7200; sarweb.org), which in 1909 moved its headquarters into the palace, restored it, and converted it into the **New Mexico History Museum**.

A century later, in 2009, the state opened a huge new history museum under the same name directly behind the palace, in what had formerly been a stable and parade ground, then a parking lot. Remarkably, the three-story museum building is so well designed it is virtually unnoticeable from the street or the nearby plaza. It contains artifacts spanning the centuries, from ancient mammoth hunters to New Mexico's unique role in World War II, as well as numerous movie and video screens, a room of albums filled with historical photographs, a cafe, and a rooftop patio with an expansive view of the downtown area. Special exhibitions are mounted each year that touch on interesting aspects of New Mexico's cultural history, including one on famed hotel and restaurant entrepreneur Fred Harvey and one on New Mexico's famed lowriders, the highly artistic, tricked-out, low-slung cars that "promenade" on Saturday nights in downtowns throughout northern New Mexico. The Governors Palace, which fronts onto the plaza, has been folded into the new history museum behind it and continues to house historical exhibits.

The daily entrance fee for the New Mexico History Museum/Governors Palace is $12 for adults ($7 for New Mexico residents with ID), $1 discount for students with ID, and free for New Mexico residents on the first Sun of each month, free for seniors every Wed, free for children age 16 and under, and most important, free for everyone on Fri evenings May through Oct and the first Fri of the month Nov through May. Open daily from 10 a.m. to 5 p.m., until 8 p.m. on Fri, closed Mon off-season; (505) 476-5200; palaceofthegovernors.org.

Note: The New Mexico History Museum/Governors Palace is the main unit of the **Museum of New Mexico** (museumofnewmexico.org), which, in Santa Fe, includes this site and the neighboring New Mexico Museum of Art in downtown Santa Fe and the Museum of International Folk Art and Museum of Indian Arts and Culture/Laboratory of Anthropology on Museum Hill, northeast of downtown (see later entry). Statewide, the Museum of New Mexico runs 7 state museums and 7 state monuments. If you plan to visit three of the four state museums in Santa Fe, and other of the state-run history museums and monuments in other parts of the state, I strongly suggest you buy the **New Mexico Culture Pass**, which, for just $30, offers admission to each of the Museum of New Mexico sites and is valid for 12 months. It is available from any of the 14 sites run by MNM and can be used immediately, or you can purchase online ahead of time.

Before leaving downtown, head toward the southwest corner of the plaza and stroll down to 211 W. San Francisco St. (almost to Sandoval) to check out the historic **Lensic Performing Arts Center** (505-988-7050; box office 505-988-1234; lensic.com).

The Lensic first opened in 1931, when West San Francisco Street was still a dirt road. It quickly became known for its elaborate faux Moorish–Spanish Renaissance architecture. In its heyday, the Lensic hosted vaudeville shows, screened films, and welcomed such guests as Errol Flynn, Rita Hayworth, Olivia de Havilland, Judy Garland, and Roy Rogers. An $8.2 million renovation, completed in 2001, took more than three years but was well worth the wait. The new Lensic is now not only beautiful but state-of-the-art as well. The 821-seat auditorium boasts a revolutionary sound system that simulates various acoustics—one of only two such systems in the US—and is home to seven different arts organizations, meaning something is going on there several nights a week (200 performances a year), a plus for visitors and residents. The Lensic is a community-based theater and presents a range of diverse, affordable programming that encompasses theater, dance, music, literary events, and film.

After decades of disappointed tourists wandering the streets of Santa Fe, wondering where they could see the paintings of New Mexico's most famous artist, the long-awaited **Georgia O'Keeffe Museum** opened in Santa Fe during the summer of 1997. Dedicated to preserving and presenting the lifework of one of America's most remarkable artists, the museum houses a permanent collection of O'Keeffe's art unequaled by any museum in the world. The museum features more than 80 of O'Keeffe's works, including some of the more famous—large-scale flowers and bleached desert bones—as well as abstracts, nudes, landscapes, cityscapes, and still lifes. Private docent tours are available for small groups by reservation for an additional fee; the museum also offers an app for smartphones that allows you to explore in greater depth. Tours of Georgia O'Keeffe's home and studio in Abiquiu are available seasonally by reservation and leave from the Abiquiu Studio Tour Office next to the Abiquiu Inn (see earlier Abiquiu entry).

Tucked away behind the Eldorado Hotel (the biggest building in downtown Santa Fe), the privately run Georgia O'Keeffe Museum is located a few blocks from the plaza at 217 Johnson St.; (505) 946-1000; okeeffemuseum.org. Admission is $13 for adults, $11 for students 18 and over with ID, and free for those under 17 and members; first Fri of the month is free for New Mexico residents. Like the Museum of New Mexico, the O'Keeffe Museum is open until 7 p.m. on Friday evenings and offers art activities for visitors the first Friday of the month; most art openings take place at galleries and museums around town on Friday evenings, so it is a popular time to visit. The museum is open daily from 10 a.m. to 5 p.m. (until 7 p.m. Fri).

To get an idea of Santa Fe's upscale appeal, take a stroll up **Canyon Road**, about 8 blocks southeast of the plaza. The most coveted address in town, this 2-mile avenue was once part of an Indian trail through the Sangre de Cristo Mountains to the trading pueblo of Pecos (Cicuye) in the Pecos River valley, east of Santa Fe. By the time an influx of artists, archaeologists, architects, and other Anglos arrived here from back east in the early 20th century, it was a poor Hispanic barrio, where farmers grew their beans and squash using irrigation water from the Acequia Madre, the Mother Ditch, which runs through the area. Nowadays, Canyon Road is synonymous with art and money, though it has remained slightly "above the fray" of rampant tourism and retained much of its authentic charm. You'll find many of the city's finer galleries along this narrow promenade, as well as a distinctive medley of restaurants and shops, intermingled with some very old Hispanic homes and businesses, such as a firewood yard on Camino del Monte Rey, halfway up Canyon Road.

Even if you can't afford to purchase anything, one of the more interesting stops along Canyon Road is **Morning Star Gallery**. Though it deals in investment-quality antique American Indian art, Morning Star seems more like a museum that allows visitors to purchase the exhibits. The gallery doesn't limit itself to Indian art from New Mexico, although you'll certainly find plenty of it here. An exquisite Acoma Pueblo pot may go for as much as $4,500, and Navajo blankets from the 1800s reach into the $45,000–$50,000 range. It's incredible to see these items up close and wonder what the potter or weaver would have done with all that money.

Morning Star is located at 513 Canyon Rd.; (505) 982-8187; morningstargallery.com. It's open Mon through Sat from 9 a.m. to 5 p.m. Its sister gallery, Nedra Matteuchi Galleries, is not far away, close to the state capitol, at 1075 Paseo de Peralta; (505) 982-4631; matteuchi.com. It is immediately opposite Kakawa Chocolate House, a popular cafe in an old adobe building that specializes in historically accurate Aztec-style chocolate drinks. You won't find a more uniquely local Santa Fe experience than sampling one of their chocolate concoctions, about as near to heaven as it comes for chocolate lovers.

If you're not especially into art, there's more to Canyon Road than painting and sculpture galleries. One of the most unusual shops, **Project Tibet**, is tucked away in a cul-de-sac at 403 Canyon Rd. Selling everything from prayer flags and incense to Tibetan clothing, it raises funds for the nonprofit group that sponsors Santa Fe's extensive Tibetan refugee community, the first in the US and still one of the largest. (Tibetans from Santa Fe were once flown to the Andes to work as extras in the film *Seven Years in Tibet*.) That explains the "Free Tibet" bumper stickers you see all over town, as well as the preponderance of prayer flags in many homes. Open Mon through Fri from 10 a.m. to 5 p.m; (505) 982-3002; tibet.org.

As an aside, if you really want to get way off the beaten path to see one of Santa Fe's most unusual places, head out Cerrillos Road to the south side of the city and turn right on Airport Road to visit the **KSK Buddhist Center of Santa Fe** (3777 KSK Ln., off Airport Road; nobletruth.org). A spiritual center for Santa Fe's Tibetan refugee community, the center hosts visiting Buddhist monks from around the world who live there while studying and lecturing. The towering gold stupa, one of the tallest in the Western Hemisphere, houses an elaborate shrine that is open to the general public. There is also a Buddhist bookshop. Donations are welcome. For more information on Santa Fe's fascinating Tibetan community, check out the Tibetan Association of Santa Fe's website at taosf.org.

All along Canyon Road, some of the most intriguing places are hidden behind the buildings that line the road. Keep an eye out for **Gypsy Alley**, an inconspicuous compound full of small galleries and studios. You'll usually find food and entertainment there during the self-guided Canyon Road ArtWalks, held every Friday afternoon from about 4:30 on during the summer months.

Following an afternoon of gallery-hopping along Canyon Road, ease into **El Farol** for a taste of the unexpected, and expect to be entertained. This fine restaurant specializes in tapas, a way of eating that has long been associated with Spain but has become very popular in cities across the US, as well as in Santa Fe, which has several Spanish restaurants, including El Meson and Boca downtown. Choose several tapas to share to make a meal from the extensive menu. They come hot or cold and run the gamut from meat and chicken to seafood and vegetarian. This is a great way to sample a variety of foods. El Farol's bar has live entertainment every night, variously featuring jazz, blues, flamenco, and folk sounds.

El Farol is at 808 Canyon Rd.; (505) 983-9912; elfarolsantafe.com. It's open daily for lunch, 11 a.m. to 4 p.m., and for dinner, 5:30 to 10 p.m.; bar hours are noon to 2 a.m.

Right across from El Farol is **The Teahouse**, a cozy and attractively furnished cafe serving over 100 different teas, warm home-baked goods, and full meals in a sprawling converted adobe home. For light refreshment after walking Canyon Road, don't miss the warm, fresh-from-the-oven cranberry-almond scone with homemade clotted cream and lemon curd; it tastes delicious with a cup of rooibos or black tea. A full sit-down menu is also served all day and includes, at breakfast, homemade oatmeal, eggs Benedict, and Confetti Eggs, creatively steam-scrambled with the espresso machine, and for lunch and dinner, a variety of soups, salads, paninis, pastas, salmon, and meat entrees; beer and wine are available. The Teahouse is at 821 Canyon Rd. (at the corner of Palace); (505) 992-0972; santafeteahouse.com. It's open daily from 9 a.m. to 9 p.m.

For a quick nature escape from gallery-hopping, continue to the top of Canyon Road, turn right onto Camino de la Cabra, pass the Church of Cristo Rey, then turn left (north) onto Upper Canyon Road, which dead-ends at the 135-acre *Randall Davey Audubon Center and Sanctuary*. An information wall outside the center's office indicates the recent sightings of some of the 190 bird species and other wildlife on the grounds of this wildlife refuge on the eastern edge of Santa Fe. The main attraction here is El Temporal Nature Trail, which winds among the native piñon-juniper vegetation of the foothills of the Sangre de Cristo Mountains. It's a great spot for a mini-hike for those who may not be inclined to take advantage of the more challenging and remote hiking trails in the mountains.

Randall Davey is located at 1800 Upper Canyon Rd.; (505) 983-4609; nm .audubon.org/center. Admission to the hiking trail is $2 for adults, $1 for children age 12 and under; guided hikes at the refuge are on Sat morning at 8:30 a.m., and tours of the historic home of artist Randall Davey (the grounds are very popular for weddings) are offered every Fri at 2 p.m., $5 per person. The center is open Mon through Sat from 8 a.m. to 4 p.m.; closed seasonally from Christmas to January 31.

The Audubon Center adjoins other more recently created natural areas that make the mouth of Santa Fe Canyon a nature lovers' paradise. Across from the center, the 188-acre *Santa Fe Canyon Preserve* was set aside by The Nature Conservancy to protect wildlife habitat around Santa Fe Reservoir; formerly owned by the local water company, parts of the preserve had been off-limits to the public for almost 70 years before it was opened to visitors in 2002. No dogs are allowed, but this is a great place for a family hike. Near the preserve's entrance is one of several trailheads for the *Dale Ball Trail System*. The 22-mile network of trails among the piñon-covered hills on the city's outskirts takes hikers and mountain bikers to hidden canyons and ridgelines with scenic vistas, from Atalaya Trail next to St. John's College on the south to the Ski Basin on the north—and also practically through the backyards of some of Santa Fe's most expensive homes. For more information, check out The Nature Conservancy's website at nature.org.

Another scenic, noncommercial spot in Santa Fe is the hill on which rests the *Cross of the Martyrs*. A brief but spirited hike takes you up a trail to the

newmexico**trivia**

Fiesta de Santa Fe, held the first long weekend in September, is the oldest continuously celebrated public event in the US.

hilltop containing the statuesque white cross commemorating the crucifixion of Jesus Christ and other religious martyrs. Although there are other trails atop the hill, the primary point of interest here is the picturesque and improbably intimate view of Santa Fe and the surrounding area—yet merely blocks from downtown. The hillside's trailhead is at Paseo del Paralta and Hillside Avenue (1 block north of East Marcy); no phone; no fee.

In contrast with the museums in downtown Santa Fe, the museums off Camino Lejo on Museum Hill, off Old Santa Fe Trail in southeast Santa Fe, have an open, contemporary feel. Alongside the privately run ***Wheelwright Museum of the American Indian*** and ***Museum of Spanish Colonial Arts***, you'll find two units of the Museum of New Mexico: the ***Museum of Indian Arts and Culture*** and the more unusual ***Museum of International Folk Art***, the largest museum of its kind in the world.

Set aside a few hours to soak up the eclectic exhibits of various folk arts from more than a hundred countries. The facility's highlight is the Girard Collection, the lifetime collection of the famous architect Alexander Girard and his wife. The brightly colored displays reflect diverse cultures' special talents at channeling their creativity into toys, textiles, costumes, masks, and more. There are no labels in the Girard Collection wing to interfere with the aesthetics of the exhibits. There is, however, a printed guide whose entries correspond to the numbered exhibits so that you can make your excursion as "left brain" as you want.

The Museum of International Folk Art is at 706 Camino Lejo; (505) 476-1200; internationalfolkart.org. As for all units of the Museum of New Mexico, admission is $12 for adults, $1 discount for students; young people age 16 and younger are admitted free. Admission is free for seniors on Wed, free for New Mexico residents on the first Sun of the month, and free for everyone Fri evenings from 5 to 8 p.m. The museum is open daily from 10 a.m. to 5 p.m., closed Mon off-season.

Note: As mentioned earlier, the ***New Mexico Culture Pass*** allows you to visit 7 state museums and 7 state monuments over the course of a year for just $30. It's a great buy even if all you plan to do is visit all 4 state museums in Santa Fe—New Mexico History Museum/Palace of the Governors, the New Mexico Museum of Art, the Museum of Indian Arts and Culture/Laboratory of Anthropology, and the Museum of International Folk Art. The pass is available from any of the Museum of New Mexico museums or online, and is valid for 12 months.

To see what's new in old Santa Fe, take a detour a few blocks west of downtown to Guadalupe Street and continue south for several blocks, past the impressive 12-foot bronze statue of Our Lady of Guadalupe in front of the

Santuario de Guadalupe (ca. 1781), to **Railyard Park and Plaza**. The old railyard, which hadn't been in use for years, had deteriorated into an eyesore. After 20 years of controversy and planning, this shopping area and park was built in less than a year and opened in 2008. Besides a large children's play area landscaped with boulders for climbing and a playground of wood beams and ropes, there's an open-air concert area, restaurants, and . . . more art galleries.

A central feature of the park is the **Santa Fe Farmers' Market Pavilion** (1607 Paseo de Peralta; 505-983-4098), which houses one of the largest and oldest farmers' markets in the country, with as many as 200 small organic farmers selling their produce during the peak summer-fall season. Also open during market hours is the **Gift Shop**, selling locally made clothing and other gifts; the **Cafe**, serving tea, coffee, baked goods, and ice cream; a wine tasting room for **Vivac**, a small local winery in rural Dixon; and **Artful Tea**, which sells a selection of loose tea. The **Railyard Artisan Market** is open in the pavilion on Sun from 10 a.m. to 4 p.m. The farmers' market is open in the pavilion year-round Sat 8 a.m. to 1 p.m., 7 a.m. to 1 p.m. June through Sept; additional markets Tues from 7 a.m. to 1 p.m. May through Nov 21 and Wed evenings from 3 to 7 p.m. June 21 through Sept 27. Also in the park, the homegrown **El Museo Cultural de Santa Fe** (1615 Paseo de Peralta; 505-992-4098) showcases changing exhibits of Hispanic art, culture, and history and has a performance venue for theater groups and lectures.

The Railyard also serves as the main Santa Fe depot for the state-run New Mexico Rail Runner Express (see Central New Mexico for details). While the attractive passenger train, which began service to Santa Fe in December 2009, was designed to serve commuters between Albuquerque and points north and south, it is enormously popular for Saturday excursions to Santa Fe.

In the past, the long commercial route into town along Cerrillos Road (US 14) may have been the place to find less expensive lodging away from the downtown core. With its bland strip malls and chains, the route offered little for tourists. Even so, with sky-high rents in Santa Fe and a low supply of affordable housing crippling the city, the newer subdivisions, loft developments, live-work studios, and regenerating neighborhoods off Cerrillos around Second Street, and increasingly farther south, have become a mecca for those on tighter budgets, including many working-class Santa Feans, young people, and artists working on large-scale projects.

That's particularly true of the grittier, slowly gentrifying, mixed-use industrial zone on the south side of the Santa Fe River between Siler Road and Cerrillos (known as **SIDI**, or Siler District), where live-work warehouses and old commercial buildings have suddenly become populated by artists, entrepreneurs, coffee shops, and local businesses.

The shift has been gradual yet inexorable, and then in March 2016, it seemed to suddenly explode with the opening of art collective **Meow Wolf**'s entrancing and decidedly psychedelic **House of Eternal Return**, a sort of futuristic Victorian haunted fun house and immersive art experience. Built in an old bowling alley, the exhibit features room after room of colorful, clever, artful, and interactive experiences that engage the senses and offer fresh perspectives.

Meow Wolf is the brainchild of a group of artists who over a number of years have been slowly incubating the very un-Santa Fe–style permanent art installation for kids of all ages, as part of Mayor Javier Gonzales's ongoing initiative to improve youth culture and contemporary art in Santa Fe. The project took off when *Game of Thrones* author and local resident George R. R. Martin,

newmexicotrivia

Each August, Santa Fe hosts Indian Market on the Plaza. It's the largest Indian art market in North America and brings together 1,200 tribal artisans from across the US, Canada, and Mexico.

The Burning of Zozobra

The burning of Zozobra, a 49-foot-tall effigy of Old Man Gloom, marks the beginning of Fiesta de Santa Fe each September, the Thursday after Labor Day. The event invites comparisons with the annual artist-driven Burning Man celebration in the Nevada desert and Mardi Gras in New Orleans.

Early in the evening locals, thrill seekers, and tourists alike stake out spots in Fort Marcy Park, a couple blocks north of the plaza, awaiting the main event. The symbolic burning is a magical catharsis, ridding gloom and misfortune, in preparation for the weekend-long celebration.

After dusk the action heats up. Led by the traditional Firedancer, other dancers perform around the base of the intricately engineered Zozobra, who begins taunting the crowd with moaning and groaning as he arrogantly awaits his fate. (The moans are provided by an amplified human voice cleverly in sync with the puppet's mouth movements.) As the crowd claps and chants, "Burn him, burn him," Zozobra moans louder. The crowd's enthusiasm builds to a frenzied crescendo as the shouting continues. Finally, the Firedancer torches Zozobra and simultaneously sets off hundreds of colorful fireworks into the clear, dark Santa Fe sky.

Zozobra continues to moan until he's completely engulfed in flames. The crowd of thousands, now thoroughly primed, cheers and begins the trek back to the plaza for music, merrymaking, and dancing in the streets—now that all the gloom has been dispelled.

a big supporter of the arts in Santa Fe, purchased the old 20,000-square-foot bowling alley complex as a home for the Meow Wolf Arts Complex. Since it opened, the project has been a massive hit with locals and tourists, and the prototype for the arts experience is likely to expand outside New Mexico.

Meow Wolf is at 1352 Rufina Circle (look for the huge iron sculpture of a robot); (505) 395-6369; meowwolf.com. It's open Mon, Wed, Thurs, and Sun from 10 a.m. to 8 p.m., Fri and Sat from 10 a.m. to 10 p.m.; admission is $18 adults, $12 kids, and $16 seniors.

An aside is appropriate here: Avoid the city of Santa Fe during summer if you can. Though many businesses depend on this tourist season, Santa Feans will heartily thank me if any of you heed this advice. You too will be grateful after you've explored this captivating city without so many people. And although there can be crowds in Santa Fe around the Christmas holidays as well, that's just such a magical time to be in Santa Fe that it's hard to tell someone to avoid December, too.

Avoiding Santa Fe in the summer is, however, impossible if you're a devout opera fan who has always dreamed of attending the world-famous **Santa Fe Opera**; (505) 986-5900 or (800) 280-4654; santafeopera.org. You guessed it; the opera season runs from the end of June (with an outrageously flamboyant Gala Opening marked by elegant, formal-dress tailgate parties in the parking lot) through August, ending with the opera's "Grande Finale Fiesta." Keep in mind, though, that it's not unheard of for tickets for specific performances to sell out months in advance. **Note:** Inexpensive standing-room-only tickets are often surprisingly easy to come by on the day of each performance; call for ticket prices and details.

The community of **Tesuque**, named for nearby Tesuque Pueblo, is about 8 miles north of Santa Fe via Highway 590 (or US 84/285 and then Highway 591). This quiet little traditional Hispanic village has become quite pricey real estate over the years as Santa Feans and others have come to appreciate the simple tree-covered beauty of this slow-paced valley. Lately the famous have joined the rich in discovering the appeal of Tesuque. Whether as residents or long-term visitors, the likes of Candice Bergen, Martina Navratilova, part-time resident Robert Redford, and full-time resident Ali MacGraw have been spotted in town, especially at the Tesuque Village Market, the congregating spot in the center of the village.

If you're into sculpture, Shidoni is the place for you. This intriguing spot is actually three spots: **Shidoni Contemporary Gallery**, **Shidoni Bronze Gallery**, and **Shidoni Sculpture Garden**. Shidoni (the word for a Navajo greeting to a friend) is not only a place for art lovers to visit but was until recently an important resource for artists. Established as a foundry in 1971 by sculptor Tommy Hicks, Shidoni evolved into an internationally known fine-art casting facility. Sadly, the foundry was forced to close its doors in early 2017, but the sculpture garden and art galleries remain open. The sculpture garden is a favorite of many visitors to Shidoni. You're immediately struck that this place is special when you pull into the parking area and are greeted by colorful shapes springing from the earth. As you gaze beyond, you'll notice that there are many more intriguing and sometimes outlandish works of art positioned among old apple trees in a spacious grassy area. A crisp, sunny fall day is perfect for examining the garden.

Shidoni is 5 miles north of Santa Fe, just south of the main village of Tesuque, on Bishop's Lodge Road; (505) 988-8001; shidoni.com. The galleries are open Mon through Sat from 9 a.m. to 5 p.m. The sculpture park is always open during daylight hours.

If you're hungry after your visit to Shidoni, grab a bite to eat at the recently upgraded **Tesuque Village Market** (505-988-8848; tesuquevillagemarket.com) on Highway 591 in the village of Tesuque. This laid-back restaurant, deli, and wineshop serves great soups and sandwiches and wine by the glass; the market is known for its wood-fired pizzas, authentic New Mexican dishes such as homemade tamales, and a selection of scrumptious desserts and cakes (all available for takeout). It's a great central spot to meet with friends and enjoy breakfast, a leisurely weekend brunch, or dinner. Patio seating is available, and is the best place to sit and watch the world go by. The market, a welcome change from some of the stuffier places in the city, is open daily from 7 a.m. to 9 p.m.

While you're in the area, stop at **Camel Rock** along US 84/285, opposite Camel Rock Casino, on Tesuque Pueblo. This dromedary-shaped rock landmark is next to the pueblo's main commercial campground and picnic area. It's a great place to get your picture taken.

Its name may sound like a family water park, but leave the kids at home when you visit **Ten Thousand Waves** (505-992-5025; tenthousandwaves.com), a truly magnificent Japanese-style spa tucked into the foothills of the Sangre de Cristo Mountains, en route to the Ski Basin, just east of Santa Fe.

From the parking lot, a series of steep wooden steps ascends to the main entrance and into the lobby/registration area, where you'll be greeted with the soft sound of water falling in a Zen fountain filled with koi. The spa offers proprietary herbal wraps, massages, salt glows, and aromatherapy, among other treatments. Santa Fe is home to a well-regarded massage school and many private bodywork and spa practices, and the Waves, as it is known locally, draws the cream of experienced and well-rounded massage therapists, so you are virtually guaranteed a good experience—although this is a spa and, thus, somewhat lacks the intimacy of a session with a therapist in private practice. Massages begin at $117 per 50-minute massage.

The main focus here, though, is on enjoying a nice, long soak in the exquisite wooden hot tubs, with their mountain views and crystal-clear water. (State-of-the-art purification systems, combined with ultraviolet light, hydrogen peroxide, and ozone, ensure this; and though some of the cold plunges are purified with bromine, chlorine is not used in any tub or plunge.) If a private tub is not available (probably the case if you didn't make a reservation), opt for either the communal bath or, if you are female, the women's bath. Both are outdoors on large wooden decks sheltered by fragrant piñon and juniper trees. A cold plunge is nearby, as is an authentic wooden sauna. Ten Thousand Waves is Santa Fe at its holistic, spiritual, sensually indulgent best. If you're not uptight about nudity (bathing suits are rarely seen) and really want to release stress, this is the place to do it.

Being pampered is part of the deal. Your bathing experience includes kimonos, towels, sandals, soap, shampoo, the spa's own cedar- or kudzu-scented skin lotion, hair dryers, and lockers. Communal baths are $24.30 per person for unlimited time. The Waves' private tubs vary in style—one includes a waterfall, rock deck, and steam room; others include saunas and decks—and range from $35 to $45 per person per hour, or $53 for 90 minutes. The Waves now has three styles of lovely Zen-style accommodations available, if you can't tear yourself away. Prices range from $249 to $299 per night in high season. Call for pricing information for other spa services.

The most recent addition to the offerings at the spa is *Izanami*, a restaurant in a beautiful airy building serving authentic, upscale Japanese izakaya small-plate pub food such as locally sourced, organic Wagyu beef, chicken, and pork (no sushi or fish), homemade pickles, and artisanal microbrewed cold sake. It has been such a big hit, it was nominated for Best New Restaurant in the James Beard Foundation culinary awards the year it opened, in 2014. Izanami is open Wed to Mon from noon to 10 p.m. and Tues from 5 p.m. to 10 p.m. Reservations are suggested; (505) 982-9304.

newmexicotrivia

Renowned San Ildefonso potter Maria Martinez is credited with the 20th-century revival of Pueblo pottery. The pottery of the late Martinez is among the most valued by collectors.

Ten Thousand Waves is open daily, and though hours of operation vary for different tubs and seasons, it's basically open from late morning until 9:30 p.m., later during summer and on Fri and Sat; on Tues, it's open from late afternoon through normal closing time. You'll find this Far Eastern–southwestern paradise 3½ miles east of Santa Fe on Artist Road (which becomes Hyde Park Road), the route to the Santa Fe Ski Basin. (By the way, if you haven't already guessed, this is the perfect place to wind down after a spirited day of skiing or hiking on nearby trails!)

Northwest of Santa Fe, on Highway 502, the road to Los Alamos through the Española Valley, you'll discover **San Ildefonso Pueblo**. Set in the Rio Grande Valley, close to the Rio Grande, and flanked by vast stands of cottonwood, the pueblo is home to 1,500 residents who live in a beautifully maintained village laid out in the traditional manner with mission church and plaza. The Jemez Mountains in the immediate background complete the scene. Similar to Santa Clara Pueblo, San Ildefonso is famous for its matte black-on-black pottery, though other types are also created here. One of New Mexico's most famous Indian artists, Maria "Poveka" Martinez, was from San Ildefonso and revived this traditional art form.

newmexicotrivia

New Mexico boasts the oldest road in the US, El Camino Real ("The Royal Road"), which roughly follows I-25 from Anthony to Santa Fe. Historically, it connected Mexico City with Santa Fe during the early days of Spanish exploration and occupation. El Camino Heritage Center, an interpretive center about the highway, is located off I-25, south of Socorro.

San Ildefonso welcomes visitors Mon through Sat from 8 a.m. to 4 p.m., but you must first register with the visitor center, where you will find a museum displaying artifacts; call ahead for specific dates of events. There's a $7 admission fee per carload, and camera and sketching/painting fees of $10 to $25 also apply. San Ildefonso is 22 miles northwest of Santa Fe: 16 miles north on US 84/285 and then 6 miles west on Highway 502; (505) 455-3549; newmexico.org/san-ildefonso-pueblo. Winter hours are subject to change; call ahead.

South of Santa Fe, just past the community of La Cienega, you'll find **El Rancho de las Golondrinas** ("The Ranch of the Swallows"). This isolated, 200-acre living-history museum is part of one of the most historic ranches in the Southwest. The ranch (of the same name) was founded in the early 1700s as a stopping place on El Camino Real, "The Royal Road" connecting Mexico City to Santa Fe. The museum has as its main focus 18th-century life on a working Spanish Colonial ranch. Every effort has been made to re-create the ranch as it was during that period: Crops are grown, orchards and vineyards are tended to, and sheep, goats, turkeys, geese, and ducks mill about. Though there's a small "traditional" indoor museum on the grounds, the joy of a visit to Las Golondrinas is walking among all the outbuildings and gardens.

Las Golondrinas really comes alive during its spring and fall festivals, especially the latter. Each October you can step back in time to all the sights and smells of an authentic fall harvest from the past. You'll witness costumed inter-preters first carding, spinning, and dyeing wool and then weaving it into rugs. You can also see sugarcane becoming molasses with the help of a burro-driven press. Then there are blacksmiths and wheelwrights at work and a wonder-ful water-driven mill spinning among the golden poplars. Gourds, sunflowers, and red chiles lie drying in the sun, while juice is crushed from freshly picked apples (samples available). The stillness and anticipation of an autumn day in the country creep into your soul and take hold at Las Golondrinas and are well worth the trek.

El Rancho de las Golondrinas is located 15 miles south of downtown Santa Fe, at 334 Los Pinos Rd. Take the exit off I-25 (exit 276 coming from Santa Fe and exit 276B coming from Albuquerque) and follow the signs; (505) 471-2261; golondrinas.org. The museum is open June through Sept, Wed through Sun from 10 a.m. to 4 p.m. Admission is $6 for adults, $4 for seniors, military personnel, and youths ages 13 to 17, and $2 for children ages 5 to 12. Spring Festival takes place the first full weekend in June, and Fall Festival is held the first full weekend in October. Festival hours are 10 a.m. to 4 p.m. Festival admission is $8 for adults, $5 for seniors and youths ages 13 to 18, and $3 for children ages 5 to 12. New Mexico residents pay $2 admission except on festival weekends and are admitted free on Wed, June through Oct. Call for information regarding Las Golondrinas's Wine Festival (first weekend in July, $13 admission), the Renaissance Fair (third weekend in September, $10), and the Civil War Weekend (first weekend in May, $8).

The ***Turquoise Trail*** starts just outside Albuquerque, in Tijeras, but the bulk of it is in Santa Fe County, tracing the route of Highway 14, commonly known as the Turquoise Trail. Designated a Scenic and Historic Area, the Tur-quoise Trail connects the revived mining ghost towns of Golden, Madrid, and Cerrillos (among others) via a leisurely behind-the-mountain road that links Albuquerque and Santa Fe. For more information, visit turquoisetrail.org.

The trail probably got its name from Mount Chalchihuitl, near Cerrillos, which contained a vast lode of the blue-green gemstones and was the only place in New Mexico where turquoise was mined. The Cerrillos turquoise mines have been famous since prehistoric times, when Puebloans traded the precious stones with Chaco and other major pueblos, and even all the way down to Mesoamerica. The mines also played a major role during Spanish Colonial times, being a major draw for self-funding conquistadores, such as Don Juan de Oñate, to travel north and seek their fortune in the otherwise dusty Southwest.

The towns along the Turquoise Trail (sometimes known as the Ghost Town Trail) have a boom-and-bust mining legacy similar to that of towns in

Traditional Food of New Mexico

Holy Guacamole!

Because avocados are native to the tropics, guacamole is not a traditional New Mexican preparation. Nevertheless, in the Mexican-influenced Southwest, it's a favorite adapted southwestern side dish. Here is one version:

2 large, ripe avocados, peeled and pitted

1 teaspoon red chile powder

1 tablespoon lemon juice

1 small clove garlic, minced

1 tomato, minced (optional)

1–2 green onions, minced (optional)

1 teaspoon salt

Mash avocados with a fork and mix with remaining ingredients. Serve with corn tortilla chips. Makes 4 servings.

the southern part of the state. Mined in this area, in addition to turquoise, were coal, lead, copper, silver, and gold.

Each of the spots along the Turquoise Trail has its own charms and history, but the revived ghost town of **Madrid** (pronounced MAD-rid, unlike its namesake in Spain) is perhaps the most fun. Originally an old coal-mining town, Madrid all but died after the last mine shut down in the 1950s, when the demand for coal declined, leaving scores of similar wooden company houses along this strip of Highway 14.

During the past 30 or so years, Madrid has been rediscovered by artistic types and former hippies drawn to its funky charm. The successful revival of this onetime ghost town was even the subject of a *60 Minutes* spot in 1982. A textile importer with unique Tibetan carpets and a New Age crystal emporium join ranks with other small shops and a dozen art galleries. The entire town was spruced up in 2006 to serve as the location for the Walt Disney movie *Wild Hogs*, starring John Travolta and other major Hollywood stars. About half the film was shot inside or in front of Maggie's Main Street Diner, attached to the Great Madrid Gift Emporium (2868 Hwy. 14; 505-471-7605; maggiesdiner .com), which sells T-shirts and memorabilia from the film, among other things.

More so than many places in New Mexico, Madrid is evolving, so although this is a quiet, rural location you can expect to find something a little different each time you visit. Then, too, the weather is not the only thing that can get quite hot during the summer in Madrid—the outdoor Madrid jazz and blues concerts have become quite a popular weekend outing for folks from Albuquerque and Santa Fe.

Midway between Madrid and Santa Fe on a side road off Highway 14, the village of **Cerrillos** feels as if it's stuck in the past. Lack of water has prevented it from growing much since the 19th century, when many of its adobe houses were built. The ghosts of signs painted on its few commercial buildings add to the Old West ambience but were actually added for the shooting of the 1988 movie *Young Guns.*

Well hidden up an unpaved road north of the village is one of Santa Fe County's newest and least-known parks, **Cerrillos Hills State Park** (505-474-0196; cerrilloshills.org). Until it was opened to the public in May 2003, signs used to strongly discourage people from entering the maze of barren gray hills concealed from view by piñon-clad ridges and deep arroyos. Many small hand-dug pit mines were in danger of collapsing and burying hikers. These were the mines made by Ancestral Pueblo miners a thousand years ago in search of sacred turquoise to be used in ceremonies and extensively traded throughout the Southwest. Artisans at Santo Domingo Pueblo, a traditional pueblo on the other side of the Cerrillos Hills, off I-25, historically used turquoise from these mines for their famous jewelry and continue to do so today. There is a good chance that turquoise used to make historic artifacts at pueblos like Chaco (where it filled whole rooms) came from these mines. They were that important.

Other mines in the area produced lead, used as a glaze by Pueblo potters between 1300 and 1700. Besides the mines, other evidence of ancient visitors includes pottery shards, stone rings, and petroglyphs. Mines close to hiking trails have now been stabilized to prevent accidents.

Within the 1,116-acre state park, you'll find a small parking lot, restrooms, information kiosks, and 5 miles of trails for hiking, mountain biking, horseback riding, and picnicking, all with great views. The visitor center is located in Cerrillos Village itself, at 37 Main St., and offers exhibits, information, brochures, and a variety of ranger programs, including star parties, guided hikes, and living-history presentations. Amigos de Cerrillos Hills State Park manages the gift shop, which sells water and snacks as well as books, postcards, and gemstones. A herbarium contains 750 specimens of plants native to Cerrillos Hills and Hyde Park State Parks and is open by appointment. The visitor center is open Thurs through Mon from 2 to 4 p.m.; the park is open daily from sunrise to sunset. Entrance is $5 per car; free for bicyclists and walk-ins.

Taos County

Taos has long been a gathering place for creative people. Its reputation for seducing artists and nurturing their works began before the end of the 19th century and continues to this day. The legacy of the Taos Society of Artists and the other artists who followed them to New Mexico lives on in Taos's many fine galleries—more per capita, in fact, than in any other city in the US. Iconic Taos Pueblo and nearby Taos Ski Valley, a popular ski destination, have also brought this lovely little town worldwide attention.

There's more to Taos County than Taos (population 5,791), but the little Hispanic town that grew up around a small central plaza is a good place to start. As with Santa Fe, exploring Taos's downtown museums, galleries, and shops is best done on foot. Taos is actually composed of three communities, all with Taos in their names: There's Taos the town, Ranchos de Taos, and Taos Pueblo. Let's start with Taos proper.

True to the northern New Mexico tradition of "wonderful things lie hidden behind adobe walls," the **Kit Carson Home and Museum** lies behind a plain, storefront-like facade. But one of the most famous residents in Taos history once lived behind these adobe walls. Oh, what stories they could tell!

Legendary trapper, mountain man, Indian scout, translator, and army officer Christopher "Kit" Carson was born in Kentucky in 1809, and lived in Taos between 1826 and 1868. At the time of Carson's arrival, Taos was known among mountain men as the center of the fur trade, due to the abundance of beaver in the nearby mountain streams, and the mountain man's plan was to become a fur trapper. In 1843, he bought this 12-room adobe home as a wedding gift for his bride, Maria Josefa Jaramillo, and the couple raised seven children here. Individual rooms in the 1825 home are given over to exhibits depicting the different periods of Taos's colorful history and celebrating the trappings of Carson's adventurous life. Even Kit Carson's cradle is on display in the museum. There are fine examples of guns and a typical camp that kids will enjoy walking through. Two of the costumed interpreters are distant relatives of Josefa Jaramillo. Carson's grave is in nearby Kit Carson Park. The Masonic Order Bent Lodge #42 of Taos, founded by Carson and fellow mountain men Charles Bent and Ceran St. Vrain, runs the museum.

The Kit Carson Home and Museum is at 113 Kit Carson Rd., ½ block east of Taos Plaza; (575) 758-4945; kitcarsonmuseum.org. Hours are daily from 10 a.m. to 5 p.m.

Seven separate museums, all run by the City of Taos, bring Taos's illustrious past to life: Hacienda de los Martinez, the Blumenschein Home and Museum, Taos Art Museum at Fechin House, Couse-Sharp Historic Site, D. H.

Lawrence Ranch, Harwood Museum of Art, and the Millicent Rogers Museum. Admission to each museum is $8 for adults, $4 for students under 16, free for children under age 5; free admission for Taos residents on Sun. These are small museums and easy to access. For more information, visit taos.org/what-to-do/arts-culture/museums. Taosmuseums.org, the new website for Taos Museums, is currently under construction; check back later.

For a view of Spanish Colonial life in Taos, **Hacienda de los Martinez**, in the community of Ranchos de Taos, south of Taos, has no rivals. This fully restored compound, the northernmost destination for trade between Mexico City and New Mexico via El Camino Real, sits defiantly on the banks of the Rio Pueblo, as it did nearly 200 years ago. The sprawling, 21-room home of Don Antonio Severino Martinez encloses two *placitas* (courtyard-type areas), has no exterior windows, and looks like a fort. In reality, it did serve as a fortress against the Apache and Comanche raids of the times.

newmexicotrivia

New Mexico's state flower, the yucca, is also known in the plural as *lamparas de Dios*, which means "lamps of God," due to the bright mass of white flowers that protrudes from a center stalk within the plant. Not only an attractive native plant, the yucca has also been an important resource in past decades, as its roots and palmlike leaves provided materials for making soap and baskets, respectively.

Today the hacienda provides a glimpse back at the many components that made up the self-contained compound. A blacksmith shop, a tack room, a granary, and a weaving room have all been restored, as have living quarters with period furnishings. It's located at 708 Hacienda Rd., off Ranchitos Road, 2 miles southeast of Taos Plaza on Highway 240; (575) 758-1000. Hours are Mon through Sat from 10 a.m. to 5 p.m. and Sun from noon to 5 p.m.

The **Blumenschein Home and Museum** is an art museum with the feel of a traditional museum inside an artist's home in downtown Taos. The furnishings of the Blumenschein family of artists—Ernest, wife Mary, and daughter Helen—together with their paintings and those of other prominent Taos artists, take visitors back to the glory days of art and culture in Taos.

Ernest Blumenschein was the cofounder of the now-legendary Taos Society of Artists. The story of how Blumenschein ended up in Taos—and thus put Taos on the art map—is well-known. Blumenschein had originally heard about Taos from a fellow artist while studying in Paris in 1895 and taken the train out to Denver with fellow artist Bert Phillips. From there, they continued south toward Mexico through New Mexico. While traveling through Taos Canyon, however, a wheel on their wagon broke and needed to be repaired in Taos.

While they were awaiting the repair, both artists became captivated by the valley, its inhabitants, and the brilliant light. They decided to stay and urged other artists to come to Taos as well. In 1912 Blumenschein and five other artists founded the Taos Society of Artists, whose purpose was to enable its members as a group to exhibit their art in galleries throughout the country. Although Phillips moved to Taos immediately, it took a bit longer for Blumenschein, who had commitments and a young family back east in New York City. However, in 1919, after spending many summers in Taos, Blumenschein and his wife and daughter moved from New York to Taos and purchased the home that was to become part of the Taos Museums.

The Blumenschein Home is at 222 Ledoux St., 2 blocks west of Taos Plaza; (575) 758-0505. Hours are from daily 9 a.m. to 5 p.m.

From the Blumenschein Home, continue walking west on Ledoux and you'll quickly come to ***Harwood Museum of Art***, the third of the Taos Museums. The Harwood is the second-oldest museum in the state: It was founded in 1923 and has been operated by the University of New Mexico since 1936. The art museum contains paintings, drawings, prints, sculpture, and photographs by Taos artists from 1898 to the present. The Taos Society of Artists is well represented in this permanent collection and occupies a full downstairs room of this beautiful museum. There's also an assortment of 19th-century *retablos* (religious paintings on wood) that were given to the foundation by arts patron and writer Mabel Dodge Luhan. Special exhibitions of Taos artists and works from the University of New Mexico's collections are also displayed during the year.

The Harwood Museum of Art is at 238 Ledoux St.; (575) 758-9826; harwood museum.org. Hours are Tues through Sat from 10 a.m. to 5 p.m. and Sun from noon to 5 p.m.

Also downtown is ***Taos Art Museum at Fechin House***, located in the spectacular former home of Russian immigrant artist Nicolai Fechin. Fechin was the son of a wood-carver and found a spiritual home among New Mexico's traditional artisans. He took woodworking to dizzying heights in this small but light-filled home, which he converted from a traditional adobe into his primary residence between 1924 and 1927. Almost everything in the home is carved, from beds, chests, chairs, and other furniture to barley sugar twisted posts and corbel beams. You'll find the brilliantly vibrant portraits that Fechin was known for downstairs among all this splendid woodwork, while upstairs are rooms containing some 300 pieces of art by 50 Taos artists.

Taos Art Museum is at 227 Paseo del Pueblo Norte; (575) 758-2690; taos artmuseum.org. Museum hours are Tues through Sun from 10 a.m. to 5 p.m. Call for winter hours.

The newest museum in Taos is only open to the public for tours by appointment in summer, but for anyone interested in the Taos Society of Artists, it's a necessity. The home and studios of two of the six founding members of the Taos Society of Artists—E. I. Couse and Joseph Henry Sharp—are on the National and State Registers of Historic Places and, to mark the centenary of the founding of the Taos Society of Artists, have been designated the *Couse-Sharp Historic Site*. The property on Kit Carson Road includes the Couse home, studio, and gardens; the workshops of Couse's son; and the two neighboring studios of fellow artist Joseph Henry Sharp.

The Couse-Sharp Historic Site is at 146 Kit Carson Rd.; (575) 751-6309; taos .org. It is open for tours by appointment only, May through Oct. Call the office for details, Mon through Fri from 8:30 a.m. to 5:30 p.m.

Like Santa Fe, Taos offers an abundance of distinctive lodging. *Taos Inn* (125 Paseo del Pueblo Norte; 575-758-2233 or 888-518-8267; taosinn.com) is the oldest hotel in town and the only hotel on both the National and State Registers of Historic Places. It was originally a Hispanic family hacienda around its own *placita*, which was bought by Dr. Thomas Paul "Doc" Martin, Taos's first physician, as a family residence in the late 1800s. Doc Martin's wife, Helen, was a gifted batik artist and the sister-in-law of Taos Society of Artists cofounder Bert Phillips. In fact, it was in the Martins' dining room that Blumenschein and Phillips founded the Taos Society of Artists in 1912.

The inn's restaurant and bar is named for Doc Martin. It specializes in innovative fish, beef, and New Mexican dishes and has been honored by *Wine Spectator* for more than 25 consecutive years for having one of the most outstanding restaurant wine lists in the world (over 400 selections). The inn's Adobe Bar is a comfortable, popular gathering place for the arts crowd; local musicians often provide entertainment, and this is by far the best place to mingle with local residents. The bar's seating area flows into the lobby so that patrons can enjoy the atmosphere there as well. For Doc Martin's restaurant, call (575) 758-1977.

The restored inn has uniquely outfitted each of its 44 guest rooms with pueblo-style furnishings, including hand-loomed Indian bedspreads; all have adobe kiva fireplaces. The rooms are spread through 4 separate buildings. Best of all, Taos Inn is not only a genuinely enjoyable historic inn but also an extremely good value for both food and lodging. Because of this, reservations are often hard to come by, so book early. Room rates range from $119 to $209 per night, depending on type of room and season.

If you don't want to worry about getting around in your car, Taos Inn is the best base from which to explore the downtown plaza area, including the shops, galleries, and cafes in the *Bent Street District*, which includes the *Governor Bent House and Museum*, across the street.

Around the corner from Taos Inn, off Kit Carson Road, is another historic inn with a fascinating past that you really should not miss experiencing. **Mabel Dodge Luhan House** offers guest rooms in Mabel Dodge Luhan's original home, as well as in a separate, more modern 8-room addition, Juniper House. But as the original estate of the Taos writer, designer, and champion of the southwestern creative arts movement, this home is also worth exploring on its own. The existing 200-year-old structure was expanded to its present size of 21 rooms in 1922 by Antonio (Tony) Luhan, Mabel's Taos Pueblo husband. Spanish Colonial and Pueblo styles shine throughout.

Stories persist that the home is haunted by either the ghost of Mabel herself or that of a young Taos Pueblo girl. Apparitions aside, if these old adobe walls could talk, present-day visitors would gladly listen: Mabel entertained such guests as D. H. Lawrence, Willa Cather, Aldous Huxley, Georgia O'Keeffe, and Carl Jung here, among many others.

A whole different set of characters frequented the estate in the late 1960s and early 1970s, after actor Dennis Hopper purchased it when filming *Easy Rider* near Taos. Peter and Jane Fonda, Jack Nicholson, and Elizabeth Taylor were among Hopper's guests. (Some visitors would no doubt rather hear the walls talk about that period!)

The inn carries on in Mabel's tradition of hosting the creative crowd—many famous contemporary writers and artists enjoy the serenity and sense of history found here, and the inn hosts regular residential workshops in this inspiring setting. Guests are served a delicious breakfast buffet, either in the spacious dining room or outside on the patio among the huge cottonwood, beech, and elm trees. Wine and cheese are often served in the afternoon.

Rates range from $145 to $200 for rooms in the historic home, and $116 for rooms in Juniper House. Mabel's and Tony's bedrooms, in the solarium area at the top of the house, rent for $220 and $145 per night, respectively, and the Solarium rents for $145. In addition to the main accommodations, the recently remodeled two-bedroom Auntie's Cottage rents for $220 per night for 3 people, and has a kitchenette and patio, and the two-bedroom Gate House Cottage, with kitchen and 3 fireplaces, rents for $275 per night for up to 4 people. Mabel Dodge Luhan House historic inn, lodging, and conference center is located at 240 Morada Ln., north of Kit Carson Road; (575) 751-9686 or (800) 846-2235; mabeldodgeluhan.com.

The village of **Ranchos de Taos**, adjoining Taos on the south, is most famous for its iconic **San Francisco de Asis Church**, built in 1850. Photographers and painters have been capturing the image on film and canvas for more than a century, including Ansel Adams and Georgia O'Keeffe, who both visited Taos and stayed with Mabel Dodge Luhan. Oddly enough, it's the back of the

Whatever Happened to Hippies?

Travelers who recall the counterculture of the late 1960s and early 1970s may remember northern New Mexico as a center of the rural hippie commune movement. Thousands of idealistic young people flocked here from San Francisco's Haight-Ashbury district and other urban havens for flower children. The New Mexico commune scene became famous, thanks to the film *Easy Rider*, in which bikers played by Peter Fonda and Dennis Hopper briefly discovered peace, creativity, and free love in one such tribal farm.

Most New Mexico hippie communes failed within the first few years as their participants' utopian quest for a new social order collided with the harsh realities of subsistence farming and the prejudices of the conservative local population. But some lived on, and their influence can still be found today. Photographs of luminaries like Wavy Gravy, Baba Ram Dass (aka Dr. Richard Alpert), and the late Timothy Leary are exhibited in trendy Santa Fe galleries. Counterculture architecture, such as geodesic domes, earthships, and straw bale houses, dots the wide-open spaces wherever there are no building codes. Experimental methods for growing crops in the high desert, originally developed by the communes, are now widely used on New Mexico's organic farms.

The Hog Farm, the commune near Black Mesa where *Easy Rider* was filmed, eventually lost its lease and migrated to several California locations, including Mendocino, where founder Wavy Gravy, now in his seventies, runs a school for clowns.

Best known as the publisher of Baba Ram Dass's cult classic *Be Here Now*, the Lama Foundation near San Cristobal has thrived since 1967 as an open spiritual community. A 1996 forest fire destroyed 24 buildings, but the central complex survived. Lama Foundation still hosts retreatants and workshops.

Near Arroyo Hondo, on the north end of Taos, New Buffalo, the largest of the old-time communes, lived on for many years as an inexpensive, nostalgia-steeped bed-and-breakfast inn. In 1996 it closed down to provide temporary shelter for refugees from Lama after the forest fire. In 2001, owner Bob Fies completely remodeled the former commune to create the New Buffalo Center, an arts and education center that still attracts artists, writers, and others dedicated to living sustainably and creatively on the land. Visitors interested in their work are welcome to visit; you can even stay overnight for a donation. The property is currently up for sale, but remains open.

As for *Easy Rider*, the late Dennis Hopper bought culture maven Mabel Dodge Luhan's home on Morada Lane, off Kit Carson Road, in Taos and lived there for almost 30 years. Costar Jack Nicholson bought land for a commune in northern New Mexico but never lived there, and the commune's occupants were run out of town by armed locals after six months. Although star Peter Fonda filmed other movies in New Mexico, he never lived here, but his sister Jane had a ranch here for many years.

church that most intrigues photographers and artists. The unusual cruciform shape of the church, together with the soft contours of buttresses that support the adobe walls, is impressive enough, but the added element of the changing shadows combines to make the sight truly inspiring. ***Note:*** Photographing the mission church's interior is not allowed, but you can click to your heart's desire outside.

The mysterious **Shadow of the Cross** painting by Henri Ault is on display in the rectory hall across from the church. The mystery of the portrait—which is of Christ on the shore of the Sea of Galilee—occurs when it is viewed in the dark: After about 10 minutes the portrait becomes luminescent, outlining the figure while clouds over the left shoulder of Jesus form a shadow of a cross.

The painting was completed in 1896, years before the discovery of radium. Moreover, no luminous paint has so far been developed that will not darken and oxidize within a relatively short time. Ault claimed he didn't know why the painting changed in the dark. He even thought he was going crazy when he first went into his studio at night and discovered the luminosity.

The painting was first exhibited at the St. Louis World's Fair in 1904 and, after more than 50 years of exhibition in galleries throughout North America and Europe, is now at its permanent home. Mon through Sat, every half hour from 9 a.m. to 3:30 p.m., except from noon to 1 p.m., the church allows viewing of the spectacle by turning out the lights for visitors. There is no admission charge to the church, but if you wish to view the "Mystery Painting," there is a small charge, with all of the proceeds going to maintain the historic church.

An adjacent gift shop sells religious articles, books, and cards. The plaza/parking area is lined with shops and galleries. The church is located at 60 St. Francis Plaza, just off Highway 68 in Ranchos de Taos; (575) 758-2754. Open daily from 10 a.m. to 4 p.m.; call for winter hours.

Falling somewhere between a bed-and-breakfast inn and a classic hotel is ***Blue Sky Retreat at San Geronimo***, the latest incarnation of the renovated San Geronimo Lodge, a historic 18-room adobe lodge with breathtaking views of Taos Mountain. Not only is it a relaxing getaway, but it's also a popular retreat destination and romantic setting for weddings. The lodge originally opened in 1925 and is Taos's oldest resort—a gathering place for Taos's art and society crowd.

In 1994, sisters Allison and Shaunessy Everett purchased the closed lodge and embarked on the painstaking process of authentically restoring the inn to its original state. The dramatic pine vigas (log ceiling beams), kiva fireplaces, and hardwood floors were all refinished by hand. Each of the small but charming guest rooms features handcrafted furniture and a completely renovated private bath; many have fireplaces. In 2015, San Geronimo Lodge was sold once again, this time to Roger and Albina Rippy, a couple who had often stayed at the lodge and whose vision was to offer yoga and meditation retreats and wellness classes and workshops, as well as individual bed-and-breakfast lodging.

All the ambience and comforts inside notwithstanding, you won't want to stay in your room for long. In addition to great views of the mountains from the inn's rambling verandas and balconies, you can also enjoy the sweeping grounds that surround the lodge, which include colorful gardens, a labyrinth, patios, an open-air hot tub, and a full-size swimming pool. There are fresh preserves for guests, made from the cherry, apricot, apple, and pear trees that line the banks of the Acequia Madre ("Mother Ditch") meandering through the grounds.

The lodge is located a little outside Taos, adjacent to Kit Carson National Forest and skiing, at 1101 Witt Rd.; (575) 751-3776 or (800) 894-4119; blueskyretreatcenter.com. Rates range from $129 for a standard queen to $179 for a room with three beds; a full country-style breakfast is included.

Two miles north of Taos you'll find **_Taos Pueblo_**, New Mexico's best-known Indian pueblo. Besides its spectacular mountainside setting, Taos Pueblo gets this distinction because of its picturesque, multistory, apartmentlike appearance, a style of architecture that was common during the classical Pueblo period but is rarely seen in modern pueblos, even the Sky City of Acoma, thought to be as old as Taos. Taos Pueblo has been continuously inhabited for centuries, and Taos Pueblo Indians have lived at or near the present site for at least 1,000 years. Taos Pueblo is the only Indian pueblo that has been designated a World Heritage Site by UNESCO, and its San Geronimo Church is a National Historic Landmark on the National Register of Historic Places.

A walking tour allows you to get a feel for the pueblo, its history, and its people. Aside from the obvious addition of tourists and the various Indian-owned shops catering to them, the pueblo looks much the way it did hundreds of years ago. The rapidly flowing, crystal-clear Rio Pueblo de Taos adds to the tranquility of the setting and is still the only source of drinking water for residents of the historic portion of Taos Pueblo (most Taos Pueblo residents live in the surrounding lands).

Only selected ceremonial dances and feast days are open to the public here, as in most pueblos, and some sacred activities are restricted to tribal members only. If you don't want to inadvertently arrive at a closed pueblo during your visit (not unusual), it's a good idea to call ahead.

Taos Pueblo is normally open to the public Mon through Sat from 8 a.m. to 4:30 p.m. and Sun from 8:30 a.m. to 4:30 p.m. Guided tours begin at 9 a.m. daily. The pueblo usually closes to the public for 10 weeks during the late winter or early spring for planting ceremonies, so plan accordingly. The following fees apply: admission—$16 for adults ($14 per person for groups of 8 or more adults), $14 for students, and free for children age 10 and younger. Fees for use of cameras, cell phones, and video vary; all professional photographers and artists wishing to photograph, paint, or sketch the pueblo must preapply for permission. Taos Pueblo is 2 miles north of Taos off Highway 68; (575) 758-1028; taospueblo.com.

Taos Indian Horse Ranch, an Indian-owned venture near the pueblo, at 340 Little Deer Horn Rd., is popular with horse-loving visitors. The ranch, with 80,000 acres of riding trails, provides various rides and excursions. In winter, traditional sleigh rides are given over breathtaking terrain and come complete with Indian storytellers, music, campfires, and marshmallow roasts.

Trail guides are Taos Pueblo Indians, who are master riders but, as with most Indian people, dry-humored and not particularly talkative. The ranch features horses selected for their ability to ride responsively to the novice rider. Beginner rides are 1 to 2 hours and 3 hours for more advanced riders, who are permitted to go at their own pace. The ranch has been owned and operated by Cesario Stormstar Gomez and his family for 42 years.

Tour prices range from $40 to $110 per person. Private sleigh-ride packages are available upon request; prices vary. Because all tours are by appointment only, call (575) 758-3212 or (800) 659-3210 for reservations, as well as to get directions.

Taos County's other pueblo, **Picuris Pueblo**, is a little more out of the way, at the top of the Taos High Road, near Peñasco. It does not see that many tourists and is more representative of most New Mexico pueblos. Some people feel it offers visitors a more authentic New Mexico Indian experience than the very visible Taos Pueblo.

Despite its relative isolation, Picuris is quite receptive to visitors, and the custodian is happy to open up the recently restored San Lorenzo de Picuris Church for you to view the beautiful interior; ask at the visitor center. The pueblo's main sources of income are raising bison on its land and its majority-Indian-owned hotel in Santa Fe, Hotel Santa Fe, the only such Indian venture in Santa Fe itself. The bison meat is a specialty at the excellent Amaya Restaurant in the hotel, one of the best-priced and most attractive hotel restaurants in Santa Fe. You can also fish for trout at the stocked pond at the pueblo for a small fee.

Because Picuris Pueblo is located in a hidden valley, it was the last of New Mexico's pueblos to be discovered by Spanish explorers. The name Picuris, derived from Pikuria, meaning "those who paint," was given to this pueblo by Spanish colonist Don Juan de Oñate, who was impressed by their artwork. Although it has a population of only around 1,800 today, Picuris was once one of the largest Tiwa pueblos in northern New Mexico. Most of the population work off the reservation, and kids attend the local schools.

If you can find it open, Picuris Pueblo Museum displays the tribe's distinctive micaceous pottery, beadwork, and weavings. A gallery and gift shop are also on the pueblo, but may or may not be open when you visit, so don't rely on it. Every August 10 the pueblo celebrates St. Lorenzo Feast Day, which is open to the public. Corn and buffalo dances are held, too.

There is no fee to visit the pueblo or the museum. There are, however, modest fees for self-guided tours to excavated sites (the old pueblo is on top of the hill and has incredible views of the surrounding mountains), as well as for fishing or camping permits. In addition, there are fees for cameras and sketching. The pueblo is generally open to visitors daily from 8 a.m. to 5 p.m. To get to Picuris Pueblo, take Highway 75 east for 13 miles off Highway 68; (575) 587-2519; picurispueblo.org.

The *Millicent Rogers Museum*, the sixth of the seven museums operated by the City of Taos, is one of the finest and most specialized museums in the area. The private, nonprofit institution celebrates the art and culture of the Native American and Hispanic peoples of the Southwest. Built around the extensive collection of the late Millicent Rogers, the museum, north of town, is a living memorial to the former society heiress, who took it upon herself to collect and preserve what she recognized as the rapidly vanishing arts of the area's people during the late 1940s and early 1950s.

In addition to a representative collection of American Indian and Hispanic arts, the museum boasts the most important public holding of the lifework of San Ildefonso Pueblo's most famous potter, Maria Martinez, and her talented

The Taos Hum

On a list of things the Taos Chamber of Commerce would want you to know, its community's infamous hum may not make the cut. Or, on second thought, maybe it would. The thing is, not everyone is convinced the Taos Hum even exists, and if it does, no one really knows what it is. According to the "Taos Hum Homepage" (amasci.com/hum/hum.html), the Taos Hum is a low-pitched, reverberating sound heard in many places worldwide, especially in the US—most notably in Taos—the United Kingdom, and northern Europe.

It's usually heard only in quiet environments and is often described as sounding like a distant diesel engine. Because it has proven undetectable by microphones or VLF antennae, its source and nature remain a mystery. Taos area residents are divided on the issue, with most claiming not to have heard the hum that bears their community's name.

family. An entire room is dedicated to the Martinez family and should not be missed. Other rooms display the stunning arts and crafts that Rogers collected.

The museum is 4 miles north of Taos, just off Highway 522; (575) 758-2462; millicentrogers.org. It is open daily from 10 a.m. to 5 p.m., except Nov through Mar, when it's closed Mon.

After absorbing some of the area's culture at the Millicent Rogers Museum, head west over to the **Rio Grande Gorge Bridge** for a spectacular though slightly unnerving experience. There's a parking area on each side of the bridge. From either one you can walk across the bridge—a narrow sidewalk runs alongside the highway—which spans the 1,200-foot-wide gorge. Midway across, a small lookout platform on each side allows you to peer down 600 feet into the gorge to the wild Rio Grande. Yes, there is a railing. There's even a movement afoot to allow bungee jumping from the bridge, which proponents feel would draw adventurers nationwide. However, the plan would need legislative approval, so until then, daredevils may only dream about taking the plunge.

The bridge is on US 64, about 11 miles west of the US 64/522 junction just north of Taos. No hours, no phone, no admission fee, no restrooms.

Just north of Taos, in a remote mountain area near San Cristobal, anyone interested in literature will want to seek out the D. H. Lawrence Memorial at **D. H. Lawrence Ranch**, the second most popular local destination after Taos Pueblo and the last of the seven Taos museums, which contains the ashes of the celebrated English writer. Lawrence, whose novels include *Sons and Lovers* and *Lady Chatterley's Lover*, died in Vence, France, in 1930, but in 1937 his widow, Frieda, brought his cremated remains back to the ranch at San Cristobal for burial.

The Lawrences lived on the 160-acre Kiowa Ranch on Lobo Mountain given to Lawrence by his patron Mabel Dodge Luhan in 1924, after he returned to Taos to start a short-lived utopian community he called Rananim. Here, they encouraged others to join them in their idealistic experiment in communal living, but in the end attracted just one convert, Lady Dorothy Brett, a fellow English artist. The trio were helped by Taos Pueblo artist Trinidad Archuleta and his wife. Trinidad Archulata was the nephew of Tony Luhan, Mabel Dodge's Taos Pueblo husband, who tried to teach the European newcomers the high-desert survival skills they needed.

The fledgling commune only lasted 14 months. Lawrence was diagnosed with tuberculosis, and after that he and Frieda moved back to Europe. Even so, Lawrence's time in northern New Mexico certainly made an impact on him. He wrote, "I think New Mexico was the greatest experience from the outside world that I ever had. It certainly changed me forever. . . . What splendour!"

A visit to this glorious memorial is one of the great literary pilgrimages in the Southwest for writers and those who love Lawrence's work.

Visitors trek up the sloped walk, bordered by remarkably tall spruce trees, to the memorial site. The small, white building houses an altarlike stone marker that contains Lawrence's ashes (Frieda claimed that she mixed Lawrence's ashes with the concrete used to create the altar to prevent anyone from stealing them). It's interesting to read the comments left by visitors in a guest book inside the memorial, because they often express moving and deeply personal opinions about Lawrence and his writing. Just outside the front door is Frieda's grave site. She gave the ranch to the University of New Mexico in 1956, specifying that her husband's memorial be perpetually maintained and kept open to the public. Note Lawrence's trademark phoenix on the roof and sunflowers on the altar.

When climbing the slope, don't look behind you until you reach the door to the memorial. Then turn and be greeted by the spectacular view: Pine and spruce forest in the foreground gives way to a vast expanse of mesa-desert-gorge beyond, north of the Taos Valley.

"Brett" and Frieda and D. H. Lawrence lived in the rough homesteader cabins behind what was for many years the main caretaker's cabin. A painting of a bison by Archuleta Trinidad adorns the Lawrence Cabin. You can't enter the cabin, but you can peek inside the windows; you can, however, go inside the tiny cabin where the loyal "Brett," who was profoundly deaf, typed Lawrence's manuscripts. She stayed in Taos and became a beloved founding member of the Taos Society of Artists. Also note the huge, gnarled ponderosa pine tree under which Lawrence wrote at a wooden table. It was depicted in 1929 by Georgia O'Keeffe, in one of her most famous paintings, *The Lawrence Tree.*

The ranch remains in UNM hands, but the university reached an agreement with the D. H. Lawrence Alliance to restore and reopen the ranch to visitors, after an extended closure. The alliance is part of the Taos Community Foundation and is a multicultural group of local residents and Lawrence admirers wishing to see Lawrence's legacy continued in Taos; a grant from the foundation has allowed for a docent program to begin and tours to be given on the property, as well as restoration of certain buildings.

D. H. Lawrence Ranch is open Thurs and Fri from 10 a.m. to 2 p.m. and Sat from 10 a.m. to 4 p.m.; there is no admission charge; (575) 770-4830; dhlawrencetaos.org. To reach the ranch, head north of Taos on Highway 522 for about 12 miles. A directional sign and historical marker at San Cristobal mark the turnoff. The ranch and memorial are about 7 miles off the highway, at the end of a dirt road that climbs into the mountains.

Fort Burgwin, an 1850s fort south of Taos, protected past residents from Apache and Comanche raids. It was rescued from ruin and restored by Southern Methodist University and opened as an external campus of the school in 1974. Fort Burgwin Research Center may be their school campus for the students fortunate enough to study here, but to the rest of us it's a great destination from June through mid-August, when it hosts several public events, including evening lectures, art exhibits, and music, theater, and dance performances. Call for the schedule. Fort Burgwin is located at the top of the Taos High Road in Ranchos de Taos, at 6580 Hwy. 518; (575) 758-8322; smu.edu/Taos/FortBurgwin.

Red River State Fish Hatchery, near the community of Questa, is one of those rare functional places that double as tourist attractions. New Mexico is fortunate to have many hatcheries, thus ensuring a steady supply of fish to stock the state's many streams, rivers, and lakes.

Located within the Carson National Forest, the hatchery offers a delightful setting. It was originally built in 1941 and then totally reconstructed during 1985–1986. Pick up a brochure in the unstaffed visitor center to follow the self-guided tour of the hatchery facilities. You'll see huge rainbow trout at the display ponds, as well as fish in various stages of growth, from their beginning as eggs to their development into fully mature trout. The hatchery, New Mexico's largest, produces 1.7 million pounds of trout annually, half of which is used to stock New Mexico ponds and streams. The hatchery is gradually returning to full operational numbers after a decade of dealing with whirling disease, which affected all New Mexico fisheries from 1999 to 2009.

Picnic tables dot the scenic 2-mile drive on Highway 515, which connects the hatchery to Highway 522, 2½ miles south of the artsy village of Questa; (575) 586-0222; wildlife.state.us.nm/fishing/fish-hatcheries. Visitors are welcome daily from 8 a.m. to 5 p.m. There's no admission charge.

Taos County also offers an array of choices for the outdoor adventurer. From world-class skiing at ***Taos Ski Valley*** to whitewater river rafting in the Rio Grande Gorge and everything in between, Taos provides an inspiring setting with incredible scenery during every season.

Taos Ski Valley is simply New Mexico's finest ski resort. Built in the European tradition and nurtured by Ernie Blake, the father of New Mexico skiing, Taos Ski Valley delivers an extraordinary ski experience. *Skiing* magazine says, "The secret of Taos is in the mixture. Take European style, southwestern flavor, perfect snow and exquisite mountains and stir. . . . Taos Ski Valley is a resort to fall in love with, whatever your ability." And the *London Times* says, "Without any argument the best ski resort in the world. Small, intimate and endlessly challenging, Taos simply has no equal." Enough said. Taos Ski Valley is just

Forest Magic Preserved with "Zero Impact" Ethics

Despite its image as a desert, New Mexico is blessed with 20 million acres of forested land, almost half of which makes up the state's five national forests. Scattered throughout its high-desert landscape, these mountainous areas are not only wildlife habitat but also green oases where human visitors can escape the summer heat and find physical, mental, and spiritual retreat among the fragrant conifers and web of life that these national treasures contain.

New Mexico forests include Gila National Forest (southwestern mountains), Cibola National Forest (central and western mountains), Santa Fe National Forest (north-central mountains), Carson National Forest (Taos and northernmost mountains), and Lincoln National Forest (southeastern mountains). In addition, within these national forests and elsewhere in the state are 26 protected wilderness areas, where no motorized activity is allowed except hiking, backpacking, camping, and horseback riding and llama trekking. To keep these backcountry areas in their wild and pristine state, it's necessary to practice zero-impact ethics by remembering two basic US Forest Service commandments: Make it hard for others to notice you, and leave no record of your visit.

minutes away from Taos on Highway 150 via Highway 522; (575) 776-2291; skitaos.com. See page 231 for ski area information.

There's no shortage of lodging near Taos Ski Valley, but the **Cottonwood Inn** in Arroyo Seco is one of the nicest properties in the area. Originally built in the 1940s, on 4 acres, the Cottonwood came into its own as the residence of the flamboyant artist Wolfgang Pogzeba, who expanded the original structure to accommodate his visiting art patrons.

Recently, the Pueblo Revival–style inn has been converted from a bed-and-breakfast inn with 8 rooms to a slimmed-down vacation rental property offering 2 large, self-contained, self-catering suites with beautiful views that can sleep four people. Each suite—the Mesa Vista and Patio—is unique in style and decor and has a private hot tub, whirlpool baths, original art, locally handcrafted furnishings, a kitchen, a fireplace, patios, and outdoor grills. The common areas of the inn display an impressive collection of Taos art and regional artifacts. The grounds encompass a grove of cottonwoods, thus the name, and extensive herb and colorful perennial gardens. The inn also has an outdoor hot tub. The owners, Shantal and Bradley Goodwin, still live on the property (in the main house) but no longer provide housekeeping or daily breakfast as part of the rate (with advance notice, it can be ordered for an extra fee). They will supply you with fresh farm eggs, locally roasted coffee beans, and homemade goodies, though.

The Cottonwood is located just off Highway 150 (Ski Valley Road) near the junction with Highway 230; (575) 776-5826 or (800) 324-7120; bnblist.com/new-mexico-bed-and-breakfast-directory/cottonwood-inn-arroyo-new-mexico. Call for rates (higher during the Christmas break).

On March 25, 2013, President Barack Obama delighted New Mexicans when he designated the 48-mile stretch of "wild and scenic river" in northern New Mexico that includes the 18,000-acre Wild Rivers Recreation Area into the expanded 242,500-acre *Rio Grande del Norte National Monument*. The area where the wild Rio Grande has carved an 800-foot-deep gorge into the volcanic plateau north of Taos was first protected when Congress passed the Wild and Scenic Rivers Act in 1968; however, environmental advocates, river-running companies, politicians, and outdoorsy New Mexicans alike had long argued that it merited greater protection.

The new national monument will remain undeveloped but be afforded greater protection of its unique natural and cultural treasures under the law. It will continue to be managed by the Bureau of Land Management, which operates 2 visitor centers in the monument: Rio Grande Gorge Visitor Center at Orilla Verde Recreation Area, south of Taos, and Wild Rivers Visitor Center in Cerro, 20 miles northwest of Questa, north of Taos. Each offers information and permits for outdoor recreation. This is also the place to view exhibits on the fascinating Rio Grande rift zone geology of the area, as well as learn about the rock art and other American Indian artifacts in the monument, the traditional homeland of the Jicarilla Apache and Utes, and the northern pueblos of Taos and Picuris.

The area of the monument between Taos and the Colorado border is quite deserted country, but when the weather is fair, canoeists and kayakers flock here. The Wild Rivers Backcountry Byway follows the rim for 22 miles and offers great scenery and photo and wildlife-viewing opportunities, as well as access to 5 developed campgrounds, primitive hike-in campsites within the gorge, and 10 hiking and mountain-biking rim and river trails. Guided hikes and regular campfire presentations are offered during summer. There are picnic facilities if you just want to peer into the vast starkness of the gorge—and you might just see a soaring bald eagle.

To get to the Wild Rivers Visitor Center (1120 Cerro Rd., Cerro; 575-586-1150; blm.gov), head 3 miles north of Questa on Highway 522, then go west on Highway 538 for 17 miles. You'll see signs. Visitor center hours are daily from 10 a.m. to 4 p.m., Memorial Day weekend through Labor Day weekend; however, the Wild Rivers area is open year-round for camping, hiking, fishing, and sightseeing. The day-use fee is $3 per vehicle; camping fees range from $5 per night for hike-in riverbank sites to $7 per night in the developed campground.

For the less active outdoor enthusiast—or for active ones just wanting a break and some breathtaking scenery—there's the **Enchanted Circle** drive. The Enchanted Circle is the name for the communities and countryside surrounding **Wheeler Peak**, New Mexico's highest spot, at 13,161 feet. The loop, which involves several highways, connects the towns of Taos, Arroyo Hondo, Questa, and Red River in Taos County with Angel Fire and Eagle Nest in Colfax County (see pages 117 and 167). Although the views of many areas in the Enchanted Circle are spectacular all year, they really shine during autumn—most specifically during late September and early October, when the aspens and Gambel oaks give their all before colder weather forces them to drop their ocher and amber leaves.

The most scenic stretch can be accessed by taking US 64 in Taos northeast to Eagle Nest and then Highway 38 north to Red River. At a leisurely pace, the drive should take less than two hours.

Red River is an unabashedly successful tourist town charmed with a beautiful storybook setting. Like so many western resort areas (Aspen and Telluride come to mind), Red River started out as a mining town in the 1800s but was savvy enough to capitalize on its mountains and snow when the mines played out. Winter visitors enjoy the family-oriented Red River Ski Area, and year-round visitors enjoy the shopping, food, and scenery. Red River has its own funky appeal, blending a European-chalet style with a big dose of the Old West. Red River is on Highway 38, between Questa and Eagle Nest.

The tiny southeastern Taos County town of **Ojo Caliente** ("Hot Spring") possesses a marvelous secret bubbling up from the earth. And **Ojo Caliente Mineral Springs**, one of North America's oldest health resorts, is here to take advantage of it. The outdoor pool, with its sandy bottom and rock grotto appeal, and basic historic accommodations at Ojo Caliente were once rather plain and limited, which was just fine with generations of New Mexico residents, who loved the funky appeal, rock-bottom prices, and authenticity of these ancient healing waters. In recent years, new owners have spiffed up the place in a bid to attract guests from farther afield with more luxurious tastes and deeper pockets, and it has become pricier. Ojo's appeal remains much the same, though: This is the place in northern New Mexico to visit if you want to relax—totally—in a lovely outdoor setting.

Separate women's and men's bathhouses open onto pools and tubs for soaking in the natural therapeutic mineral waters that have been attracting folks to this area for probably 2,000 years, starting with the ancestors of New Mexico's Pueblo Indians. The Spanish explorer Cabeza de Vaca described his journey to Ojo Caliente this way: "The greatest treasure that I found these strange people to possess are some hot springs which burst out at the foot of a mountain that gives evidence of being an active volcano. So powerful are the chemicals contained in this water that the inhabitants have a belief that they were given to them by their gods. These springs I have named Ojo Caliente."

Hotel and cabin accommodations are available, and the excellent Artesian Restaurant specializes in healthful, globally inspired, spa-style meals featuring fish, chicken, and vegetarian fare as well as New Mexican foods. But the mineral waters are the focus at the resort: iron and arsenic for soaking; iron, arsenic, lithia, and soda for drinking. (***Note:*** The arsenic mineral water has only a trace of arsenic and is said to benefit persons with arthritis, rheumatism, and stomach ulcers as well as to promote relief of burns and eczema.) Various massages, herbal wraps, facials, and rubs are also available; the Milagro Wrap, the most famous of the treatments, involves swaddling the guest in woolen blankets and relaxing in a darkened room. Massages here are very good, with all of the therapists seasoned bodyworkers with healing hands.

The resort is located at 50 Los Banos Dr., Ojo Caliente, off Highway 285; (575) 583-2233 or (800) 222-9162; ojospa.com. Hours are daily from 8 a.m. to 10 p.m.; private pools from 9 a.m. to 10 p.m. Accommodations range from $149 to $169 for rooms without baths in the historic hotel (guests bathe in the bathhouse) to $329 to $399 for the new luxury cliffside suites with private patios and hot tubs. Room rates include use of hot springs; soaks, including wraps, are variably priced. Call for details. Day rates for bathing in the different pools are $20 weekdays, $32 weekends; sunset rates (after 6 p.m.) are $16 weekdays and $28 weekends. Private pools are also available. Rates start at $45 for two for 50 minutes during the day; $55 evenings. Bathing suits must be worn in the public pools, but the 3 private pools are clothing optional.

Where to Stay in the Santa Fe & Taos Region

SANTA FE COUNTY

Hotel Santa Fe
1501 Paseo de Peralta
Santa Fe
(505) 982-1200
(800) 825-9876
hotelsantafe.com
Expensive to very expensive

Inn & Spa at Loretto
211 Old Santa Fe Trail
Santa Fe
(505) 988-5531
(800) 727-5531
innatloretto.com
Expensive to very expensive

Inn of the Anasazi
113 Washington Ave.
Santa Fe
(505) 988-3030
(888) ROSEWOOD
rosewoodhotels.com/en/
inn-of-the-anasazi-santa-fe
Very expensive

La Fonda
100 E. San Francisco
Santa Fe
(505) 982-5511
(800) 523-5002
lafondasantafe.com
Very expensive

La Posada de Santa Fe
330 E. Palace Ave.
Santa Fe
(505) 986-0000
(855) 278-5276
laposadadesantafe.com
Very expensive

Santa Fe Sage Inn
725 Cerrillos Rd. (next to Whole Foods)
Santa Fe
(505) 982-5952
santafesageinn.com
Moderate

Silver Saddle Motel
2810 Cerrillos Rd. (next to Jackalope Furniture)
Santa Fe
(505) 471-7663
santafesilversaddlemotel
.com
Inexpensive
Note: Dog-friendly—weekly rates also available for select studio units; rooms with dog-friendly kitchenettes are suitable for longer stays.)

Ten Thousand Waves
Hyde Park Road
Santa Fe
(505) 992-5025
tenthousandwaves.com/
lodging
Very expensive

TAOS COUNTY

Blue Sky Retreat at San Geronimo
1101 Witt Rd.
Taos
(575) 751-3776
(800) 894-4119
blueskyretreatcenter.com
Moderate to very expensive

Cottonwood Inn
Off Highway 150 (Ski Valley Road)
Near junction with Highway 230
Arroyo Hondo
(575) 776-5826
(800) 324-7120
Expensive

Mabel Dodge Luhan House
240 Morada Ln.
North of Kit Carson Road
Taos
(575) 751-9686
(800) 846-2235
mabeldodgeluhan.com
Moderate to very expensive

Taos Inn
125 Paseo del Pueblo Norte
Taos
(575) 758-2233
(888) 518-8267
taosinn.com
Moderate to very expensive

Where to Eat in the Santa Fe & Taos Region

SANTA FE COUNTY

Amaya
1501 Paseo de Peralta
(inside Hotel Santa Fe)
(505) 982-1200
(800) 825-9876
hotelsantafe.com
Moderate to very expensive
Modern southwestern
cuisine with American
Indian influences; excellent-
value 3-course prix fixe
dinner

Cafe Fina
624 Old Las Vegas Hwy.
Santa Fe
(505) 466-3886
cafefina.com
Inexpensive to moderate
Modern American comfort
food in a converted gas
station at I-25 and US 285

Cafe Pasqual's
121 Don Gaspar Ave.
Santa Fe
(505) 983-9340
pasquals.com
Expensive to very
expensive
Superb organic, Mexican
fusion cuisine from
Katherine Kagel, a cohort
of California's Alice Waters

El Farol
808 Canyon Rd.
Santa Fe
(505) 983-9912
elfarolsantafe.com
Moderate
Tapas and other Spanish
dishes

Gabriel's
US 285 (15 minutes north
of Santa Fe,
2 miles north of Camel
Rock Casino)
(505) 455-7000
gabrielsofsantafe.com
Moderate to expensive
Innovative New Mexican
and Mexican

Harry's Roadhouse
96 Old Las Vegas Hwy.
Santa Fe
(505) 989-4629
Inexpensive to moderate
Globally inspired comfort
food, including homemade
pies

Izanami
21 Ten Thousand Waves
Way
Santa Fe
(505) 982-9304
tenthousandwaves.com/
food
Moderate
Upscale izakaya small-plate
Japanese bar food in a
James Beard–nominated
restaurant at the foothills
spa

Jambo Cafe
2010 Cerrillos Rd. (College
Plaza)
Santa Fe
(505) 473-1269
jambocafe.net
Inexpensive to moderate
Award-winning West
African cuisine

Restaurant Martin
526 Galisteo St.
Santa Fe
(505) 820-0919
restaurantmartinsantafe
.com
Moderate to very expensive
Award-winning progressive
American cuisine

Rio Chama Steakhouse
414 Old Santa Fe Trail
Santa Fe
(505) 955-0765
riochamasteakhouse.com
Moderate to very expensive
Steaks, seafood (small and
large plates)

The Teahouse
821 Canyon Rd.
Santa Fe
(505) 992-0972
teahousesantafe.com
Inexpensive to moderate
Sit-down teahouse serving
over 100 teas, homemade
scones and preserves, and
hot meals

Tune-Up Cafe
1115 Hickox St.
Santa Fe
(505) 983-7060
tuneupcafe.com
Inexpensive
New Mexican and
Salvadoran specialties

SELECTED CHAMBERS OF COMMERCE/ VISITOR BUREAUS IN SANTA FE & TAOS REGION

Santa Fe Convention & Visitors Bureau
201 W. Marcy St. (in the Santa Fe Convention Center)
Santa Fe, NM 87501
(505) 955-6200
(800) 777-2489
santafe.org

Taos County Chamber of Commerce
1139 Paseo del Pueblo Sur
Taos, NM 87571
(575) 751-8800
taoschamber.com

TAOS COUNTY

Doc Martin's
125 Paseo del Pueblo Norte
Taos
(575) 758-1977
taosinn.com
Moderate to expensive
Innovative southwestern

Gutiz
812B Paseo del Pueblo Norte
Taos
(575) 758-1226
gutiztaos.com
Moderate
Latin American–French country dining

Los Vaqueros
(at Sagebrush Inn)
1508 Paseo del Pueblo Sur
Taos
(575) 758-2254
(800) 428-3626
sagebrushinn.com
Moderate to expensive
Prime rib, steaks, seafood, New Mexican cuisine

The Love Apple
803 Paseo del Pueblo Norte
Taos
(575) 751-0050
theloveapple.net
Moderate to expensive
Regional organic country dining in a former church

Michael's Kitchen
304 Paseo del Pueblo Norte
Taos
(575) 758-4178
michaelskitchen.com
Inexpensive to moderate
New Mexican and American (a favorite with locals for breakfast)

Orlando's New Mexico Cafe
Paseo del Pueblo Norte
(1.8 miles north of Taos Plaza)
Taos
(575) 751-1450
orlandostaos.com
Inexpensive
Authentic New Mexico cuisine in a charming family-run courtyard restaurant

Central New Mexico

Compared with the other five regions in the state, central New Mexico is small in area but big on influence. Boasting the state's only true urban area (but also very rural sectors), central New Mexico combines facets of all the other regions in the state because it borders them all. That there's much to experience in this region is partly why the largest chunk of the state's population calls central New Mexico home.

Bernalillo County

Because the Albuquerque metropolitan area contains approximately one-third of New Mexico's residents, it tends to dominate Bernalillo County. And as the state's largest city, **Albuquerque** has its share of attractions to please a variety of interests.

Albuquerque was founded in 1706 by Don Francisco Cuervo y Valdes in honor of the Duke of Alburquerque, Viceroy of New Spain. The first "r" was later dropped, but Albuquerque is still known as the Duke City. The place Valdes actually designated "San Francisco de Alburquerque" is **Old Town**, just west of downtown.

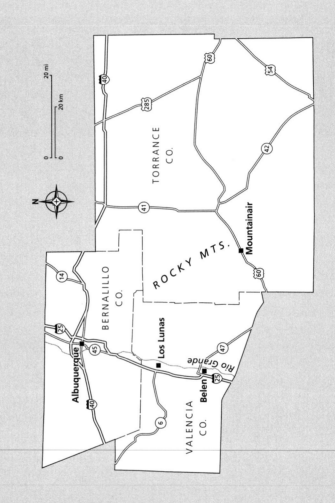

In addition to its status as a historic zone of Albuquerque, anchored by the picturesque San Felipe de Neri Chapel, Old Town is home for many families whose ancestors settled the area. On the surface, the shops around Old Town's plaza seem to cater only to tourists, but the fun part of exploring Old Town is venturing off the plaza into the side streets. There you'll find an array of fun-to-explore shops, galleries, and restaurants.

If your friends want to shop but you're in the mood for something non-commercial and contemplative, make arrangements to meet them in an hour at the plaza's gazebo, then walk over to the ***Capilla de Nuestra Señora de Guadalupe*** (Our Lady of Guadalupe Chapel). Despite its obvious Catholic character, this tiny chapel has a decidedly nonreligious yet very spiritual feel. Coupled with its beautifully landscaped courtyard, the chapel is a welcome break from the sometimes overwhelming presence of tourists.

You'll find no pews inside, but rather two small rooms. The first contains a shrine to the chapel's namesake, complete with candles burning in brightly colored holders, but it's the second room that evokes more philosophical musings. Thought-provoking verses that are not obviously biblical are carved into wooden panels on the walls. No matter what your spiritual leanings are, it's a

FAVORITE ATTRACTIONS/EVENTS IN CENTRAL NEW MEXICO

Albuquerque BioPark
Albuquerque
(505) 768-2000
cabq.gov/culturalservices/biopark

Petroglyph National Monument
Albuquerque
(505) 839-0205
nps.gov/petr

Rio Grande Nature Center State Park
Albuquerque
(505) 344-7240
rgnc.org

Sandia Peak Tramway
Albuquerque
(505) 856-7325
sandiapeak.com

University of New Mexico campus
Albuquerque
(505) 277-1918
unm.edu

EVENTS

Gathering of Nations Powwow
April, Albuquerque
(505) 836-2810
gatheringofnations.com

Albuquerque International Balloon Fiesta
October, Albuquerque
(888) 422-7277
balloonfiesta.com

very welcoming place. You'll find the chapel at the end of Patio Escondido, off San Felipe Avenue.

Old Town's plaza is the site of the annual ***Christmas Eve Luminaria Tour***. Here, tens of thousands of luminarias (lighted votive candles set in a bed of sand at the bottom of brown paper bags—called *farolitos* in northern New Mexico and luminarias in the south) create a golden glow on this special night at the place where Albuquerque began.

Parking is free around the plaza, if you can find a spot, but off the plaza are several parking lots that offer parking for a fee. Old Town is located near the intersection of Central Avenue and Rio Grande Boulevard. Most retail establishments are open seven days a week and maintain regular business hours, whereas others stay open later. As with many destinations in New Mexico, Old Town is most crowded during tourist season, which basically means summer. If your schedule is flexible, fall and winter (after Christmas) are the most pleasant times to visit.

newmexicotrivia

Actress Vivian Vance of *Lucy* fame was from Albuquerque, and occasionally she would mention her then-small hometown on the *I Love Lucy* TV sitcom of the 1950s.

If you're interested in buying Indian jewelry and crafts, two nearby stores, in addition to the shops around Old Town's plaza, offer discount pricing on jewelry, pottery, kachina dolls, drums, and other authentic crafts. ***Gus's Trading Company*** is near Old Town's plaza, at 306 San Felipe St. SW (505-843-6381), and ***Palms Trading Company*** is also close, at 1504 Lomas NW (505-247-8504; palmstrading.com).

Casas de Sueños ("Houses of Dreams") ***Old Town Historic Inn*** opened near Old Town in 1990. The inn, which has several garden areas and courtyards, is within walking distance of many Old Town and downtown attractions, such as the ***New Mexico Museum of Natural History***, the Albuquerque Museum (which connects to the Old Town shopping district via its sculpture garden), and the ***Rio Grande Zoo***. The futuristic entry building, designed by noted Albuquerque architect Bart Prince, contrasts with the traditional old adobe structures that compose the inn. The 21 Southwest-style casitas range from studios to one- and two-bedroom hot tub suites, many with kitchens and fireplaces. Casas de Sueños is at 310 Rio Grande SW; (505) 247-4560; casasdesuenos.com. Rates range from $139 to $209, less off-season.

In late 1996 the ***Rio Grande Botanic Garden*** and the ***Albuquerque Aquarium*** joined the Rio Grande Zoo to form the ***Albuquerque Biological Park***, or BioPark for short. "Tingley Beach," a favorite urban fishing spot, features pedal-boat rentals, a brick-paved promenade for bicyclists, and a narrow-gauge railroad linking the BioPark's north and south facilities. The BioPark was the first in the nation to have facilities that are physically connected and under consolidated management. The 100-acre site extends north from the zoo along more than 3 miles of the Rio Grande *bosque*, which, like the Sandia Mountain foothills, is the closest thing to wilderness within the city.

Planning and construction of the BioPark went on for years, but the wait was worth it. The clean lines and modern architecture of the botanic garden's conservatory blend well with the more traditional features of the park's other structures. From the peaceful entry complex to the Spanish-Moorish court, the botanic garden exudes the best of southwestern garden influences. A children's fantasy garden offers a "through the looking glass" magnified look at the world of plants and gardening.

The 45,000-square-foot aquarium complex, which includes a gift shop and restaurant, interprets the story of a drop of water as it enters the upper Rio Grande high in the San Juan Mountains of southern Colorado and flows through the canyons, deserts, and valleys of New Mexico, Mexico, and Texas,

Albuquerque's Central Avenue

If the Rio Grande is the lifeblood of Albuquerque, then Central Avenue is the city's soul. While the river may divide the city geographically into east and west, Central Avenue divides the city in another way. Far from its simple north-south division, the leisurely long avenue—Albuquerque's vestige of historic Route 66—also divides the city psychically. Either residents fear "Central" because their image of the area is outdated or limited, or they're quite fond of the reemerging neon-lit historic strip and the urban delights it now offers.

For years after I-40 started diverting travelers from the old route in the mid-1960s, much of it fell out of favor and into decay. While there remain several sections of Central that many a suburbanite might consider unsavory, the revitalizations and innovations occurring on the more prominent stretches since the mid-1990s have been especially heartening, considering the route's illustrious past. For pedestrian quests in search of culinary, shopping, and entertainment adventures, you won't find a better urban venue in the state.

In addition to the renovations made to Central along its border with the University of New Mexico (University Avenue through Girard) and its passage through downtown (2nd through 8th Streets, the most recent area to be revitalized), the Nob Hill area (Girard to east of Carlisle) has emerged as the preeminent see-and-be-seen district, boasting some of the city's best restaurants and most interesting shops. And for a tranquil change of pace, the wonderfully landscaped and architecturally significant UNM campus is just minutes away by foot.

through the subtropical forests of the lower Rio Grande Valley, and finally into the Gulf of Mexico. A 285,000-gallon shark tank with floor-to-ceiling viewing contains various species of Gulf sharks as well as giant groupers, moray eels, manta rays, and skates, in addition to schooling fish and various invertebrates. (Kids can enjoy an overnight Sleep with the Sharks pajama party in this exhibit, an obviously popular offering.) There are several great aquariums in the US (California's Monterey Bay Aquarium comes to mind), but it is quite a trip to see one of this scale in the high desert of the Southwest.

Because the BioPark is evolving, please call (505) 768-2000 for up-to-date visitor information, or check its website, cabq.gov/culturalservices/biopark. To get to the botanic garden/aquarium complex, take Central Avenue west from Old Town, about ½ mile, to Tingley Drive. You'll see it on your right. Admission to either the zoo or the botanic park and aquarium complex is $12.50 for adults, $5.50 for seniors, $4 for children ages 3 to 12; under 3 is free. Combined admission to all 3 units is $20 for adults, $10 for seniors, and $6 for children ages 3 to 12. Access to Tingley Beach is free. All are open daily from 9 a.m. to 5 p.m., until 6 p.m. on Sat and Sun in the summer months.

The Indian-run *Indian Pueblo Cultural Center* near Old Town is the place to go to experience the art, history, and culture of New Mexico's 19 pueblos (and one, Hopi Pueblo, in Arizona) before venturing out to explore any of them (or as an excellent single stop if you don't have time to visit). The center is owned and operated by the Pueblo Tribes of New Mexico and houses a fine museum and Pueblo Harvest Restaurant, which features New Mexican and Pueblo Indian dishes.

The museum is divided into three main historic periods of Indian occupation: prehistoric, historic, and contemporary. Pueblo House Children's Museum offers hands-on contact with ancient artifacts and modern craft works, aimed at grade school (K–5) children. It's open Tues, Thurs, and half-day Wed, as well as by group appointment. The center also contains gift shops and art galleries that offer authentic Indian pottery, sculpture, paintings, rugs, sand paintings, kachina dolls, and jewelry. Traditional Indian dance performances, alternating among the pueblos, are held on weekends in summer at 11 a.m. and 2 p.m.

The Indian Pueblo Cultural Center is at 2401 12th St. NW, just north of I-40; (505) 843-7270; indianpueblo.org. Admission to the cultural center and museum is $8.40 for adults, $6.40 for seniors, military, and New Mexico residents, and $5.40 for students; children under age 5 are free. Museum and gift shops are open daily from 9 a.m. to 5 p.m., and the restaurant is open Mon through Thurs from 7 a.m. to 9 p.m. and Sun from 7 a.m. to 4 p.m.

The *National Hispanic Cultural Center*, which opened in 2000, is located on a 16-acre site along the banks of the Rio Grande in the Albuquerque

South Valley community of **Barelas**. This world-class facility was conceived to preserve, interpret, and showcase Hispanic arts and culture. Born out of the vision of a handful of artists and community members in 1983, the center is a complex of buildings around a large central plaza and includes several impressive gallery spaces and performing arts venues, among other educational and cultural offerings. A *torreon*, or fortified watchtower, serves as the entry point and information center.

The historic community of Barelas was originally settled for its proximity to a natural ford in the Rio Grande and El Camino Real, the Spanish Colonial–era "Royal Road" connecting Mexico City with Taos. Later the railroad yards made Barelas a vibrant and economically important neighborhood in Albuquerque. However, as one of the opening art exhibits, "A Pictorial History of Barelas," explained, although the traditional Hispanic neighborhood that surrounds the center was once part of Albuquerque's vibrant core, it fell out of favor as Albuquerque grew and the greater downtown area declined. Now, along with recent streetscape improvements to the South 4th Street corridor, the center is the chief catalyst for a renaissance of the Barelas community, just as the adjacent downtown district also continues its own revitalization.

The center is located at 1701 4th St. SW (at Avenida César Chávez, also known as Bridge Street); (505) 246-2261; nhccnm.org. It's open Tues through Sun from 10 a.m. to 5 p.m. Admission is $6 for adults, $5 for seniors and New Mexico residents, and free for children under age 16; free for seniors on Wed and free for all on Sun. There are two restaurants: **M'tucci's Cocina Grill** serves a buffet of varied Latino traditional dishes and bar cocktails and is open Fri only, 11 a.m. to 8 p.m. for lunch and dinner; **Pop Fizz Paleteria** serves lighter fare, such as sandwiches, ice cream, and drinks and is open Tues through Sun from 11 a.m. to 8 p.m.

As with many cities throughout the past two decades, Albuquerque's downtown area—particularly the neon-lit Route 66 (Central Avenue), which, along with I-40, cuts right through Albuquerque—has been experiencing a renaissance of sorts, as citizens once again take pride in their city center and patronize areas of dynamic urban renewal. One historic attraction well worth a look in the regenerated downtown is the **KiMo Theatre**, built in 1927 in the Pueblo Deco style and later restored by the city. This great little theater hosts a wide range of performances, especially alternative and

newmexicotrivia

Though there is now more speculation about his alleged guilt, convicted Cold War spy Julius Rosenberg was officially arrested at a residence on High Street near Copper in downtown Albuquerque.

cultural performances, which are often more suitable to the ambience of the venue. The KiMo Theatre is at 423 Central Ave. NW; (505) 768-3522, event information (505) 768-3544; cabq.gov/culturalservices/kimo.

The **New Mexico Rail Runner Express** is a very popular, state-run passenger train service that links Albuquerque's South Valley with communities in the North Valley, including Belen, Los Lunas, Isleta Pueblo, Albuquerque, Los Ranchos, and Bernalillo, on a 100-mile corridor. The passenger trains were conceived as a weekday commuter train to help alleviate Albuquerque's rush-hour traffic. The train tracks were extended to Santa Fe in 2009, with stops at Kewa Pueblo (Santo Domingo) and the junction of I-25 with Highway 599, to allow workers in the capital commuting from Albuquerque to take advantage of the train. So many people enjoyed riding the train between Albuquerque and Santa Fe as a tourist experience, as well as an easy and inexpensive commuter train during a time of high gas prices, that service was extended to weekends.

The Rail Runner dead-ends in Santa Fe in the historic depot right in the heart of Railyard Park. From here it's an easy few blocks' walk to boutiques, restaurants, museums, and galleries along Guadalupe Street and the plaza area, or if you wish, you can take the free Santa Fe Pickup shuttle to destinations around Santa Fe.

Downtown Albuquerque's main Rail Runner station is located at the intersection of Central Avenue and 1st Street SW, just east of I-25; (866) 795-7245. Northbound trains between Albuquerque and Santa Fe on weekdays begin at 4:32 a.m., with the last train at 8:38 p.m.; 12 trains run throughout the day. Five trains run on Saturday from downtown Albuquerque starting at 8:58 a.m. to 11:09 p.m.; and Sunday there are just 3 trains, at 8:58 a.m., 1:42 p.m., and 6:27 p.m. Check the schedule for return service and to make sure of precise times due to changing schedules and new stations coming. Fares are low and based on the number of zones you are traveling through. The fare between Albuquerque and Santa Fe is $10 one-way, or $11 for a day pass offering unlimited travel; kids under 10 years of age ride free. Discounted tickets are available. Check online at nmrailrunner.com.

College campuses and the areas surrounding them are usually some of the most interesting places in a city (with the cheapest and most interesting food options, too). The **University of New Mexico in Albuquerque**, the largest university in the state, is no different. UNM is located along Central Avenue (old Route 66) east of downtown. A stroll around the campus reveals perhaps the finest examples of Pueblo Revival architecture, as buildings here were designed by New Mexico's most famous architect, John Gaw Meem of Santa Fe, who served as consulting architect for UNM from 1933 to 1959. Zimmerman

Library, Scholes Hall, and Alumni Chapel are three of the Meem firm's most striking designs on campus and are worth a look and a few photographs. The beautifully landscaped duck-pond area in the campus's center, adjacent to Zimmerman Library, is an idyllic spot for a country picnic in the middle of the city.

The UNM Visitor Center is in an old adobe tucked away on the corner of Redondo Drive at 1700 Las Lomas Blvd.; (505) 277-1989; unm.edu; open Mon through Fri from 8 a.m. to 5 p.m.

Tamarind Institute, housed in a nondescript building across Central Avenue from the university, is much more than a division of UNM; it's a unique educational facility dedicated to the fine art of collaborative lithography. And it gives the best tour in Albuquerque. The good news is that the tour is free. The bad news is that it happens only once a month—usually the first Friday of each month at 1:30 p.m. (may vary in summer). Reservations are strongly recommended.

Traditional Food of New Mexico

Calabacitas

Calabacitas ("baby squashes") is a favorite New Mexican side dish that is traditionally made in late summer, when the first baby squashes, corn, baby garlic, onion, and green chiles are harvested.

2 cups whole kernel corn

4 tablespoons corn oil

¼ teaspoon black pepper

½ onion, chopped

2 cups chopped fresh green New Mexico chiles (more or less, according to taste)

½ cup water

1 clove garlic, minced

1 teaspoon salt

4 medium yellow and/or zucchini squashes, sliced

¾ cup grated Monterey Jack cheese

Combine all ingredients, except cheese, in a large saucepan. Cook at medium heat until squash is tender, approximately 20 minutes. Garnish with cheese before serving. Makes 4–6 servings. **Note:** Although it is not traditional, to make a more substantial one-pot main-course dish, you can add chopped cooked chicken and substitute chicken broth for the water the veggies cook in.

If you didn't know a thing about collaborative lithography before your visit to Tamarind, you'll be an expert after the two-hour tour, which includes a viewing of an Emmy-nominated documentary produced by the institute, a briefing by the director, and a staff-guided tour of the facility.

Tamarind began in 1960 in Los Angeles as the Tamarind Lithography Workshop. Its purpose was to rescue collaborative lithography from becoming a lost art in the US by training a pool of master printers to work with artists. After 10 years in Los Angeles, Tamarind, supported by substantial Ford Foundation grants, moved to Albuquerque in 1970 to become self-sustaining and continue the goals established in California.

If your visit doesn't coincide with a tour, you can still view some of the finished works—a small gallery at the institute displays selected lithographs. Some are available for purchase, and once you understand the lengthy collaborative lithography process, you'll understand the prices.

Tamarind Institute is at 110 Cornell Ave. SE, and its workshop and gallery are at 2500 Central Ave. SE; (505) 277-3901; tamarind.unm.edu. Gallery hours are Mon through Fri from 9 a.m. to 5 p.m.

To immerse yourself in the flavor of campus life, you'll definitely want to stop for a meal at the *Frontier Restaurant*, across the street from the main entrance to UNM. This 1970s diner, with its incongruous art gallery of images of actor John Wayne, sprawls over an entire city block. It serves up humongous portions of budget-priced huevos rancheros, breakfast burritos (which you can smother yourself with red or green chile from vats on the buffet), green chile stew, and homemade cinnamon rolls the diameter of a dinner plate, and does it from 5 a.m. to 1 a.m. every day—to the accompaniment of shouted orders, tapping laptop keyboards, the murmur of intellectual discourse, and the din of video games. Located at 2400 Central Ave.; (505) 266-0550; frontierrestaurant .com.

The *Nob Hill–Highland District*, just east of UNM along Central Avenue, near Carlisle Boulevard, re-creates that old Route 66 ambience. This revived and continually evolving section of Albuquerque showcases antiques shops, vintage-clothing stores, and other shops; theaters; and some of Albuquerque's best restaurants and cafes, all interspersed among more practical businesses to create an eclectic mix perfect for a Saturday afternoon stroll. Among the places to seek out are popular eateries—Flying Star Cafe, Two Fools Tavern, and Scalo Italian Restaurant.

Although individual antiques stores abound in and around the Nob Hill District (mostly along Central and Morningside Avenues), the largest selection of antiques and collector items under one roof is at *Classic Century Square*. This old department-store building houses 3 levels of antiques, collectibles, furniture, glassware, books, jewelry, and other items in more than 125 wall-less shops. There's an exceptionally large collection of vintage dolls in one section of the complex. You could spend a whole afternoon browsing and still not see everything.

Classic Century Square is at 4616 Central Ave. SE, just west of San Mateo Boulevard; (505) 349-5659; classiccenturysquare.com. It's open Mon through Sat from 10 a.m. to 6 p.m. and Sun from noon to 5 p.m.

Albuquerque's rural North Valley, situated near the Rio Grande, contains some of the area's most fertile land, planted with apple orchards, alfalfa fields, extensive gardens—and grapes for wine. There are now 9 family-run estate wineries in Los Ranchos and nearby Corrales. Of these, one of the most enjoyable places to sample award-winning handcrafted wines is ***Casa Rondeña*** (733 Chavez NW; 505-344-5911; casarondena.com), off Rio Grande Boulevard. Try the Viognier; a blended Merlot, Cabernet Franc, and Cabernet Sauvignon; a Founder's Reserve Cabernet Sauvignon; or a blended Riesling and Gewürztraminer. The tasting room is open Sat and Sun from noon to 7 p.m.

For a glimpse of Albuquerque's rich farming history in a splendid and elegant setting, don't miss ***Los Poblanos Historic Inn and Organic Farm***, a 25-acre estate that includes an art-filled bed-and-breakfast, a large organic farm, and an adjoining historic cultural center rented out for special events. With its lush river-irrigated farmlands, historic buildings, art collection, views, and strolling peacocks, there is no more atmospheric place in central New Mexico.

The estate was developed by Congresswoman Ruth Hanna McCormick and her husband in 1934, when, with the help of Santa Fe Style architect John Gaw Meem and the contributions of some of New Mexico's most famous artists and artisans of the time, they remodeled the 19th-century Armijo homestead, which had been built on a former pueblo. Among the many highlights are a formal English garden laid out by famed landscape artist Rose Greeley, dotted with whimsical rock paths created by folk artist Pop Shaffer, and the adjoining La Quinta Cultural Center, which has a mural by artist Peter Hurd and unusual wooden doors carved by printmaker Gustave Baumann. The Rembe family, who own the property, have a remarkable collection of New Mexico *santos* (representations of saints), all on display throughout the inn.

The 16-acre working organic farm is remarkable in and of itself. It grows more than 75 varieties of fruit, veggies, and flowers, which are on sale weekly at Los Ranchos Growers' Market and make their way into the inn's well-regarded food offerings. Los Poblanos is an experimental farm and offers work-study programs and workshops. It specializes in growing lavender, which is used to make the lavender spa products found in the inn's guest bathrooms, on sale in the farm shop in the original Creamland Dairy building, and in many stores throughout New Mexico selling local products. A Lavender Festival takes place here annually. This is a wonderful place to visit if you want to understand the intersection of food and culture in New Mexico.

The original ranch house is one of the most successful iterations of John Gaw Meem's classic Santa Fe style, with its adobe walls, vigas, wood-burning fireplaces, and New Mexico art collection. After Penny and Armin Rembe's son, Matthew, took over running the property in 2004, new guest rooms and suites were added to the original six in the ranch house and adjoining casita. The expanded inn now has 20 lovely, light-and-bright guest rooms and suites in the original ranch house and weathered clapboard former dairy buildings. All retain their southwestern ambience and views, but now have clean, modern lines and many luxury touches, including hardwood floors, Hispanic weavings and rugs, contemporary four-poster beds, high-thread-count white linens, private bathrooms, sleeper sofas, fridges and wet bars, lavender toiletries, and flat-screen TVs.

As you can imagine, the food at Los Poblanos is farm-to-fork fresh and a locavore's dream. The delicious hot breakfasts included in the room rate feature unique egg dishes such as Eggs Shakshouka, eggs poached in a spiced tomato stew broth over chickpeas with blue corn bread; frittata with chorizo; New Mexico chilaquiles; steak and eggs; and other hearty fare, depending on the day of the week. Popular Los Poblanos farm dinners featuring the inn's local Rio Grande cuisine are offered Wed through Sat from 5 to 9 p.m. and are open to nonguests (guests receive priority reservations; book early). Meals are served in a spacious dining room, with views of the gardens and strolling peacocks.

Los Poblanos Historic Inn and Organic Farm is located at 4803 Rio Grande Blvd. NW, Los Ranchos; (505) 344-9297; lospoblanos.com. Room rates range from $210 for a Meem Classic Queen to $480 per night for one of the new North Field double suites that can sleep four; rates include hot breakfast for two. A variety of room-and-tour packages are available, including bicycling, microbreweries, and hot-air ballooning.

Hot-air ballooning is extremely popular in New Mexico because of the state's predictably pleasant fall weather and clear skies. To celebrate this colorful sport, New Mexico's largest city hosts the *Albuquerque International Balloon Fiesta* each October.

Balloonists and spectators come from all over the world to take part in the nine-day event, which draws more than 100,000 spectators. The mass ascensions on the four weekend mornings during the fiesta are worth an early rising (while it's still dark out) for the trek to Balloon Fiesta Park, located on Alameda Boulevard off I-25. Up to 600 balloons take off to thousands of "oohs and ahs," while amateur and professional photographers click away at what has surpassed Pasadena's Tournament of Roses Parade as the most photographed annual event in the world.

In addition to the mass ascensions, the yearly Balloon Glow has become quite a popular event. After sunset, hundreds of inflated hot-air balloons fire up in synchronized patterns to create huge spheres of colorful, glowing light. If you make it to Albuquerque for the fiesta, don't miss the Balloon Glow. Check weather forecasts; if it's too windy, the glows are often postponed. Another fun ballooning event during the fiesta is the Special Shapes Rodeo, limited to those balloons tailored a bit differently from the usual inverted teardrop configuration. You'll see Mickey Mouse, Planters' Mr. Peanut, a Pepsi can, a cow jumping over a moon, and scores more of the huge floating representations of familiar items.

The nine-day fiesta begins the first weekend of each October. For more information, contact 4401 Alameda NE, Albuquerque; (505) 821-1000 or (888) 422-7277; balloonfiesta.com. Balloon Fiesta takes place at 5000 Balloon Fiesta Pkwy. NE.

The history of hot-air and gas ballooning is presented through art, technology, and history exhibits at the nearby ***Anderson–Abruzzo Albuquerque International Balloon Museum***. The 60,000-square-foot museum is named for Albuquerque balloonists Maxie Anderson and Ben Abruzzo, who set a world's record by crossing the Atlantic Ocean in a gas balloon in 1978. Exhibits include more than 50 historic and contemporary balloon gondolas, from 19th-century wicker baskets and World War I observation balloons to gondolas and complete balloon systems used in world-record attempts during the 1980s. There are also rare books and magazines containing accounts of early ballooning exploits, including eyewitness reports of the first balloon ascent in 1783, and a huge collection of ballooning memorabilia such as buttons, postage stamps, commemorative plates, jewelry, decorative boxes, and souvenir curios. And if that's not enough, the museum shop sells more balloon-motif gift items than you can imagine.

For more information, call (505) 880-0500; balloonmuseum.com. The museum is at 9201 Balloon Museum Dr. NE (off Alameda Boulevard near Balloon Fiesta Park). Hours are Tues through Sun from 9 a.m. to 5 p.m., with special hours during the International Balloon Fiesta. Admission is $4 for adults (with $1 discount for New Mexico residents), $2 for seniors, $1 for children ages 4 to 12, and free for children under 4.

Though not as well-known as the Albuquerque International Balloon Fiesta, the ***Gathering of Nations Powwow***, held annually the last full weekend of April (Thurs through Sat), is also a significant event for Albuquerque. Billed as the largest Native American powwow, or social get-together, in North

America, the cultural gathering attracts more than 3,000 dancers and singers—representing more than 700 indigenous tribes from Canada and the US—who participate socially and competitively. In addition to various forms of entertainment, such as ceremonial dances, drumming, singing, and other musical performances, the event includes Native American foods and shopping at the Indian Traders Market, as well as the annual crowning of Miss Indian World. And though the powwow is staged primarily for Native Americans, everyone is welcome at the family-oriented event, as evidenced by the tens of thousands of nonnatives who attend each year.

The gathering is held at Tingley Coliseum at Expo New Mexico; entrance fees vary; (505) 836-2810; gatheringofnations.com.

New Mexico is a nature lover's paradise, and Albuquerque fits right in. **Rio Grande Nature Center State Park** in Albuquerque's North Valley lies, as its name implies, along the Rio Grande and adjoining acequia (irrigation ditch) and is a wonderful place for leisurely walks or brisk hikes. Outside the center you'll find 270 acres of *bosque* and meadows that include stands of hundred-year-old cottonwoods, among other trees, as well as a 3-acre pond that attracts abundant riparian wildlife. The *bosque* is threaded with 2 miles of trails, where unobtrusive signs identify the various forms of plant life.

The nature center itself contains self-guided exhibits that provide insight into the natural, historical, and social implications of the Rio Grande. Don't miss the glassed-in viewing room in the library, from which you can observe (and listen to, via a microphone) the wildlife at the pond without being noticed. A sign hanging here, "This Week's Visitors," lists the species of birds and other animals that have been spotted recently.

Nature walks and children's hikes are scheduled, and you can borrow a pair of binoculars if you have a photo ID. Although the center makes for an enjoyable outing throughout the year, weekdays during fall and winter are especially tranquil. As a sign at the center's entrance prominently points out, this is *not* a place to have a picnic, ride your bike or horse, run or jog, or walk your dog.

Rio Grande Nature Center State Park is at 2901 Candelaria Rd. NW (where Candelaria dead-ends); (505) 344-7240; rgnc.org. The visitor center is open daily from 10 a.m. to 5 p.m., and the grounds are open from 8 a.m. to 5 p.m. (And they mean it: Cars left in the parking lot after 5 p.m. or 4 p.m. on weekends will be locked in.) Admission is $3 per vehicle.

The west side of Albuquerque is often referred to as the West Mesa because, well, it is a volcanic mesa. It was formed by ancient lava flows erupting from cinder cones in the volcanically active Rio Grande rift zone. Aside from the conical remnants of these cinder cones, the West Mesa forms a wonderfully flat horizon, perfect for the setting sun to sink into—frequently the first thing that strikes visitors arriving at the Albuquerque Sunport at sunset.

It's on the West Mesa that you'll find 11-square-mile **Petroglyph National Monument**, one of the most impressive collections of Indian and Hispanic rock inscriptions in the world, as well as more than 350 archaeological sites and a variety of volcanic features associated with the Rio Grande rift zone—all within city limits. At a distance, the park is a barren, unimpressive pile of dark basaltic lava rocks on a hill. But look a little closer and you'll see why the place got its name—the lava escarpment is incised with ancient Indian petroglyphs, or images carved in rock. The variety is simply staggering and includes symbols and images, such as reptiles, birds, insects, four-legged animals, geometric designs, anthropomorphs, Kokopelli flute players, mysterious masked serpents, and strange star beings.

The oldest petroglyphs may be almost 3,000 years old, dating to the Archaic and early Basketmaker era, when people in the Rio Grande Valley were still living in pit houses. About 90 percent of the petroglyphs are Rio Grande style, carved by later Ancestral Pueblo people between AD 1300 and 1650. There was a tremendous commingling of Pueblo people during this period, when refugees from the Four Corners pueblos at Mesa Verde joined existing pueblos along the Rio Grande. The petroglyphs were probably used in ceremonies and are still sacred to local Puebloans today. You will also see Hispanic inscriptions and carvings made by ranchers in the 1800s at this location.

newmexicotrivia

Approximately one-third of New Mexico's population of 2,081,015 (est. 2016) resides in the Albuquerque metropolitan area.

The monument has 3 units managed by the National Park Service—Boca Negra Canyon, Rinconada Canyon, and Volcanoes Day Use Area—and 1 managed by the City of Albuquerque. Stop at Las Imagines Visitor Center at 6001 Unser Blvd. to plan your visit; other units are located at different points along the West Mesa and on top of it, in the Volcanoes Day Use Area, a good place to hike and visit the cinder cones and volcanic features, such as geological windows.

The visitor center (505-899-0205; nps.gov/petr) is housed in the 1948 adobe home of archaeologist Dr. Sophie Aberle and is located 3 miles north of I-40, adjoining Boca Negra Canyon, the most popular unit of the park. It's open daily from 8 a.m. to 5 p.m. The park does not charge admission fees; however, there is a small parking fee at the Boca Negra Canyon unit, the most popular and accessible area of the park: $1 per car weekdays, $2 on weekends.

Although most of the unique places lie near the older parts of town—Old Town, downtown, the university area, the North Valley—there's much to see in the "newer" parts of Albuquerque. The Heights, specifically the Far Northeast Heights, are blessed with the Sandia Mountains, which form a lovely backdrop for the city while bordering its east side. The Spaniards named the mountains Sandia, which means "watermelon," because of the red color they turn when hit by the setting sun.

To explore the Sandias from Albuquerque, consider a hike on *La Luz Trail*. The name of this scenic 8-mile trail means "the light." The trail, known as the site of La Luz Trail Run held each August, begins at the Juan Tabo Recreation Area and follows the western slope of the Sandias. The well-marked trail averages a 12 percent grade over the 3,700-foot rise; thus, the three- to five-hour (or more!) hike is quite a workout and you'll need to be in superb shape to do it.

Always be prepared whenever you venture out hiking in the desert, but particularly in exposed mountainous areas like this trail, where there is almost no shade. Wear a broad-brimmed hat and light, breathable clothing that can be rolled down to cover exposed skin; keep the neck covered to avoid sunstroke—a bandanna is a good idea, as it can be wetted down to keep you cool. Be sure to drink plenty of water (a gallon of water for the day is advised) and eat salty, high-energy snacks to avoid hyponatremia (too much water/too little food, causing serious metabolic imbalance). Carry the following in a day pack: topographical map, waterproof matches, mirror (for signaling), flashlight, first-aid kit, Swiss army knife, warm clothing, and waterproof gear. It gets quite brisk at the higher elevations, even during the summer months, so layered clothing is your best bet. Wear sturdy hiking boots with nonslip soles. Avoid being out on this prominent rock face during summer lightning storms; hike in the morning and be off the mountain before the afternoon monsoon arrives. Snow and ice on the steep trail in winter make it too dangerous. Spring and fall are your best bets.

You must be prepared and use common sense when hiking or climbing in the Southwest desert. Every year several hikers fall or become stranded in locations like La Luz, the most famous of the Sandia trails. For this reason, be sure to tell someone where you are going when you hike, or leave a note with your itinerary in your parked car at the trailhead. The ever-changing views and scenery along this trail are amazingly beautiful. For a less strenuous hike, take the tram (see below) to the top and hike down. If you're careful to time the last leg of your descent at sunset, you'll see why the trail is called La Luz—incredible!

A Glimpse of Central New Mexico: Impressions of the Bosque, the Mountains & the Volcanoes

By using Albuquerque as a gateway to New Mexico's more far-flung nature adventures, visitors often ignore what many Albuquerqueans also take for granted: its vast wonderland of hiking opportunities, minutes from any neighborhood in town. The three most impressive are the *bosque*, the foothills, and the volcanoes. And the best part is that they're free to enjoy anytime and they're usually quite deserted, despite their proximity.

The *bosque*, or wooded area that stretches along the Rio Grande and its tributaries throughout New Mexico, has always been a beautiful place through which to hike or bike. It can be reached at various points via 4,300-acre Rio Grande Valley State Park Open Space, managed by the City of Albuquerque and the Middle Rio Grande Conservancy District (it is *not* actually a state park, despite its name). This urban open space offers a system of trails through cottonwood groves along the river, from Sandia Pueblo on the north through Albuquerque all the way to Isleta Pueblo on the south. It's a great place for morning and evening walks, especially during spring and fall, because of the activity among the native birds that nest, and migratory birds that rest, in the sanctuary of the *bosque*. Rio Grande Nature Center State Park, off Rio Grande Boulevard, is one good place to explore the *bosque* and the wildlife in it.

The foothills of the Sandia Mountains, which form Albuquerque's eastern border, provide another welcome nature escape. In addition to the celebrated La Luz Trail (see page 152), there are many other well-marked trails, such as the Piedra Lisa Trail, which begins east of Tramway Boulevard. Trail maps are available from the US Forest Service at 333 Broadway SE in Albuquerque; (505) 842-3292. And as you might imagine, the sunsets are always quite spectacular from the foothills.

Albuquerque's West Mesa, with its five dormant volcanic peaks and its shrubby high-desert vegetation, provides an austere contrast to the *bosque* and the foothills, but the views of the Sandia and Manzano mountain ranges are quite spectacular and unobstructed, due to the mesa's elevation above the city. To get to the volcanoes, drive west on I-40 for about 9 miles, take the Paseo del Volcan exit, and head north for a couple of miles until you find primitive parking areas and trailheads.

To reach La Luz trailhead from I-25 in north Albuquerque, exit at Tramway Boulevard, then go 4 miles east to the Juan Tabo turnoff. Follow the road to the trailhead.

The foothills of the Sandias provide a wonderful vantage point from which to view the spectacular sunsets for which New Mexico is famous. And a comfortable spot for the nightly show is ***Sandiago's Mexican Grill*** (505-856-6692) nestled in the foothills at the base of the ***Sandia Peak Tramway***, the world's longest aerial tramway, which will smoothly transport you to 10,400 feet in about 15 minutes. The free **New Mexico Ski Museum**, located at the base of the tramway, is an interesting place to while away a little time while waiting for your tram ride.

Tram rides are popular at all times of the year, but be aware that winter temperatures can be more than 30 degrees colder at the top, which doesn't make for very comfortable sightseeing. If you're lucky, you might see a brave hang-glider pilot take the plunge—harnessed in his or her glider, we hope—toward the Rio Grande Valley 1 mile below.

The tramway (505-856-7325; sandiapeak.com) is at 38 Tramway Rd. off Tramway Boulevard. Although there's no set schedule, the tram departs about every 20 to 30 minutes daily, starting at 9 a.m. and continuing until 9 p.m. (last tram is 8 p.m. in winter). Round-trip tickets are $25 for adults, $20 for seniors, students, and active-duty military personnel, and $15 for children ages 5 to 12; children under 5 are free. Each tram departure is announced in the adjacent restaurant, so you can wait for your "flight" in the bar if you like.

The summit and east side of the Sandias are also worth exploring. It's amazing that although most Albuquerque residents see the Sandias every day, many of them still don't realize that they can drive to the very top—**Sandia Crest**, at 10,678 feet—in less than an hour via I-40 and Highway 14 (the Turquoise Trail) at Cedar Crest, turning west on Sandia Crest Highway (Highway 536), which has been designated a National Scenic Byway and is also the highest scenic drive in the Southwest. At the top, you'll find things a lot different than they were back "on the ground." Here, it's a lot cooler, which is refreshing during summer; even so, you might want to bring a sweater or light jacket.

The views from Sandia Crest are incredible. It's hard to imagine that the "small town" over the edge is bustling Albuquerque. The city becomes a distant, twinkling fairyland after sunset. From the observation deck at the summit, you can see more than 15,000 square miles of central New Mexico. Double Eagle II Cafe in the Double Eagle Day Lodge at the base of Sandia Peak Ski Area is open seasonally for breakfast, lunch, and snacks. In winter this is a wonderful place to get in some skiing, if you've just arrived in Albuquerque and are taking a day to get acclimated before heading to Santa Fe and Taos.

Once you've conquered the crest, check out **Tinkertown Museum** on your way back down the mountain. The museum is subtitled "Wood-Carved Miniature Village and Glass Bottle House," and is a place not to be missed. Even for people who don't think they like this sort of thing, I repeat, it's a place not to be missed!

Billed as "a collection of collections," Tinkertown explores a world gone by, as well as a slightly skewed one that never existed. You'll get a month's worth of smiles after an hour of following the arrows directing you through the displays of miniature exhibits, including a general store and three-ring circus. Some displays involve mechanical action that brings the figures to life. You'll see ghost-town relics from New Mexico's Billy the Kid Country, as well as "The Wishing Buddha," accompanied by a sign that reads "Wish for peace on earth, not just a piece of the action." The self-guided tour takes you through a structure built out of glass bottles as the sounds of old-time frontier music further remove you from time and place.

Tinkertown is the result of more than 40 years of tinkering by the late painter Ross Ward, a lover of circuses and traveling shows. And just when you're wondering when he found the time to do all this, you'll see his motto posted on the wall: "I did all this while you were watching TV."

Tinkertown is at 121 Sandia Crest Rd., about 1¼ miles up Highway 536 off Highway 14; (505) 281-5233; tinkertown.com. It's open daily from 9 a.m. to 6 p.m. (last admission at 5:30 p.m.) Apr through Oct. Admission is $3 for adults, $2.50 for seniors, and $1 for youths ages 4 to 15, while children age 3 and younger get a free peek at Ward's world.

One beautifully constructed and maintained bed-and-breakfast inn perched in the Sandias is *Elaine's* (702 Snowline Rd., Cedar Crest; 505-281-2467 or 800-821-3092; elainesbnb.com). Elaine Nelson O'Neil built this lodgepole pine home for herself and turned the top two floors into a bed-and-breakfast in 1988. There are 5 guest rooms, all with cozy western furnishings. The common area of the no-smoking-permitted inn has a vaulted ceiling, a huge stone fireplace, and an upright piano, all with a fantastic alpine view through floor-to-ceiling windows.

Rates run from $109 to $159 per night. To get to Elaine's, take the Tijeras/Cedar Crest (Highway 14) exit and, as you drive under I-40, check your odometer, then go slightly over 4 miles north on Highway 14. Turn left at the Turquoise Trail Campground (approximately 1 mile past Bella Vista Restaurant).

STATE PARKS IN CENTRAL NEW MEXICO

Online at emnrd.state.nm.us/spd

Manzano Mountains State Park
13 miles northwest of Mountainair
(southeast of Albuquerque)
(505) 847-2820

Rio Grande Nature Center State Park
in Albuquerque
(505) 344-7240

Go straight on the dirt road approximately ½ mile. Turn left at the T. As you enter the gate marked "Snowline Estates," you'll see Elaine's on your right at the top of the hill. Follow the road up the hill and around the corner.

For many years, the ***National Museum of Nuclear Science and History*** (formerly the National Atomic Museum) was located on Kirtland Air Force Base, a key distribution and collection point for America's nuclear weapons. Due to heightened security following the 9/11 terrorist attacks, Kirtland is now off-limits to the general public. The museum is now located at 601 Eubank at Southern Boulevard SE.

Even devout pacifists can enjoy this fascinating display, which objectively portrays New Mexico's nuclear heritage: the development of the first atom bombs during the 1940s in Los Alamos (see the Los Alamos County entry in the North-Central New Mexico chapter) and, subsequently, the first atomic blast at the Trinity Site (see the Socorro County entry in the Southwestern New Mexico chapter). The museum takes you through these historical developments and displays nuclear artifacts. New exhibits on nuclear science and medicine reflect the museum's change of focus away from military applications. Showings of two documentaries, *10 Seconds That Shook the World* and the newer *Commitment to Peace*, alternate throughout the day. Open daily from 9 a.m. to 5 p.m.; (505) 245-2137; nuclearmuseum.org. Admission is $12 for adults, $10 for seniors and young people ages 6 to 17, $7 for active-duty military personnel, and $8 for veterans; children age 5 and younger are admitted free.

In extreme western Bernalillo County, near the Cibola County line, you'll find truly remote yet thoroughly modern lodging at the ***Apache Canyon Ranch Bed and Breakfast Inn***. Ava and Theron Bowers converted their 3,600-square-foot home into a southern-style bed-and-breakfast in 1996; guests can now share with them the austere beauty of the landscape and endless mountain and mesa views. Grazing cattle and wild horses are the Bowerses' nearest neighbors, and in the late evening, while enjoying the cool high-desert air on the patio, guests will likely be serenaded by distant coyotes. The ranch borders both To'hajiilee Navajo lands and the Laguna Indian Reservation.

Ava is a talented host and good southern cook, and she has combined the art and antiques from American Indian, Hispanic, and her own African American culture to create a welcoming, unique decor. The largest of the inn's 3 guest rooms is the Sky City Suite, which includes a fireplace, a king-size bed, and a whirlpool bath; a self-contained casita, Casa Kokopelli, has its own kitchen and offers complete privacy. Rates range from $195 to $245, which includes breakfast, dinner, and use of the sauna and exercise room. To get to Apache Canyon Ranch, head west from Albuquerque on I-40 (about 30 minutes) to the

To'hajiilee exit, then head north for about 3 miles. The bed-and-breakfast is located at 4 Canyon Dr., Laguna; (505) 377-7925; apachecanyon.net.

Valencia County

South of Albuquerque, along I-25, you'll find the rural communities of Valencia County: Belen, Los Lunas, Bosque Farms, Jarales, and Tomé, among others. Many of the residents of this area enjoy the rural solitude of life along the Rio Grande, while benefiting from the big-city advantages of Albuquerque, only a half-hour's commute to the north.

Settled by the Spanish in 1741, **Belen** (Bethlehem in Spanish) became a major New Mexico railroad center in the 1880s. Though the railroad remains important to Belen, the heyday of passenger trains carrying travelers out west is long gone. But the **Valencia County Historical Society's Harvey House Museum** remembers. Located in the 1910 Belen Harvey House, the small museum, named for British immigrant railroad entrepreneur Fred Harvey, takes up just a part of the historic dining stop; the rest of the restored Mission-style building is occupied by the Belen Model Railway Club.

In addition to displaying a variety of antique items donated by or on loan from area citizens, the museum pays homage to Fred Harvey and the days when his Harvey House restaurants and hotels were scattered along the railway stops throughout the West. Impeccable service, fine food, and the young, gracious Harvey Girls (waitresses) helped tame the wild frontier from the turn of the 20th century until World War II, when other forms of travel took hold. One room in the museum is outfitted with furnishings typical of the Harvey Girls' boarding rooms, which usually were upstairs from the dining area.

While most of these oases of civility no longer exist, the citizens of Belen fought to save their Harvey House in the early 1980s, when it faced demolition. The railroad sold the structure to the city of Belen, and residents rallied to preserve the legacy of Fred Harvey in their town.

The museum is at 104 N. 1st St. in Belen; (505) 861-0581; belen-nm.gov. It's open Tues through Fri from noon to 5 p.m. and Sat from 10 a.m. to 5 p.m. Admission is free.

The **Luna-Otero Mansion** was once the headquarters of a livestock and land dynasty, but since 1977 the stately home has been serving up appetizing entrees as the **Luna Mansion** restaurant. A National Historic Landmark, this is a restaurant with a story.

Domingo de Luna and Don Pedro Otero both came to New Mexico from Spain on land grants near the end of the 17th century. After nearly 200 years of amassing fortunes in land, livestock, and political influence, descendants of the two men's families were united by marriage in the late 1800s to create what is known as the Luna-Otero Dynasty.

The Luna-Otero Mansion was built by the Santa Fe Railroad in 1881 in exchange for right-of-way privileges through the Luna property (which meant the existing Luna home had to go). The Southern Colonial architectural design of the mansion is said to have been inspired by trips through the South by the Luna family. Though the design certainly seems out of place in New Mexico, the building material is not. You guessed it—it's constructed out of adobe. It's said that this mansion is haunted.

newmexicotrivia

"Christmas" is not only a holiday in New Mexico; it's also the proper response to a local waiter if you want your New Mexican entree topped with both green and red chile sauce.

Perhaps ironically, the restaurant serves up just about everything except New Mexican food—steaks, chicken, prime rib, pasta, and seafood dishes dominate the menu. The closest thing to New Mexican is the Red Chile Linguini.

Luna Mansion is at the junction of Highways 6 and 314 in Los Lunas; (505) 865-7333; lunamansion.com. It is open Tues through Thurs from 11:30 a.m. to 3:30 p.m., Fri and Sat from 11 a.m. to 9 p.m., and Sun from 10 a.m. to 2:30 p.m.

Torrance County

Torrance County attaches to Bernalillo County's southeast side and is therefore a quick drive from Albuquerque. Many city residents enjoy a Sunday afternoon drive along the back of the Sandia and Manzano Mountains on Highway 337 (old South 14) and Highway 55, dubbed the Salt Mission Trail because it was used by the residents of the three Salinas Pueblo missions that you will find on and near this highway. The atmosphere is decidedly rural and dotted with small towns along the route—Chilili (Bernalillo County), Tajique, Torreon, Manzano, and Mountainair.

One particular bypass along the way is the *Tajique–Torreon Loop*, an incredibly scenic, unpaved 17-mile stretch of road that indirectly connects the two towns. In Tajique, head east on FR 55 (the road directing you to Fourth of July Campground off Highway 55). Unless you're in a four-wheel-drive vehicle, don't attempt to go past the Fourth of July Campground at the 7-mile mark—the road is clearly marked "primitive" at this point. Manzano Mountain Wilderness, which is what the loop takes you through, is one of the few places in New Mexico where oak, maple, and aspen trees are interspersed with the usual mountain evergreens. It's a beautiful autumn drive. And if you're into camping or just want to have a picnic, the **Fourth of July Campground** (commonly known as Fourth of July Canyon) at the midway point is a great spot.

Old Catholic churches are the historic highlights of the towns along Highway 55 and attest to the rich Spanish traditional values of the villages. If you plan your visit during harvesttime, check out the area apple orchards. (Manzano means "apple tree" in Spanish, you know.) In recent years, the creative set has discovered some of the communities. You'll find artists, weavers, potters, and wood-carvers if you take the time to explore the area.

The ruins of 3 impressive 17th-century Spanish mission churches and earlier pueblos—Abó, Quarai, and Gran Quivira—are the focal points of **Salinas Pueblo Missions National Monument**, one of the major destinations in this area. The pueblo missions are located in the Estancia Basin, which once held a huge lake that attracted paleohunters following mammoth and other big game at the end of the Ice Age. As the climate warmed, the lake dried up, leaving behind salt flats, or *salinas*, as they were known to Spanish conquistadores, who, like the local Puebloans before them, understood the importance of salt, a mineral that is essential to human health, as a precious trade item.

In the early 1600s, Spanish friars built missions at many pueblos in the basin, including the major trading pueblo of Gran Quivira, the southernmost unit, which lay on a major cultural frontier between the Apache, Mogollon, and Ancestral Pueblo domains. But drought, famine, and Apache raids caused both the Spaniards and the Pueblo Indians to abandon the sites by the 1670s. Over the years, the pueblos and missions were vandalized and started to collapse. These ruined missions are now protected by the monument.

The most beautiful and photogenic of the ruins is **Quarai**, located on a well-marked road 1 mile west of the village of Punta de Agua on Highway 55, 8 miles north of Mountainair. The church here, Nuestra Senora de la Purisima Concepcion, was founded in 1626 atop the Tewa-speaking pueblo of Cuarac, now only outlined under nearby grassy hummocks. Its 5-foot-thick red, tapering sandstone walls reach heights of 40 feet; next to the church is the *convento*, the living quarters for the monks, which has a *porteria* (waiting room), patios, *ambulatarios* (cloisters), cells, kitchens, and livestock corrals. Although it is peaceful now, it wasn't during Spanish Colonial times: This was the base for the local branch of the Spanish Inquisition, which collected evidence of impropriety against the Church by colonists.

The modest ruins at **Abó**, 9 miles west of Mountainair on US 60, are similar to those at Quarai, in that they are made out of red sandstone, and they are also located on a natural spring, which allowed the residents to farm. It may not look like much now, but Abó's strategic location on a hillside between the Rio Grande pueblos and the Estancia Basin meant that it was an important gateway pueblo. Spanish missionaries recognized the pueblo's useful location. Abó's small church of San Gregorio de Abó was the first to be built in the area in 1622; it was replaced by a larger church in 1851. Using Abó as their base, priests served the *visitas*, or satellite parishes, of neighboring Tenabo and Tabira (outside the park), and Gran Quivira to the south.

Twenty-six miles south of Mountainair on Highway 55, you'll find **Gran Quivira**, the most extensive of the Pueblo and Spanish mission church ruins in the monument and the most important culturally and politically to both the Ancestral Pueblo and mission stories in the Estancia Basin. Of the three ruins, this is the one you should not miss.

In the 1400s the powerful Pueblo de las Humanas ("Pueblo of the People with the Stripe-Painted Faces"), as it was known to the Spanish conquistadores arriving in the area, was once an important trading pueblo (farming was not possible here, so it served as a redistribution and ceremonial center) serving the southernmost frontier between the Rio Grande pueblos to the north, the Plains Indians to the east, the Pacific cultures to the west, and the Mesoamerican cultures to the south. Gran Quivira was firmly established when the Spaniards colonized New Mexico in the 1600s, and missionization never fully took here. In 1630 Fray Francisco Letrado oversaw the construction of the church and *convento* of San Isidro but left the structure incomplete when he moved to Zuni Pueblo, where he was subsequently killed. A new church, San Buenaventura, was begun in 1659 but was not completed before the whole pueblo was devastated and eventually wiped out by severe famine, Apache raiding, and sheer overwork from the impossible competing demands of Spanish missionaries and military and colonial masters, in addition to pueblo duties.

Gran Quivira's gray limestone structures are hauntingly lonely and beautiful today, their silence belying their rich human history and fascinating glimpses of the different people who once called this dry and desolate area home. Gran Quivira was set aside as one of the first national monuments under the Antiquities Act in 1906; it was absorbed into the newly created national historical park in the 1980s.

Each unit of the Salinas Pueblo Missions Monument has a visitor center, picnic tables, and restrooms, but camping is not allowed. They're all open daily from 9 a.m. to 6 p.m. during summer and 9 a.m. to 5 p.m. the rest of the year. There's no admission charge. Monument headquarters and the main visitor center for the park is centrally located between the 3 units of Quarai, Abó, and Gran Quivira, on US 60, in the ranching and farming community of Mountainair; (505) 847-2585; nps.gov/sapu. It is open daily from 8 a.m. to 5 p.m.

While you are in Mountainair, until the 1950s the "Pinto Bean Capital of New Mexico" but increasingly known as an arts town, don't miss taking a look at the 19-room historic ***Shaffer Hotel*** (103 W. Main St.). It was built by industrial artist Clem "Pop" Shaffer out of reinforced and highly decorated cast concrete in 1923, employing a style that has been dubbed "Pueblo Deco." Pueblo Deco is a brightly painted southwestern take on stylized art deco, with Spanish mission and Indian art influences. Sadly, this hotel has a history of multiple very short-term owners—some say the place is haunted—and is once again closed for business. If you pass through, it's worth checking to see if it's been reopened; it is a sight not to be missed, and a meal, if the hotel dining room has reopened.

It may seem modest and remote, but quiet and easygoing Mountainair sits at the exact center of the state, at the crossroads of Highway 55 and US 60, making it a good base for artists who like room to stretch out (think Marfa, Texas, a remote ranching town with a popular artist community). Hollywood filmmakers often use the iconic Shaffer Hotel for location shoots. Several members of the very active Manzano Mountain Arts Council run businesses in the area, including the excellent little ***Alpine Alley Coffee Shop*** ("Serving Coffee, Conversation, and the Mountainair Spirit since 2007") at 210 Summit Ave; (505) 847-2478, and the elegant ***Casa Manzano Bed-and-Breakfast Retreat Center*** in Tajique (103 FR 321; 505-384-0689; home.earthlink.net/~casa.manzano), an unexpectedly luxurious hacienda open seasonally along the Salt Mission Trail. If you're visiting Mountainair in August, check out the community's Sunflower Festival, held the last weekend of that month. Contact the Manzano Mountain Arts Council (mountainairarts.org) for details.

From Mountainair to the White House

Mountainair's all-time most prominent citizen, Clem "Pop" Shaffer earned an international reputation as a folk artist. Shaffer started as the town blacksmith, but when his shop burned to the ground, he decided to build a hotel and restaurant on the site instead. The **Shaffer Hotel** may be closed when you visit, but from the outside, you can still admire Shaffer's unique handcrafted ornamentation, from the colorful roof trim and American Indian motifs to the bright stones embedded in the outside walls to form animal-shaped mosaics.

After Shaffer finished building the hotel, his wife ran it while he turned his talents to wood carving. His fanciful animals fashioned from tree roots became so well-known that the State of New Mexico gave one as an official gift to each newly elected US president. Many of his carvings are still stored in his studio at **Rancho Bonito**, a mile down the road. For more information, contact Mountainair Chamber of Commerce (505-847-2795; discovermountainairnm.com).

Where to Stay in Central New Mexico

BERNALILLO COUNTY

Apache Canyon Ranch Bed and Breakfast Inn
To'hajiilee
(505) 377-7925
apachecanyon.net
Very expensive

Best Western Rio Grande Inn
1015 Rio Grande Blvd. NW
(Old Town area)
Albuquerque
(505) 843-9500
(800) 959-4726
riograndeinn.com
Moderate

Casas de Sueños Old Town Historic Inn
(bed-and-breakfast)
310 Rio Grande SW
Albuquerque
(505) 247-4560
(800) 665-7002
casasdesuenos.com
Expensive

Elaine's
(bed-and-breakfast)
Sandia Mountains
(505) 281-2467
(800) 821-3092
elainesbnb.com
Moderate to expensive

Hacienda Vargas
1431 Hwy. 313
Algodones
(505) 867-9115
haciendavargas.com
Moderate to expensive

Hotel Albuquerque at Old Town
800 Rio Grande Blvd. NW
Albuquerque
(505) 843-6300
(800) 237-2133
hotelabq.com
Moderate

Los Poblanos Historic Inn and Organic Farm
4803 Rio Grande Blvd. NW
Albuquerque
(505) 344-9297
lospoblanos.com
Expensive to very expensive

The Mauger Estate Bed and Breakfast Inn
701 Roma Ave. NW
Albuquerque
(505) 242-8755
(800) 719-9189
maugerbb.com
Moderate to very expensive

Sandhill Crane Bed and Breakfast
389 Camino Hermosa
Corrales
(505) 898-2445
sandhillcranebandb.com
Moderate to expensive

SANDOVAL COUNTY

Hyatt Regency Tamaya Resort
1300 Tuyuna Trail
Santa Ana Pueblo
(505) 867-1234
tamaya.hyatt.com
Expensive to very expensive

TORRANCE COUNTY

Casa Manzano Bed-and-Breakfast Retreat Center
103 FR 321
Tajique
(505) 384-0689
home.earthlink.net/~casa.manzano
Moderate (open May–Nov only)

Sunset Motel
501 E. Central Ave.
Moriarty
(505) 832-4234
sunseton66.com
Inexpensive

VALENCIA COUNTY

Days Inn Los Lunas
1919 Main St. SW
Los Lunas
(505) 865-5995
wyndhamhotels.com/days-inn
Inexpensive

Quality Inn
1711 Main St. SW
Los Lunas
(505) 865-5100
choicehotels.com/new-mexico/los-lunas/quality-inn-hotels
Inexpensive to moderate

Super 8 Motel
428 S. Main
Belen
(505) 864-8188
super8.com
Inexpensive

Where to Eat in Central New Mexico

BERNALILLO COUNTY

Chez Axel
6209 Montgomery NE (at San Pedro)
Albuquerque
(505) 881-8104
chezaxelrestaurant.com
Expensive
Authentic cuisine of Provence, France

Corrales Bistro Brewery
4908 Corrales Rd.
Corrales
(505) 897-1036
cbbistro.com
Inexpensive
Globally inspired pub grub, microbrews, and a pottery next door

El Patio de Albuquerque
142 Harvard SE (university area)
Albuquerque
(505) 268-4245
elpatioabq.com
Inexpensive to moderate
Traditional New Mexican with some heart-healthy choices

Farm & Table
8917 4th St.
Albuquerque
(505) 503-7124
farmandtable.com
Moderate to very expensive
Seasonally inspired, farm-fresh local cuisine

Flying Star Cafe
4026 Rio Grande Blvd. NW
Los Ranchos
(505) 344-6714
flyingstarcafe.com
Inexpensive to moderate
Locally sourced New Mexican and American comfort food
(several branches in Albuquerque, including Nob Hill)

Frontier Restaurant
2400 Central Ave.
Albuquerque
(505) 266-0550
frontierrestaurant.com
Inexpensive
Classic New Mexican and American

SELECTED CHAMBERS OF COMMERCE/ VISITOR BUREAUS IN CENTRAL NEW MEXICO

Albuquerque Convention & Visitors Bureau
20 First Plaza NW, Suite 601
PO Box 26866
Albuquerque, NM 87125-6866
(800) 284-2282
visitalbuquerque.org

Greater Belen Chamber of Commerce
712 Dailies Ave., Box 6
Belen, NM 87002
(505) 864-8091
belenchamber.org

Mountainair Chamber of Commerce
PO Box 595
Mountainair, NM 87036
(505) 847-2795
discovermountainairnm.com

Valencia County Chamber of Commerce
3447 Lambros Rd.
Los Lunas, NM 87031
(505) 352-3596
loslunasnm.gov

Kai's Chinese Restaurant
138 Harvard SE (university area)
Albuquerque
(505) 266-8388
kaischineserestaurant.com
Inexpensive to moderate
The best Chinese food in New Mexico

Monte Vista Fire Station
3201 Central NE (Nob Hill–Highland area)
Albuquerque
(505) 255-2424
montevistafirestation.com
Moderate to very expensive
Upscale, creative New American cuisine, emphasizing southwestern ingredients

Vinaigrette Bistro
1828 Central Ave. SW
Albuquerque
(505) 842-5507
vinaigretteonline.com
Inexpensive to moderate
Hearty and delicious main-course salads sourced daily from the young owner's organic farm in Nambé (branch of the popular Santa Fe restaurant)

Yanni's and Lemoni Bar and Grill
3109 Central NE
(Nob Hill–Highland area)
Albuquerque
(505) 268-9250
yannisandlemonibar.com
Moderate to expensive
Award-winning Mediterranean cuisine

Zacatecas Tacos and Tequila
3423 Central Ave. NE
Albuquerque
(505) 255-8226
zacatecastacos.com
Inexpensive to moderate
Authentic Zacatecas-style Mexican taqueria and tequila bar from Santa Fe's Compound chef and owner, Mark Kiffin

SANDOVAL COUNTY

The Corn Maiden
At Hyatt Regency Tamaya Resort
1300 Tuyuna Trail
Santa Ana Pueblo
(505) 771-6060
tamaya.regency.hyatt.com/en/hotel/dining/corn-maiden
Expensive to very expensive
New western cuisine with American Indian influences

VALENCIA COUNTY

Luna Mansion
Junction of Highways 6/304
Los Lunas
(505) 865-7333
lunamansion.com
Moderate to expensive
Innovative southwestern

Pete's Cafe
105 1st St.
Belen
(505) 864-4811
Inexpensive to moderate
New Mexican

Teofilos Restaurante
144 Main St. NW
Los Lunas
(505) 865-5511
Inexpensive to moderate
New Mexican
(sister restaurant to Pete's)

TORRANCE COUNTY

Alpine Alley Coffee Shop
210 N. Summit Ave.
Mountainair
(505) 847-2478
alpinealley.com
Inexpensive
Artist-owned cafe serving breakfast burritos, pastries, burgers, soups, salads, and "customerized" sandwiches and wraps

El Rey's Comedor
1005 Old Hwy. 66
Moriarty
(505) 453-2660
Inexpensive to moderate
New Mexican and American (with a famous revolving Route 66 neon sign)

Northeastern New Mexico

The scenery found in New Mexico's northeastern quadrant is quite different from that usually associated with the state.

Grasslands upon rolling hills and plains dominate the landscape, giving it a softer quality in comparison with the state's expansive desert regions. Some of New Mexico's oldest and largest ranches share this area with modern ski resorts.

The historic **Santa Fe Trail** snakes through northeastern New Mexico and figures prominently in the region's geography and history. The 900-mile trail connecting Old Franklin, Missouri, to Santa Fe was the lifeline linking the New Mexico Territory to the eastern US from 1821 to the coming of the railroad to New Mexico in 1879. Not only did the trail bring much-needed goods and prosperity, but it also brought a new people, language, skills, and customs—for better or worse, Anglos had come to New Mexico.

A decisive battle of the Civil War was also fought in this region on March 28, 1862, at the summit of Glorieta Pass, between Santa Fe and Pecos. In the Battle of Glorieta Pass, Union troops defeated the Confederates, thus destroying Southern hopes for taking over New Mexico.

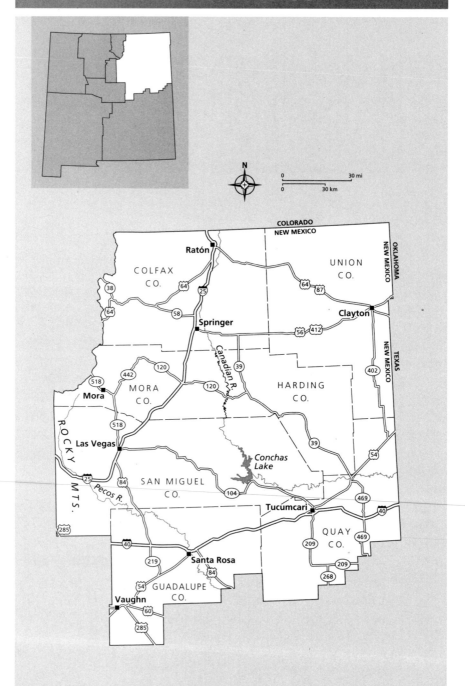

Colfax County

The quiet community of **Springer**, with its tree-lined main street, Maxwell Avenue, would seem more at home in the Midwest than in the plains of New Mexico. Here you'll find a slower pace, a couple of old antiques shops, and the **Santa Fe Trail Museum**, housed in the 1881 Colfax County Courthouse, which at first glance resembles a church.

Built in 1879, when Springer sat in the county seat before Ratón took over almost 20 years later, what is now the Santa Fe Trail Museum served as a New Mexico reform school for boys, a public library, the town hall, and the city jail, before townsfolk transformed it into a museum in 1967. It commemorates Colfax County's pioneers during the time when the Santa Fe Trail was an active route crossing the region.

The museum, which now also houses the Springer Visitor Center, is at 606 Maxwell Ave.; (575) 483-2682; santafetrailnm.org. It's open Memorial Day through Labor Day, daily from 9 a.m. to 4 p.m. Admission charge is $2 for adults and $1.50 for seniors and children.

As far as one-horse towns go, this one's got most others beat. It has its own livery stable—now known as **R. H. Cowan Livery Stable Antiques**—which is

FAVORITE ATTRACTIONS IN NORTHEASTERN NEW MEXICO

Capulin Volcano National Monument
Union County
(575) 278-2201
nps.gov/cavo

Fort Union National Monument
Mora County
(575) 425-8025
nps.gov/foun

Montezuma Castle
United World College campus
Las Vegas
(505) 454-4200

Pecos National Historical Park
San Miguel County
(505) 757-2421
nps.gov/peco

Philmont Ranch
north of Cimarron
(575) 376-2281
philmontscoutranch.org

Ratón Arts and Cultural District
Ratón
(575) 445-3689
ratonmainstreet.org

St. James Hotel
617 S. Collison
Cimarron
(575) 376-2664
(888) 376-2664
exstjames.com

a Springer landmark and houses a wonderful, cluttered mishmash of antiques for sale. Hidden treasures abound. Built in 1880, the stone stable is definitely from the horse-and-wagon days and in excellent shape, considering its age and lack of restoration. Avoid this place if a little dust and dirt offend you. Livery Stable Antiques is at the corner of Maxwell Avenue and 3rd Street; (575) 483-2825. Open by appointment only.

A 37-mile drive northeast of Springer brings you to the grand, 36-room *Dorsey Mansion*, a place of pure rustic opulence in the middle of New Mexico's high plains. The log-and-stone home was built by US senator Stephen W. Dorsey of Arkansas in 1880. An addition several years later produced the castlelike structure with likenesses of Dorsey, his wife, and his brother carved in stone on the tower.

In addition to his role as a politician, Dorsey was a railroad financier and up-and-coming cattle baron who liked to throw elaborate parties at his mansion, now listed on the National Register of Historic Places. Highlights of the interior include the black marble fireplace from Italy, the cherrywood staircase brought from Chicago, and the artificial pond with three islands, one of which once boasted a gazebo.

Though closed to tours until further notice, the mansion can be seen from a distance by following the unpaved 12-mile road that starts at the Dorsey Mansion Scenic Historical Marker on Highway 56. The grounds are home to the largest llama herd in New Mexico—more than 250 of them; (575) 375-2222; dorseymansion.com.

newmexicotrivia

The Santa Fe Trail Museum in Springer boasts New Mexico's first and only electric chair. The death penalty was abolished in New Mexico in 2009, though only one prisoner had been executed in the previous 40 years.

Just 7 miles south of the Colorado border, the city of *Ratón* evolved along the Santa Fe Trail around three main influences: coal mining, railroading, and ranching. The days of the first two are pretty much in the past. Ratón's Spanish Mission Revival–style depot, built in 1903, served the city well until 1990, when Amtrak suspended its last scheduled stop (en route to Albuquerque from Chicago).

The depot is the focal point of the *Ratón Arts and Cultural District*, which centers on 1st Street just across from the railroad tracks. Listed on the National Register of Historic Places since 1977, the district includes some 70 buildings. Businesses originally sprang up in this area in the 1880s to serve the needs of railroad workers. Today this strip is a great place to check out

STATE PARKS IN NORTHEASTERN NEW MEXICO

Online at emnrd.state.nm.us/spd

Cimarron Canyon State Park
3 miles east of Eagle Nest
(575) 377-6271

Clayton Lake State Park
15 miles north of Clayton
(575) 374-8808

Conchas Lake State Park
34 miles northwest of Tucumcari
(575) 868-2270

Coyote Creek State Park
south of Angel Fire near Guadalupita
(575) 387-2328

Morphy Lake State Park
southwest of Mora near Ledoux
(575) 387-2328

Santa Rosa Lake State Park
7 miles north of Santa Rosa
(575) 472-3110

Storrie Lake State Park
6 miles north of Las Vegas
(505) 425-7278

Sugarite Canyon State Park
10 miles northeast of Ratón
(575) 445-5607

Ute Lake State Park
3 miles west of Logan
(575) 487-2284

Villanueva State Park
31 miles southwest of Las Vegas
(575) 421-2957

antiques shops and admire the diverse architecture. You can also travel back in time at *Ratón Museum*, which chronicles the area's history of mines, rails, and cattle through artifacts and photographs.

Ratón Museum is located at 108 S. 2nd St.; (575) 445-8979; theratonmuseum.org. It's open Tues through Sat from 10 a.m. to 4 p.m. Memorial Day through Labor Day and Wed through Sat from 10 a.m. to 4 p.m. the rest of the year. There's no admission charge.

Nearby, at 131 N. 2nd St. (575-445-4746; shulertheater.com), the restored *Shuler Theater* continues to stage theatrical productions and is the permanent home for the *Santa Fe Trail School for the Performing Arts*, with monthlong summer theater workshops for youth from second grade through high school. It opened in 1915 and was named for Dr. J. J. Shuler, Ratón's mayor when the grand structure was built. The theater's exterior, described as European rococo architecture, pales in comparison with its interior, with its ornate woodwork, sky-painted ceiling, and gold-trimmed box seats. Eight Works Progress Administration (WPA) murals commissioned by the federal government during the Great Depression enhance the lobby and trace Ratón's history.

The theater welcomes visitors during office hours—call ahead, as they vary—and on weekends when a show is scheduled. There's no cost to look or take a photo.

Heart's Desire Inn opened in 1998 and, following the closure of the Red Violet Inn, is now the only bed-and-breakfast in Ratón itself. Located in the heart of historic downtown Ratón, the 1885 Victorian-style home is the perfect setting for a romantic getaway to northeastern New Mexico. Innkeeper Barbara Riley pampers her guests by welcoming them with fruit baskets in their rooms, providing evening hors d'oeuvres such as fresh-baked breads and cheeses, and preparing breakfasts tailored to her guests' preferences. Four theme rooms (the Lodge Room, Patriotic Room, Blue Willow Room, and Victorian Room), each with its own sink, are appointed with antique furnishings, as is a suite, with kitchen, private bath, and living area.

Heart's Desire doubles as an antiques shop, with antiques and collectibles featured throughout the inn's first floor. It's open to the public Mon through Fri from 8 a.m. to noon, and Sat and Sun from 9 a.m. to 6 p.m.

Heart's Desire Inn is located at 301 S. 3rd St.; (575) 445-1000 or (866) 488-1028; heartsdesireraton.com. Room rates range from $69 to $90. (Discounts are offered for seniors and government employees.)

From Ratón, head 38 miles southwest on US 64 to discover the hidden Old West romance of ***Cimarron*** (roughly meaning "wild" or "unbroken" in Spanish). This is Marlboro Country, in all its iconic, wide-open glory. Quite literally, too, for those famous cigarette ads featuring the iconic cowboy were photographed on the CS Cattle Company ranch near Cimarron. All of Old Cimarron is ripe for exploring and centered on Santa Fe Trail (that's the name of the street here; it's also the trail, though it becomes Highway 21 south of town).

The ***St. James Hotel*** in Cimarron once attracted the most famous and infamous guests in the Wild West. Located on the Santa Fe Trail, the St. James retains its air of mystery and intrigue, right down to the ghosts that are said to waft around its rooms and hallways.

Built in 1873 by Henri Lambert, a former cook for Ulysses S. Grant and Abraham Lincoln, the stately, pale-pink adobe hotel was once considered one of the finest in the West. Jesse James, Black Jack Ketchum, Wyatt Earp, Buffalo Bill Cody, Annie Oakley, and Zane Grey were among the hotel's early patrons. The hotel was restored and reopened in 1985.

The entire hotel, including lobby, 22 guest rooms (12 in the old hotel and 10 in the annex), and dining area, is outfitted with authentic Victorian furnishings, mounted game, and large paintings. Individual rooms are named after some of the celebrated figures who stayed in them. Every old hotel worth its salt has one or several resident ghosts, and it's common knowledge that the St.

James was not shortchanged. The room that once belonged to Mary Lambert, Henri's second wife (no. 17), is frequently strongly scented with roses, her favorite perfume, while a nearby room belonged to a gambler who lost the hotel in a card game and came to a sticky end. That one does not get rented out.

Evidence of the hotel's rough-and-tumble past is apparent in the bullet holes visible in the pressed-tin ceiling of the Restaurant and Bar (previously Lambert's Saloon and Gambling Hall). Instead of red-eye, the newly renovated restaurant now serves reasonably priced hearty western fare. A large breakfast is served to guests daily from 7 to 10:30 a.m. It's included in the room rate for guests; $9.95 per person for nonguests. Inexpensive lunch specials of New Mexican favorites and sandwiches are served daily from 11 a.m. to 5 p.m. A dinner menu consisting of bison burgers, steaks, trout and other seafood, chicken, and other fare is available Mon through Sat from 5 to 9 p.m.

The St. James is on Highway 21, just north of US 64 in the center of Cimarron's historic district; (575) 376-2664 or (888) 376-2664; exstjames.com. Room rates range from $85 to $135.

Just down the lane, across from the St. James, you'll spot the **Old Mill Museum**, guarded by the thick rock walls of the Aztec Mill. The mill was built in 1864 by Lucien B. Maxwell, who, with his 1.7 million acres, was purported to be the single largest landowner of all time in the Western Hemisphere. Maxwell brought an engineer, a millwright, and a chief mason from back east to take on the $50,000 project. In its time, the mill could turn out 300 barrels of flour per day. Though the three-story building was converted to a museum in 1967, the stone structure itself is just as impressive as its contents, which include exhibits chronicling late 19th-century northern New Mexico.

The museum is run by the CS Cattle Company and opens on an irregular schedule in summer only. Contact Cimarron Visitor Center at (575) 376-2417 for hours; cimarronnm.com/visitor-center.

About 5 miles south of the St. James, on Highway 21, you'll find the headquarters to the vast **Philmont Ranch**, now owned by the Boy Scouts of America (BSA). Here's where the buffalo really do roam and the deer and the antelope are known to play. The jewel of the 137,493-acre ranch is **Villa Philmonte**, the Mediterranean-style mansion built as a summer home by Oklahoma oilman Waite Phillips, of Phillips 66.

Phillips gave the ranch to the BSA in 1938 "for the purpose of perpetuating faith, self-reliance, integrity, and freedom, the principles used to build this great country by the American Pioneer." And each summer since, thousands of scouts have convened at Philmont for the ultimate camping adventure.

Visitors can also enjoy much of the Boy Scout ranch. Tours of Villa Philmonte are given daily by reservation during spring, summer, and fall. The home and most of its furnishings have been restored to their original grandeur. In addition to the living room, with its custom-built piano, the most impressive room is the trophy room, highlighted by the huge buffalo mounted above the fireplace.

Reservations to tour Villa Philmonte can be made on-site at the **Philmont Museum** and **Seton Memorial Library** (or by calling the museum at 575-376-1136), just past the driveway that loops around the mansion. Both are open to visitors year-round (daily in summer, weekdays only in winter). The museum displays exhibits of those persons who influenced this area—cowboys, Indians, miners, mountain men, and settlers. The library contains the books, art, and natural history collection of Ernest Thompson Seton, an author, artist, and naturalist and the first chief scout of the Boy Scouts of America. The museum and library are open daily from 8 a.m. to 5 p.m. There's no admission charge; tours cost $3 for adults, and children under age 12 are free.

Seven miles south, in Rayado, you'll find another feature of the Philmont Ranch, the **Kit Carson Home and Museum**. It's built in the adobe hacienda style and finished with 1850s period furnishings. Living-history demonstrations are given here. It's open June through Aug, daily from 8 a.m. to 5 p.m.; call the Philmont Museum number for specific schedules.

If you're no Boy Scout and the St. James is booked, consider the **Casa del Gavilan** ("House of the Hawk") bed-and-breakfast for a weekend hideaway. The gracious Pueblo Revival–style inn was built in 1912 by the eastern industrialist J. J. Nairn, who often hosted famous artists and writers in his gleaming white adobe home tucked into the foothills of the Sangre de Cristo Mountains. Only those with confirmed reservations are allowed on the premises, though, because guests' privacy is highly regarded here. Casa del Gavilan is 6 miles south of Cimarron on Highway 21; (575) 376-2246 or (800) 428-4526; casadelgavilan.com. Rates for the 4 elegant rooms range from $116 to $182, which includes breakfast.

Heading west on US 64 from Cimarron, you'll come across the community of Eagle Nest—along with its attractive namesake lake—and the village of Angel Fire.

The meadows meeting the mountains in the countryside surrounding **Angel Fire** give new meaning to the enchantment of New Mexico. Atop a small hill you'll find the country's first memorial dedicated to all Vietnam veterans. Originally built in 1971 by Dr. Victor Westphall in memory of his son, who was killed in the war, the memorial was expanded and taken over by the Disabled American Veterans in the early 1980s; however, the memorial disaffiliated with the DAV in 2000 and is now run privately by the David Westphall Veterans Foundation.

Harvesttime

New Mexico has played a pivotal role in the development of independent, organic farms in recent years. Because the dry, rugged countryside does not lend itself to large-scale agribusiness, about 93 percent of the farming in the state takes place on single-family farms less than 1 square mile in size. The economics of agriculture are such that small farms cannot make a profit competing for sales to conventional supermarkets. Instead, the new breed of farmers produces premium products through organic farming and cuts out middlemen by selling crops directly to the public. Among the most important of these economic outlets are farmers' markets, which you'll find in every corner of the state.

If you are a traveler in New Mexico, you may find it impractical to buy much in the way of fresh produce and take it along on the road (although I encourage you to pack a cooler and do so). Even so, farmers' markets also sell many foodstuffs that make great souvenirs and gifts, such as raspberry jam, green chile jelly, garlic oil, southwestern chutney, and bags of ground red chile, roasted piñon nuts, and pistachios. Farmers' markets are also a wonderful place to mingle with the local people.

Farmers' markets usually operate from June through October, although the Santa Fe Farmers' Market operates year-round in its own custom-built pavilion in the Railyard. They are open only one or two days a week in any single locality, but there are farmers' markets somewhere in the state every day of the week. The list below shows which communities have farmers' markets on each day. Most markets operate from about 7 a.m. to noon or 1 p.m. Those marked with asterisks (*) below operate in the afternoons, typically from 4 to 7 p.m.

Monday: Española*, Portales*

Tuesday: Albuquerque (7605 Central Ave. NE), Clovis*, Elephant Butte, Farmington*, Roswell, Santa Fe, Silver City*, Socorro*, Tucumcari*

Wednesday: Corrales*, Aztec*, Carlsbad, Clayton, Dixon*, Las Cruces, San Felipe*, Santa Fe

Thursday: Albuquerque (South Valley)*, Bloomfield*, Los Alamos, Portales,* Santa Fe*

Friday: Bernalillo*, Belen*, Sunland Park

Saturday: Alamogordo, Albuquerque (downtown), Albuquerque (7605 Central Ave. NE), Albuquerque (Los Ranchos), Carlsbad, Chaparral, Clayton, Clovis, Elephant Butte, Farmington, Gallup, Grants, Las Cruces, Questa, Ramah, Roswell, Santa Fe, Socorro, Tierra Amarilla, Tucumcari, Tularosa

Sunday: Corrales, Cedar Crest, Mesilla*, Pecos, Silver City, Taos

For information on exact schedules and locations, as well as what crops are in season at any specific time, visit the New Mexico Farmers' Marketing Association website at farmersmarketsnm.org.

The small, nondenominational chapel at the ***Vietnam Veterans Memorial*** at Angel Fire is breathtakingly simple as it sits in harmony with the land. The tallest wing of this dovelike structure rises 64 feet, gracefully curving downward to the ground. The accompanying visitor center is just as contemporary and displays banners and poster-size photographs of wide-ranging scenes from the war.

Completed years before the celebrated memorial in Washington, DC, the Angel Fire structure differs in the feeling it leaves within when visitors depart. There is no turbulence or divisive political statement associated with this memorial. Though powerful in the emotions it elicits, the memorial allows visitors to come away with their own reactions, rather than forcing any particular ones.

The Vietnam Veterans Memorial is just off US 64 at the Angel Fire turnoff; (575) 377-6900; vietnamveteransmemorial.org. The visitor center is open daily from 9 a.m. to 5 p.m. The chapel never closes, and there's no admission charge.

Union County

The perfectly shaped cinder cone rising from the plains, known as Capulin Volcano, was once a fiery volcano in the extensive Ratón-Clayton Volcanic Field that last erupted some 10,000 years ago. It's now protected within the fascinating and scenic ***Capulin Volcano National Monument***, about 30 miles east of Ratón. As one of the remotest of the New Mexico units in the National Park System, Capulin is a quiet joy to visit. It rarely gets crowded, is easy to ascend via a paved road, and has a level trail to wander on top for extraordinary views of several surrounding states. What's more, Capulin is highly photogenic. The surrounding short-grass prairie is dotted with wildflowers in summer, while brilliant turning oak and aspen leaves on this and other mountains make it a great photography destination in fall.

A road from the visitor center winds 1,000 feet up the cinder cone to the volcanic caldera. You can see four states—New Mexico (obviously), Texas, Colorado, and Oklahoma—if you hike the mile-long Crater Rim Trail around the caldera. Another short trail actually leads inside the volcano—one of the few places in the world where you can do this (Haleakala National Park on Maui is another). Although Capulin hasn't erupted in 10,000 years, it's considered dormant, not extinct. Scientists say volcanoes 25,000 years old or less are potentially active, so no one knows whether Capulin will ever erupt again. Not knowing—for certain, anyway—adds to the thrill.

To get to Capulin Volcano National Monument from Ratón, take US 64/87 east for about 30 miles to the community of Capulin and then head north on

Highway 325 for a few miles to the monument; (575) 278-2201; nps.gov/cavo. The visitor center is open daily from 8 a.m. to 4 p.m. Labor Day through Memorial Day; during summer, hours are daily 7:30 a.m. to 6:30 p.m. Admission is $7 per carload and $5 per person for motorcycles and bicycles; Golden Age Passports are accepted for seniors, as well as federal multiagency passes.

In extreme northeastern New Mexico (mere miles from the Oklahoma and Texas borders), you'll find the thriving community of **Clayton**, Union County seat and regional trading hub—and home base for exploring several notable area attractions, including Capulin Volcano, Clayton Lake, Rabbit Ear Mountains, authentic dinosaur tracks on an ancient mudflat, Santa Fe Trail ruts, and Folsom Falls.

Along the Dry Cimarron River, 4 miles northeast of the small community of **Folsom** on Highway 456, you'll find **Folsom Falls**, a natural spring-fed waterfall on the river, which forms a favorite fishing spot as well as a great place for a picnic.

The postage stamp–size community of Folsom (population 57) was named for President Grover Cleveland's bride, Frances Ruth Folsom, for whom the Baby Ruth candy bar was also named. Remarkably, Folsom was once the largest stockyard west of Fort Worth but declined when the railroad arrived in 1880 and has never recovered. A flash flood on the Dry Cimarron River nearly wiped out the town in 1908, but led to an important find for African American cowboy George McJunkin: a beautiful fluted arrow point embedded in the ribs of a long-extinct bison. Archaeologists were excited by the discovery, for it heralded tangible proof of a 10,000-year-old Paleo-Indian culture they dubbed, naturally, the Folsom, then thought to be the oldest in North America. Although the discovery of an earlier Paleo-Indian culture, the Clovis (named for Clovis in eastern New Mexico), quickly supplanted this one at Folsom as the oldest known culture in the US, McJunkin's discovery of Folsom-era artifacts put this village on the archaeological map forever.

They don't make much fuss about Folsom Man here. The dusty **Folsom History Museum** in the old Doherty Mercantile building has a few exhibits alongside the requisite pioneer artifacts, and that's about it. Nearby Capulin Volcano National Monument sometimes offers ranger-led archaeological excursions to the Folsom area, and if you are really interested in the archaeology, it's best to inquire there.

Folsom History Museum is right in the center of the village; (575) 278-2122; folsomvillage.com/folsommuseum. It's open Memorial Day weekend through September, daily from 10 a.m. to 5 p.m.; weekends in May and Oct; and the remainder of the year by appointment only. Admission is $1.50 for adults, 50 cents for children ages 6 to 12, and free under age 6.

Back in Clayton, be sure to check out the landmark *Hotel Eklund* (15 Main St.; 575-374-2551; hoteleklund.com), which was built in 1882 and was a famous hangout for outlaws. Its most famous resident was Tom "Black Jack" Ketchum, who was hanged here on April 26, 1901. The specialty in the restaurant is, naturally, Union County beef (steaks), and like that of the St. James Hotel, the Old West ambience includes a well-worn wooden bar and bullet holes in the pressed-tin ceiling. The restaurant is open daily from 7 a.m. to 9 p.m.; a buffet is served at breakfast, and there's full meal service at lunch and dinner. The hotel has 26 attractive rooms with handmade furnishings and all standard amenities; rates range from $90 to $135 per night.

newmexicotrivia

Notorious outlaw Black Jack Ketchum is buried in the Clayton Cemetery.

Mora County

Fort Union National Monument is at its best when visited on a crisp, sunny autumn day. Though it's quite isolated, Fort Union is easily accessible via I-25, which brings a steady stream of visitors during summer. When you approach the remains of the fort, the vision of redbrick and adobe ruins jutting up from the grassy plains is at once attractive and a little odd. Once you get to the fort site along the Santa Fe Trail, with its incredibly expansive views, you sense why this spot was chosen.

Established in 1851 by Lieutenant Colonel Edwin V. Sumner to protect the Santa Fe Trail and the New Mexico Territory from Indian raids, Fort Union was the largest military depot in the Southwest. There were actually three Fort Unions, the last of whose ruins constitute the park. The fort was abandoned in 1891, after which residents from nearby communities scavenged most of its usable materials, thereby hastening its deterioration.

The visitor center provides a walking-tour map to help interpret the fort's layout. If you visit on a sunny day, follow the trail to the fort's sundial, just across from the quartermaster's lodging. It's still intact and quite accurate. The park service has done a great job preserving the frontier feeling and dignity of the fort. Interpretive audio stations at selected stops along the trail emit dialogues indicative of the situation, that is, soldier to commander and soldier to soldier. Recorded bugle calls sporadically echo across the grounds from loudspeakers hidden by the adobe walls. Fort Union is also one of the best places to see the wagon-wheel ruts of the Santa Fe Trail; those wagons last cut through the plains more than a century ago.

To get to Fort Union, take I-25 north of Las Vegas to exit 366, then head north on Highway 161, which dead-ends at the fort after 8 miles; (575) 425-8025; nps.gov/foun. A tree-shaded picnic area is available. The park is open daily from 8 a.m. to 5 p.m. Memorial Day through Labor Day and from 11 a.m. to 4 p.m. the remainder of the year. Admission to Fort Union is now free.

Just east of the village of Cleveland, northwest of *Mora*, you'll come across the *Cleveland Roller Mill Museum*. Like other, earlier flour mills in the area, the Cleveland Roller Mill, built in 1901, helped satisfy the growing demands for wheat flour in the region around the turn of the 20th century. The two-story adobe mill was the last of its kind to be built in northern New Mexico—and the last to cease operations, around 1954; as such, it's the only roller mill in New Mexico of any size to have its original milling works intact.

The mill's restoration began in 1979, when it was placed on the National Register of Historic Places and the New Mexico Cultural Properties Register. Providing a glimpse into the agricultural past of the area, the museum features historical and cultural exhibits focusing on the Mora Valley. On Labor Day weekend, the museum hosts Millfest, during which the operation of the mill is demonstrated. The usual food, fun, and frolic round out the event.

The museum is open weekends only, Memorial Day weekend through Labor Day weekend. Hours are 10 a.m. to 3 p.m. but subject to change, so please call ahead. Admission is $3 for adults and $1 for youth age 18 and under. The grounds are always open; (575) 387-2645; clevelandrollermill museum.com.

Just outside the small community of Mora, you'll encounter *La Cueva Mill*, another beautifully rustic old structure, now part of Mora County's famed Salman Ranch, a raspberry-growing business. The mill was built by Vicente Romero in the 1870s, partly in response to the heavy demand for flour, owing to the establishment of Fort Union and to the steadily increasing Santa Fe Trail traffic. Though Mora County is now one of New Mexico's most economically depressed areas, during the late 1800s it was one of the most prosperous.

The old adobe and stone buildings of the mill are not accessible, for safety reasons; nevertheless, you can pull off the road for an exterior look at one of New Mexico's more impressive old water-driven mills. The cold, clear water from the acequia still flows around the mill, though it's now diverted from the wheel.

Although the mill has not been used for grinding wheat and generating electricity since 1949, during late summer through early fall *Salman Raspberry Ranch* sets up shop at the mill to sell its produce, including vegetables, herbs, cut flowers, and, most notably, farm-fresh raspberries. You can buy them by the flat or pick them yourself. You can also stock up on the ranch's prized raspberry jam. Its raspberry vinegar is perfect for dressing a salad. They also have a cafe.

Salman Raspberry Ranch was started by one of New Mexico's most prominent families. Colonel William Salman was a Jewish refugee from Poland who had lost most of his family in the Nazi death camps during World War II and fled to the United States. He bought the ranch as a safe haven for his family on his return from serving in Europe in World War II. He went from working as a stevedore on the Houston, Texas, docks to owning his own steamship business, which he then ran from the isolated location of Mora from the 1940s on.

His children grew up on the ranch and, like their father, were dedicated to tending the land. Salman's son, David, a state representative with a strong conservation record, ran the Salman Raspberry Ranch and Santa Fe Greenhouses for 40 years and developed the property's ponds as a flyover for wintering birds. He died in 2010. William Salman, the eldest son, helped found Santa Fe Greenhouses and the raspberry fields. Frances Salman Koenig, a clinical psychologist in Albuquerque, ran the berry ranch until 2016. When the next generation declined to take over, surviving family members decided to sell the ranch to a Texan rancher and property developer who had already bought a section of the historic Romero land grant with the intention of reuniting it. He has vowed to maintain the integrity of the land and much-loved ranch operation as it has always been for visitors.

The mill is located 6 miles south of Mora near the junction of Highway 518 and Highway 442. In-season produce sale hours are generally 9 a.m. to 5 p.m. daily. For more information, contact the ranch at (575) 387-2900; salmanraspberryranch.com.

San Miguel County

Not to confused with the glitzier and much younger gambling capital of Nevada, the community of **Las Vegas**, New Mexico, has a charm all its own. During its railroad heyday in the 1880s, Las Vegas ("The Plains") was the largest and most exciting city in New Mexico, and in 1900, had the largest population in New Mexico, largely as a result of its location on the main railroad line. Today, Las Vegas is quieter but has mellowed into a captivating community enhanced by a rich architectural heritage—half the state's registered historic buildings, more than 900, are located here.

To get a sense of Las Vegas's past, stop by the **City of Las Vegas Museum and Rough Rider Memorial Collection**. The main draw at the museum is the Rough Rider collection, which displays exhibits associated with the heroic group of men Teddy Roosevelt organized in 1898 for his acclaimed Cuban campaign during the Spanish-American War. Many of the volunteers came from New Mexico, and even though the Rough Riders were commissioned for just 150 days, they held a reunion in Las Vegas every year from 1899 (when the event was attended by Roosevelt while he was governor of New York) until 1967, when it was attended by only one veteran, Jesse Langdon, who died in 1975. Roosevelt even announced his candidacy for president in Las Vegas, and twice stayed at the Plaza Hotel (see below).

Las Vegas Museum began with mementos brought home by the Rough Riders and now includes a great variety of artifacts relating to Las Vegas's history and New Mexico's past. It is located at 725 Grand Ave.; (505) 426-3205; lasvegasmuseum.org. It's open year-round, Tues through Sat from 10 a.m. to 4 p.m. There's no admission charge, but a $2 donation is suggested.

Many native New Mexicans consider Las Vegas's **Old Town Plaza** the most beautiful plaza in the state because of its large size, abundance of trees, and gazebo. Anchored by the 1882 **Plaza Hotel**, the plaza and surrounding streets are dotted with shops and restaurants.

In 1982, a hundred years after it was built, the Plaza reopened in its present iteration following a $2 million renovation by new owner William "Wid" Slick, who with his partners was involved in restoring many of the historic buildings around the Las Vegas plaza to their former Victorian glory and jump-starting New Mexico's Main Street Program. In 2006, Slick added on to the hotel the 1891 Ilfeld Department Store next door in a $5 million renovation, which increased the number of hotel guest rooms to 35 and added on a ballroom and meeting space for business use.

In 2014, the Plaza was purchased by historical property enthusiast and entrepreneur Allen Affeldt, owner of the historic La Posada hotel in Winslow, Arizona. Affeldt and his team have been renovating the hotel, room by room, and have doubled the size of the bar and expanded the ballroom. At the same time, Affeldt also bought the Castaneda Hotel across the street. Designed by Mary Elizabeth Jane Colter, architect of La Posada in Winslow and many hotels at the Grand Canyon for hotelier Fred Harvey, the Castaneda has been derelict for some years and will require a complete overhaul. But for Affeldt and his artistic team, made up of college friends and spouses, this is just the kind of challenge they love. All lived on-site at La Posada over years of renovation and were determined to do things slowly and carefully; the plan is to effect the same award-winning transformation at the Castaneda.

From the worn hardwood of the lobby floor to the towering twin staircases connecting the lobby to the second floor, the Plaza Hotel has an air of history and elegance. Except for the modern comforts of queen-size beds and new bathrooms, the high-ceilinged guest rooms are appointed in period antiques with wall and window treatments consistent with the Victorian era (new furnishings and linens have now been brought over from La Posada in Winslow to improve the guest experience). Unlike many historic hotels, the guest rooms are surprisingly well insulated and thus quiet, with each offering its own thermostat.

Byron T's Saloon, the lobby bar, is named after former Plaza Hotel owner Byron T. Mills, who's also the hotel's resident ghost. It's a comfortable place to have a drink while enjoying a street-level view of Old Town Plaza.

A favorite with locals as well as guests, the hotel's renovated restaurant, the **Gilded Age**, offers breakfast (free for guests), lunch, and dinner and features local farm-sourced ingredients in a menu inspired both by the traditional cuisine of Spanish settlers in the 1700s and dishes from the Victorian era. Chef Amaury Torres, a veteran of the Santa Fe food scene, was lured to the restaurant in 2016 and has jump-started the menu, which now combines a good balance of New Mexico favorites. For breakfast, there are traditional selections such as porridge or huevos rancheros. Lunch includes club sandwiches, green chile stew, a taco plate, a local organic salad dressed with raspberry vinaigrette from nearby Salman Ranch, and the popular half-pound burger with green chile in a local bun. Dinner is where the restaurant really shines. Entrees include Chef Amaury's mariscada (a Portuguese/Brazilian seafood stew), aged grilled rib eye, pan-seared salmon, a Spanish vegetable pasta that includes green chile, Victorian chicken fricassee, and blue corn enchiladas. Spanish guitar on Sunday mornings accompanies the popular brunch.

The Plaza Hotel has 71 reasonably priced, updated rooms and suites, and many have plaques showing celebrities who have stayed in each one. It's located at 230 Plaza; (505) 425-3591; plazahotellvnm.com. Room rates range from $99 to $149.

Head out of Las Vegas about 5 miles on Hot Springs Boulevard (which borders the streetside corner of the Plaza Hotel) and you'll be in the small community of **Montezuma**, at the mouth of Gallinas Canyon. Imposing **Montezuma Castle** looms on a hilltop as the focal point for the **Armand Hammer United World College of the American West** (505-454-4221; uwc-usa.org). Built in 1884 as a showpiece resort by the Santa Fe Railroad, Montezuma Castle was abandoned as a hotel, run by Fred Harvey, during the financial depression at the turn of the 20th century. The castle was purchased in 1981 by Dr. Armand Hammer—billionaire philanthropist and former chairman of Occidental Petroleum Corporation—with the intention of starting the college. It was completely renovated in 2000–2001. The small college now has more than 200 students from more than 60 nations and is one of 16 United World Colleges worldwide begun by Armand Hammer.

On campus, the unusual and striking **Dwan Light Sanctuary** is the result of a collaboration among conceptualizer Virginia Dwan, artist Charles Ross, and architect Laban Wingert. The project grew out of Dwan's dream of creating a quiet space for contemplation for people of all beliefs. According to Dwan, the sanctuary "revolves around the spiritual and temporal universality of the number 12." Integral to her vision, the Light Sanctuary incorporates

newmexicotrivia

Tom Mix shot his silent Westerns in the Las Vegas, New Mexico, area.

12 angles of light within its circular space, and 12 large prisms in the apses and ceiling create a progression throughout the year of unique spectrum events. In addition, the sanctuary's orientation and geometry were designed so as to align the prisms of the building to the sun, moon, and stars, as well as to capture their light rays from sunrise to sunset. The interacting spectrums create broad, moving ribbons of color on the walls, ceiling, and floor of the sanctuary.

Dwan Light Sanctuary is open for quiet reflection daily from 6 a.m. to 10 p.m. Yoga classes, concerts, and other events are sometimes staged here. Admission is free. (**Note:** United World College is a closed campus. Visitors to the campus must first stop at Moore Welcome Center to register and be accompanied around campus by a UWC guide.) Once inside the sanctuary, please remove your shoes. Find more information on the sanctuary at uwc-usa .org/page.cfm?p=528.

Just past the castle on Hot Springs Boulevard (Highway 65), you'll find **Montezuma Hot Springs**, nondescript holes that dot the banks of the Gallinas River. Located on the property of the United World College, these natural hot tubs are fed from 112-degree mineral springs that bubble up from the ground. The springs are a great place to relax and enjoy the view—Montezuma Castle, the river, the rock cliffs—especially when it's a little nippy outside. A brown sign that reads "Hot Springs Baths" marks the spot.

There's no charge to enjoy the therapeutic waters, but it's a first-come, first-soak arrangement. Early morning and late night are the best times to find them vacant. You may encounter naked people milling about, so if this offends you, consider yourself warned.

About ½ mile farther on Highway 65 toward the mountains, veer left on a gravel road and you'll immediately come across **Gallinas Pond**, or **City Pond**, as it's also known. During most times of the year, the pond is nothing more than a small body of water bordered by shimmering, sheer cliffs on one side. But during the dead of winter, when the water has frozen and the ice skates

A Sampling of Movies and TV Shows Filmed in New Mexico

Batman v Superman: Dawn of Justice
(2016)
Ben Affleck, Henry Cavill
(Deming)

The Space Between Us (2016)
Gary Oldman
(Santa Fe, Albuquerque, Truth or
Consequences)

Whiskey, Tango, Foxtrot (2016)
Tina Fey
(Santa Fe)

Sicario (2015)
Emily Blunt, Josh Brolin, Benicio Del Toro
(Albuquerque)

Longmire (TV; 2012–2016)
Robert Taylor, Lou Diamond Phillips
(Santa Fe, Las Vegas, Valles Caldera,
Pecos, Taos)

Breaking Bad (TV; 2008–2013)
Bryan Cranston
(Albuquerque)

Crazy Heart (2010)
Jeff Bridges
(Santa Fe)

My One and Only (2009)
Renée Zellweger, Kevin Bacon
(Shaffer Hotel, Mountainair)

Appaloosa (2008)
Ed Harris, Viggo Mortensen, Renée
Zellweger
(Abiquiu, Galisteo, Santa Fe, Lamy)

No Country for Old Men (2007)
Tommy Lee Jones, Javier Bardem, Josh
Brolin
(Albuquerque, Santa Fe, Las Vegas, Taos)

3:10 to Yuma (2007)
Russell Crowe, Christian Bale
(Abiquiu, Santa Fe)

Wild Hogs (2007)
Tim Allen, John Travolta, William H. Macy,
Martin Lawrence
(Madrid, Santa Fe, Pojoaque)

Brokeback Mountain (2005)
Jake Gyllenhaal, Heath Ledger
(La Mesilla)

The Missing (2003)
Tommy Lee Jones, Cate Blanchett
(Santa Fe County)

All the Pretty Horses (2000)
Matt Damon, Penelope Cruz
(Santa Fe, Las Vegas)

Contact (1997)
Jodie Foster, Matthew McConaughey
(Socorro County)

have been brought out, the pond turns into a winter wonderland reminiscent of the Northeast and Midwest. It's one of only a few places open to the public in New Mexico where you can pond-skate.

Heading south and west from Las Vegas on I-25, plan a stop at ***Pecos National Historical Park***, near the community of Pecos, which preserves the ruins of a Spanish mission church and the abandoned ancient pueblo of Cicuye, at one time one of the largest and most powerful trading pueblos in New Mexico.

Wyatt Earp (1993)
Kevin Costner, Dennis Quaid, Gene Hackman
(Santa Fe, Rancho de las Golondrinas, Chama, Las Vegas, Zia, Tesuque, Santa Clara Pueblo)

City Slickers (1991)
Billy Crystal, Jack Palance, Daniel Stern
(Ghost Ranch, Santa Fe, Abiquiu, Nambé Pueblo, Santa Clara Pueblo)

Lonesome Dove (1989)
Robert Duvall, Tommy Lee Jones, Danny Glover, Anjelica Huston
(Santa Fe, Angel Fire)

The Milagro Beanfield War (1988)
Ruben Blades, Sonia Braga, Daniel Stern
(Truchas)

Young Guns (1988)
Emilio Estevez, Charlie Sheen, Lou Diamond Phillips, Kiefer Sutherland, Terence Stamp, Jack Palance
(Cerrillos, Galisteo, Ojo Caliente, Rancho de las Golondrinas)

Silverado (1985)
Kevin Kline, Danny Glover, Kevin Costner, Rosanna Arquette, Linda Hunt
(Galisteo, Abiquiu, Santa Ana Pueblo)

Superman (1978)
Christopher Reeve, Margot Kidder
(in and around Gallup)

My Name Is Nobody (1973)
Henry Fonda, Terence Hill
(Acoma Pueblo, Mogollon)

The Cowboys (1972)
John Wayne, Bruce Dern, Colleen Dewhurst
(Chama, Galisteo, Santa Fe)

The Cheyenne Social Club (1970)
James Stewart, Henry Fonda, Shirley Jones
(Santa Fe)

Butch Cassidy and the Sundance Kid (1968)
Paul Newman, Robert Redford, Katharine Ross
(Taos, Chama)

Hang 'Em High (1968)
Clint Eastwood, Inger Stevens, Ben Johnson
(Las Cruces)

Source: New Mexico State Film Office (nmfilm.com)

The park's attractive log-and-glass E. E. Fogelson Visitor Center, named for the husband of late actress Greer Garson, who donated the land for the national park, is an essential first stop. Be sure to view the short film narrated by Garson, which dramatically presents the history of the pueblo site. The film will put you in the right frame of mind to better appreciate what you'll see later. It's screened every 20 minutes or so.

The park includes a mile-long trail through the ruins of the pueblo and the lovely Spanish mission church and adjoining *convento*. The visitor center has an excellent museum, containing artifacts relating to the pueblos, Spanish settlement, Anglo pioneers, the battlefield at Pecos that played an important role in the Civil War in New Mexico, and the Santa Fe Trail, which passed through here (you can still see the wagon ruts). The park also protects Kozlowski's Santa Fe Trail trading post; Greer Garson's spectacular Forked Lightning Ranch, originally designed for rodeo entrepreneur Tex Austin by Santa Fe–style architect John Gaw Meem in 1926; and the smaller 14th-century Arrowhead Pueblo ruin. All told, 12,000 years of history is on display at Pecos, one of the most fascinating parks in New Mexico.

Of particular interest is the extensive collection of pottery on display, some of the 80,000 artifacts excavated at this site in the early 1900s by archaeologist A. V. Kidder, known as the "father of Southwest archaeology." Kidder and fellow archaeologists convened at Pecos annually and developed the important Pecos Classification, which uses comparative differences in regional ceramic making over a long period of time to date different periods in Pueblo culture.

While exploring the trail that winds among the ruins, you can climb down a ladder into a restored kiva (underground ceremonial chamber) and see the *sipapu*, the small hole in the ground believed to connect to the lower spirit world in Pueblo creation stories. The scenery is inspiring, as it varies from plains, mesas, and mountains in the distance.

Van tours of Greer Garson's off-site 10,000-acre Forked Lightning Ranch along the Pecos River and the 1862 Civil War battlefield site are offered on weekends (Sat to the Civil War battlefield site and Sun to Forked Lightning Ranch). Tours depart at 1:30 p.m. from the visitor center. On the ranch tour, the first stop is Kozlowski's Santa Fe Trail trading post, the final stop along the Santa Fe Trail before travelers from the East reached Santa Fe, and from there, the tour continues to the ranch. The Glorieta Pass Battlefield unit, 8 miles to the west, will be of interest to Civil War history buffs. It is the site of a battle in March 1862 between Confederate troops on an expedition from Texas to Colorado hoping to seize gold mines and a Union patrol from Santa Fe's Fort Marcy that accidentally happened across them. As reinforcements arrived, the battle lasted three days and involved more than 1,500 soldiers.

To get to the park from Las Vegas, take I-25 south about 40 miles to the Pecos exit (exit 307) and proceed to the park on Highway 63; (505) 757-2421; nps.gov/peco. (***Note:*** For travelers coming from the west, the park is 25 miles east of Santa Fe, exit 299 off northbound I-25, via Highways 50 and 63.) From Memorial Day through Labor Day, the monument is open daily from 8 a.m. to 6 p.m.; the rest of the year, the park is open daily from 8 a.m. to 4:30 p.m. Admission to Pecos National Historical Park is now free.

Harding County

Kiowa National Grasslands (714 Main St., Clayton; 575-374-9652; fs.usda
.gov/detail/cibola/home) preserves thousands of acres of short-grass prairie
on New Mexico's northeastern plains as part of a federal grasslands restoration
project designed to bring back lands devastated by the Dust Bowl of the 1930s.
The quiet and lonesome grasslands offer an interesting contrast to the more
popular mountainous areas of the state. This is a place where you are likely
to be all alone, surrounded by nature, with just the whistling sound of wind in
the rustling grasses.

The grasslands are divided into two units, both off Highway 56 near Clayton. McKnee's Crossing, just south of Clayton, is the easternmost unit. It protects a 2-mile section of the Dry Cimarron Cutoff route of the Santa Fe Trail. In
the distance is Rabbit Ear Mountain, named for a Cheyenne chief who died in
a fight between Indians and Hispanic settlers in 1717; it was an important landmark along the trail. The Mills Canyon unit, in the western section, is reached
via Highway 39, from Abbott, off Highway 56. This unit comprises most of
northwest Harding County and is more impressive due to its location in scenic
Canadian River Canyon. Highway 39 bisects the grasslands and thus serves as
a convenient route for a road tour, from which you just may encounter grazing pronghorn antelope, among other wildlife. This is a superb place to camp,
hike, and mingle with wildlife in a trailless area.

Mills Canyon is named for a once-prosperous farmer, lawyer, and busi-
nessman named Melvin Mills, who tended thousands of fruit and nut trees in
the late 1800s before they were wiped out by the great flood of 1904. Mills's
misfortune and eventual financial ruin ultimately led to his farm becoming
public lands. If you've got a sturdy, high-clearance vehicle (four-wheel drive
recommended, just in case) and want to
explore one of the remotest, most hidden river valleys in the state, then a trip
to Mills Canyon may be just what you're
looking for.

After you turn off the highway,
psych yourself up for the 2-mile, 800-
foot descent into the rugged Canadian
River valley. In addition to the natural
beauty of the area, you'll also see the ruins of the great Mills estate—including
a few of the hardier fruit trees that have barely survived decades of inattention
and the unforgiving extremes of New Mexico weather.

newmexicotrivia

Five New Mexico counties were
named for US presidents: Harding, Grant, Lincoln, Roosevelt, and
McKinley.

To get to Mills Canyon, take the Wagon Mound exit off I-25 north of Santa Fe/Las Vegas; head east on Highway 120 to Roy, then north on Highway 39 for 10 miles until you see a sign at the turnoff.

Guadalupe County

Just southeast of downtown **Santa Rosa**, you'll find northeastern New Mexico's most fascinating hidden jewel: the city-owned **Blue Hole Dive and Conference Center**, a true oasis that has been developed into a destination for business travelers as well as recreationalists.

Well-known in scuba-diving circles across the country as the diving mecca of the Southwest, the Blue Hole is a tiny, bell-shaped lake prized among divers for its clarity.

A mere 60 feet in diameter (though it widens to 130 feet across the bottom) and 81 feet deep, Blue Hole is well named—it's more of a hole than a lake. The crystal-clear freshwater, which appears to glow a turquoise color with the light reflecting from the limestone below, is replaced every six hours, at a rate of 3,000 gallons per minute, by a subterranean river. Often called Nature's Largest Fishbowl because of its wide variety of fish, snails, plants, and sands, the Blue Hole remains a constant 64 degrees.

If you're a diver, avoid the crowds by visiting during the week. If you just want to see what all the fuss is about, you'll see the most action on weekends. You'll need to buy a permit either at the **Blue Hole Center** (575-472-3763; santarosabluehole.com) or the **Blue Hole Dive Shop**, or ahead of time online. Permits cost $20 and are valid for one week; annual permits are $50. You must be certified or accompanied by a certified, insured instructor. Blue Hole Dive Shop has locker rooms for 65 divers.

Santa Rosa Dive Center (575-472-3370) is located next to the Blue Hole and open Sat and Sun from 8 a.m. until the last diver is served. The shop rents gear and tanks and offers air fills but does not provide instruction. Contact the Santa Rosa Visitor Center at (575) 472-3763 for more information.

Santa Rosa is also home to the **Route 66 Auto Museum**, where you can see more than 30 classic and vintage cars and hot rods, polished 'til they gleam, along with historical photos and assorted Route 66 memorabilia. You can't miss the bright yellow hot rod perched on a metal tower 20 feet above the museum entrance. The museum is located at 2766 Will Rogers Ave.; (575) 472-1966. It's open daily from 7:30 a.m. to 5:30 p.m. Admission is $5 per person.

If your travels take you through the quiet, crossroads town of **Vaughn** (37 miles southwest of Santa Rosa via US 54) and your stomach is grumbling, **Penny's Diner** is just the spot. The squeaky-clean eatery's 1950s rock-and-roll

Selected New Mexico Authors

Robert Creeley
Poet

Tony Hillerman
author of many murder mysteries

Oliver LaFarge
Pulitzer Prize winner for *Laughing Boy*

George R. R. Martin
author of *Game of Thrones*

Cormac McCarthy
author of *All the Pretty Horses* and
The Road

Mark Medoff
playwright, author of *Children of a Lesser God*

N. Scott Momaday
Jemez Pueblo author of *House Made of Dawn*

John Nichols
author of *The Milagro Beanfield War*

Sam Shepard
actor, author, and playwright

Leslie Marmon Silko
Laguna Pueblo author of *Ceremony*

Luci Tapahonso
Navajo poet

theme is reflected in the decor and music, and its menu includes American diner classics such as burgers and roast beef, as well as fajitas and several New Mexican dishes. A friendly waitstaff and a smoke-free environment round out the appeal. What more could you want? Penny's Diner is affiliated with the adjacent Oak Tree Inn and is located at the junction of US 54, 60, and 285 at 1005 Hwy. 285; (575) 584-8733; oaktreeinn.com/pennys-diner; open daily 24 hours.

If Penny's doesn't ring your bell, just mosey on 17 miles farther west on US 285/60 to Encino, where you'll find the delightful ***Encino Firehouse Mercantile and Deli***, a friendly, family-run cafe in a rescued 1930s firehouse that opened in 2016. This backroads place is a nice find in the sticks if you like fresh-made comfort food using locally sourced ingredients at a bargain price. They win high marks for their burgers, pizza, barbecue, sandwiches, handmade tamales and tacos, and fresh pie. Try the barbecue brisket sandwich or perhaps the taco plate with pulled pork. The Encino Firehouse is 54 miles southwest of Santa Rosa at 121 W. US 285; (575) 584-9111; theencinofirehouse.com; open Mon through Fri from 10 a.m. to 7 p.m.

Quay County

The town of ***Tucumcari*** is the gateway to New Mexico from the east. But if you've driven through New Mexico along I-40 from the west, chances are your curiosity has been piqued about Tucumcari because of the stark red billboards proclaiming "Tucumcari Tonight—1,500 Hotel Rooms," along with the mileage from the sign to this model Route 66 town. The town, named after nearby Tucumcari Mountain, is proud of its abundance of lodging.

While in Tucumcari, check out the **Tucumcari Historical Museum**. As far as New Mexico's community-based museums go, this is one of the finer ones. Situated in a three-story 1903 schoolhouse, it contains thousands of old relics, including such large-scale ones as a 19th-century windmill and a 1926 fire truck. Several "reenactment" exhibits are featured, such as a 1920s hospital room, an early post office, a cowboy room complete with barbed wire and gun collections, and an old moonshine still. The museum also has a worthy collection of musical instruments.

Traditional Food of New Mexico

Biscochitos

(Anise-flavored shortbread cookies)

Traditionally enjoyed around the Christmas holiday, the *biscochito* also has the distinction of being designated New Mexico's official state cookie.

6 cups flour

3 teaspoons baking powder

¼ teaspoon salt

1 pound (2 cups) lard

1½ cups sugar

2 teaspoons anise seeds

2 eggs

¼ cup brandy

¼ cup sugar

1 tablespoon cinnamon

Sift flour with baking powder and salt. In a large mixing bowl, cream lard with sugar and anise seeds until fluffy. Beat in eggs one at a time. Mix in flour mixture and brandy until well blended. Turn dough out onto floured board and pat or roll to ¼- to ½-inch thickness. Cut into shapes. (The fleur-de-lis is traditional.) Dust with mixture of sugar and cinnamon. Bake 10 minutes at 350°F or until lightly browned. Makes approximately 5 dozen cookies.

The museum is located at 416 S. Adams St.; (575) 461-4201; cityoftucumcari.com/museum. It's open Tues through Sat from 9 a.m. to 3 p.m. Admission charges are $2 for adults and 50 cents for children ages 6 to 15.

The **Dinosaur Museum**, on the campus of Mesalands Community College, houses the world's largest collection of bronze dinosaur skeleton replicas. Actual fossilized dinosaur bones are rarely exhibited in museums because they are fragile and irreplaceable. Until recently, the "bones" on public display were plaster of paris castings of the skeletons; today, most are made of epoxy resin. The community college has a bronze foundry, which is normally used by the art department in sculpture classes. Students and staff, along with enthusiastic community volunteers, developed a technique for casting fossils in bronze, resulting in replicas that are more durable—though much heavier—than those created by traditional methods. Unlike other museums, this one invites children to touch most of the dinosaurs. Exhibits range from tiny dinosaur footprints to the only complete skeleton on public display of a Torvosaurus, a rare 40-foot-long Jurassic predator related to *Tyrannosaurus rex*. The museum facility also includes a paleontology laboratory and a large collection of fossils that are not on display but are available for study by appointment, as well as a museum shop full of dinosaur-themed books and gift items.

Located at 222 E. Laughlin St. in Tucumcari, the museum is open Tues through Sat from 10 a.m. to 6 p.m. March 1 through Labor Day and Tues through Sat from noon to 5 p.m. the rest of the year. Admission is $6.50 for adults, $5 for seniors, $4.50 for students and teachers with ID, and $4 for children ages 5 to 11. For more information, call (575) 461-3466; mesalands.edu/community/dinosaur-museum.

If you enjoy cheese, you might like to know that Tucumcari has its own award-winning artisan cheese plant, and its cheeses are available throughout New Mexico and beyond. Founded in 1995 by Charles Krause, a fourth-generation cheese maker from Wisconsin with 40 years of cheese-making experience under his belt, **Tucumcari Mountain Cheese Factory** (823 E. Main St.; 575-461-4045) is an unexpected find in this rather homely Route 66 town. In recent years, though, Tucumcari has begun to attract a variety of older folks looking to escape the rat race and indulge their passions—whether that be Route 66 hostelries like the Blue Swallow Motel, recently bought by Route 66 fans, or gourmet cheeses. Using milk from the local Schaap Dairies, the company makes organic cheeses under its Native Pastures label and a variety of artisanal cheeses ("The cheese with the enchanting taste"), such as green chile jack, a delicious New Mexico variety, and feta, which won silver and bronze medals in world competition and has become so popular it now accounts for 10 percent of all feta cheese sold in the US. The cheese factory received several grants to expand and is in the process of ramping up production and adding jobs. You can tour the plant, if you call ahead.

Where to Stay in Northeastern New Mexico

COLFAX COUNTY

Casa del Gavilan
Highway 21
south of Cimarron
(575) 376-2246
casadelgavilan.com
Moderate to expensive

Casa Lemus Inn and Restaurant (formerly America's Best Value Sands)
350 Clayton Rd.
Ratón
(575) 445-2737
casalemus.com
Inexpensive

Heart's Desire Inn
301 S. 3rd St.
Ratón
(575) 445-1000
(866) 488-1028
heartsdesireraton.com
Moderate

St. James Hotel
Highway 21
Cimarron
(575) 376-2664
(888) 376-2664
exstjames.com
Moderate

UNION COUNTY

Best Western Kokopelli Lodge
702 S. 1st St.
Clayton
(575) 374-2589
(800) 392-6691
Moderate

Holiday Motel
Highway 87 North
Clayton
(575) 374-2558
Inexpensive

Hotel Eklund
15 Main St.
Clayton
(575) 374-2551
hoteleklund.com
Moderate to expensive

Super 8 Motel
1425 S. 1st St.
Clayton
(575) 374-8127
wyndhamhotels.com/
super-8/clayton-new
-mexico/super-8-clayton
Inexpensive

SAN MIGUEL COUNTY

Comfort Inn
2500 N. Grand Ave.
Las Vegas
(505) 425-1100
Moderate

Plaza Hotel
230 Plaza Park
Las Vegas
(505) 425-3591
plazahotellvnm.com
Moderate to expensive

Regal Motel
1809 N. Grand Ave.
Las Vegas
(505) 454-1456
Inexpensive

GUADALUPE COUNTY

Best Western Adobe Inn & Suites
1501 Will Rogers Dr.
Santa Rosa
(575) 472-3446
(800) 528-1234
Moderate

La Quinta Inn & Suites
1701 Will Rogers Dr.
Santa Rosa
(575) 472-4800
Moderate

Oak Tree Inn
Junction of US 54, 60, and 285
Vaughn
(575) 584-8733
oaktreeinn.com/hotels/
vaughn-new-mexico
Moderate

SELECTED CHAMBERS OF COMMERCE/VISITOR BUREAUS IN NORTHEASTERN NEW MEXICO

Angel Fire Chamber of Commerce
3407 Mountain View Blvd.
Angel Fire, NM 87710
(575) 377-6353
angelfirechamber.org

Cimarron Chamber of Commerce
356 9th St.
Cimarron, NM 87714
(575) 376-2232
cimarronnm.com

Clayton/Union County Chamber of Commerce
1103 S. 1st St.
Clayton, NM 88415
(575) 374-9253
(800) 390-7858
claytonnewmexico.org

Eagle Nest Chamber of Commerce
50 E.Therma St.
Eagle Nest, NM 87718
(575) 377-2420
eaglenestchamber.org

Las Vegas–San Miguel Chamber of Commerce
500 Railroad Ave.
Las Vegas, NM 87701
(505) 425-8631
lasvegasnewmexico.com

Logan Chamber of Commerce
PO Box 277
Logan, NM 88426
(575) 403-6255
logannm.com

Ratón Chamber of Commerce
100 Clayton Rd.
(inside New Mexico Visitors Center)
Ratón, NM 87740
(575) 445-3689
raton.info

Red River Chamber of Commerce
101 W. River St.
Red River, NM 87558
(575) 754-2366
redriverchamber.org

Santa Rosa Chamber of Commerce
244 S. 4th St.
Santa Rosa, NM 88435
(575) 472-3763
santarosanm.org

Springer Chamber of Commerce
PO Box 323
Springer, NM 87747
(575) 483-2998
springerchamberofcommerce.com

Tucumcari/Quay County Chamber of Commerce
404 W. Route 66
PO Drawer E
Tucumcari, NM 88401
(575) 461-1694
tucumcarinm.com

QUAY COUNTY

Blue Swallow Motel
815 E. Route 66
Tucumcari
(575) 461-9899
blueswallowmotel.com
Moderate

Motel Safari
722 E. Route 66
Tucumcari
(575) 461-1048
Inexpensive to moderate

Pow Wow Inn
801 W. Route 66
Tucumcari
(575) 461-0500
powwowlizard.com
Inexpensive

Route 66 Motel
1620 E. Route 66 Blvd.
Tucumcari
(575) 461-1212
rte66motel.com
Inexpensive

Where to Eat in Northeastern New Mexico

COLFAX COUNTY

Casa Lemus Restaurant
350 Clayton Rd.
Ratón
(575) 445-2737
casalemus.com
Inexpensive to moderate
American and Mexican
food in a pleasant setting
adjoining the inn

Enchanted Grounds Espresso Bar and Cafe
111 Park Ave.
Ratón
(575) 445-2219
Inexpensive
A local favorite in historic downtown for coffee, homemade pastries, soup, salad, pasta, paninis, and sandwiches

Patchwork Phoenix
228 S. 1st St.
Ratón
(575) 445-8000
patchworkphoenix.com
Inexpensive
Local gifts and fresh-roasted fair-trade organic coffee, a large selection of looseleaf teas, natural sodas, and locally made ice cream in an art gallery/quilting shop opposite the train station

UNION COUNTY

Hatcha's Cafe
Highway 518
Mora
(575) 387-9299
Inexpensive
Traditional New Mexican

Hotel Eklund Dining Room and Saloon
15 Main St.
Clayton
(575) 374-2551
hoteleklund.com
Inexpensive to expensive
American, featuring steaks and seafood, and New Mexican

Mock's Crossroads Coffee Mill
2 S. Front St.
Clayton
(575) 374-5282
mocksmill.com
Inexpensive
Fresh-roasted coffee, pastries, and hot breakfast and lunch specials in a quaint downtown location

Rabbit Ear Cafe
402 N. 1st St.
Clayton
(575) 374-3277
Inexpensive
Mexican

SAN MIGUEL COUNTY

Charlie's Spic and Span Bakery and Cafe
715 Douglas Ave.
Las Vegas
(505) 426-1921
Inexpensive
A Las Vegas institution for New Mexican food and fresh doughnuts

El Rialto Restaurant and Lounge
141 Bridge St.
Las Vegas
(505) 454-0037
Inexpensive to moderate
New Mexican

Gilded Age
Plaza Hotel
230 Plaza
Las Vegas
(505) 425-3591
plazahotellvnm.com/dining
Moderate to expensive
American and southwestern

Hillcrest Restaurant
1106 Grand Ave.
Las Vegas
(505) 425-7211
hillcrestlv.com
Inexpensive to moderate
American and Mexican

World Treasures and Travelers Cafe
1814 Plaza
Las Vegas
(505) 426-8638
Inexpensive
Excellent coffee, croissants, scones, sandwiches, and quiche in back of Tapetas de Llana, a weaving cooperative shop in a historic building on the plaza

GUADALUPE COUNTY

The Encino Firehouse Mercantile and Deli
121 W. US 285
Encino
(575) 584-9111
theencinofirehouse.com
Inexpensive
BBQ brisket, pizza, local burgers, tacos, and breakfast burritos in a 1930s firehouse

Joseph's Bar and Grill
1775 Historic Route 66
Santa Rosa
(575) 472-3361
Inexpensive to moderate
New Mexican and American

Penny's Diner
1005 US 285 (junction of 285, 54, 60)
Vaughn
(575) 584-8733
oaktreeinn.com/pennys-diner
Inexpensive
American

Silver Moon Cafe
3501 Will Rogers Dr.
Santa Rosa
(575) 472-3162
Inexpensive to moderate
American

QUAY COUNTY

Branding Iron
3716 Tucumcari Blvd.
Tucumcari
(575) 461-3780
Inexpensive to moderate
American and New Mexican

Circa Espresso Bar & Gift Shop
Route 66 Motel
1620 E. Route 66 Blvd.
Tucumcari
(575) 461-6099
rte66motel.com/circa-espresso-bar/coffee-bar.htm
Inexpensive
Contemporary coffeehouse attached to retro motel

Del's Restaurant and Gifts
1202 E. Route 66
Tucumcari
(575) 461-1740
delsrestaurant.com
Inexpensive to moderate
American steaks and burgers, Mexican, and salad bar

Kix on 66
1102 E. Route 66
Tucumcari
(575) 461-1966
kixon66.com
Inexpensive
Build-your-own omelet and salads in a fun retro diner owned by Del's; pet-friendly patio

Pow Wow Restaurant
801 W. Route 66
Tucumcari
(575) 461-2587
powwowlizard.com
Moderate to expensive
American steaks and burgers and New Mexican

Watson's BBQ
502 S. Lake St.
Tucumcari
(575) 461-9620
tucranchsupply.com/watsons-bbq
Inexpensive
Authentic Texas-style BBQ brisket, pulled pork, and smoked turkey in a family-run country hardware store

Southeastern New Mexico

Probably the most diverse region of the state, southeastern New Mexico can't be pigeonholed. Its varying landscape ranges from the harshness of the Chihuahuan Desert, the decorated limestone subterranean caves at Carlsbad Caverns National Park, and the glistening gypsum dunes of White Sands National Monument near Alamogordo to the cool, high peaks of the Sacramento Mountains and evergreen Lincoln National Forest, sacred to the Apache. Fertile river basins like the Hondo Valley, between Ruidoso and Roswell, produce pastoral scenes of horses grazing on green fields of oats, as well as vistas of orchards teeming with crisp red apples, and attract artists. And vast areas of rich, irrigated cropland help feed the nation, thanks in part to the legendary Pecos River (as in "the law west of the Pecos").

De Baca County

De Baca County is home to **Fort Sumner**, and Fort Sumner will forever be associated with outlaw **Billy the Kid**. Without a doubt, William Bonney, also known as Billy the Kid, is the most famous New Mexico legend who actually lived. Though

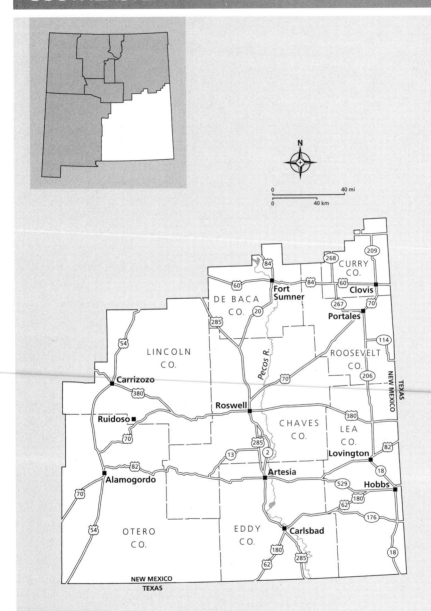

only 21 when he died, the Kid created a legacy and a legend that just won't die. The community of Fort Sumner is one of several locales in New Mexico where the Kid left his mark. It's also where his remains remain.

In the *Old Fort Sumner Cemetery*, you can visit the grave of Billy the Kid. Graves are few and scattered in the small military cemetery, but the most prominent site is encaged in metal—it's a three-person grave, Billy's alongside those of two of his pals, Tom O'Folliard and Charlie Bowdre.

The Kid's tombstone has a history of its own. It was first stolen in 1950, and its whereabouts remained a mystery until 1976, when Joe Bowlin, owner of the Old Fort Sumner Museum adjacent to the cemetery, recovered it in Granbury, Texas. Several years later it was stolen again, but this time it was recovered within days, in California. The Kid's tombstone, now shackled in iron for protection, has an epitaph that reads: "The Boy Bandit King / He Died as He Had Lived."

Each summer during the second weekend in June, Fort Sumner hosts *Old Fort Days*. Here a favorite event is, appropriately enough, the World's Richest Tombstone Race, where participants run while carrying a replica of Billy's tombstone.

To get to the cemetery (which is just behind the Old Fort Sumner Museum), head east on US 60/84 from Fort Sumner for 3 miles, then take a right onto Billy

FAVORITE ATTRACTIONS/EVENTS IN SOUTHEASTERN NEW MEXICO

Bosque Redondo Memorial at Fort Sumner State Monument
(575) 355-2573
bosqueredondomemorial.com

Carlsbad Caverns National Park
Eddy County
(575) 785-2232
nps.gov/cave

Lincoln State Monument
Lincoln
(575) 653-4025
nmmonuments.org/lincoln

Old Fort Sumner Cemetery
Fort Sumner

White Sands National Monument
Alamogordo
(575) 679-2599
nps.gov/whsa

EVENTS

Smokey Bear Stampede
July, Capitan
(575) 354-2202
smokeybearstampede.com

Old Lincoln Days
August, Lincoln
(575) 653-4025

the Kid Road (Highway 272) and proceed for 4 miles. There's no admission charge to enter the cemetery, and it's always open.

The **Old Fort Sumner Museum** (3501 Billy the Kid Rd.; 575-355-2942), in front of the Old Fort Sumner Cemetery, contains artifacts from the town's past, including Billy the Kid's spurs and chaps and letters from both Pat Garrett and the Kid. Historical paintings line the walls, and Billy the Kid newspaper clippings and photos are posted on easels throughout. If you have time on your hands, you can learn a lot about the Kid by reading the news items. Otherwise, check out the barbed-wire collection, the US Army swords and rifles, and the old Apache moccasins and articles of Indian ceremonial dress. The museum also has items that were purchased from La Paloma Museum when it closed down in Lincoln many years ago.

Old Fort Sumner Museum is open daily from 9 a.m. to 4 p.m. Admission is $3 for adults, $2 for young people ages 7 to 14, and free for children age 6 and younger. Group rates are available.

About ¼ mile down Billy the Kid Road, the gravel road in front of the museum, you'll find **Bosque Redondo Memorial at Fort Sumner State Monument** (575-355-2573; bosqueredondomemorial.com), the place where Billy the Kid was gunned down by Lincoln County sheriff Pat Garrett on July 14, 1881, years after the 1869 abandonment of the fort.

Fort Sumner State Monument's grounds include the ruins of the old US Army fort, as well as a small but very powerful memorial to the most infamous events of the Navajo Long Walk, which occurred between 1863 and 1868. A small visitor center tells the story of Fort Sumner and showcases items excavated from the fort. Late autumn is a great time to visit, for instead of seeing other people you can take a gander at the migratory birds making patterns in the blue sky above nearby Bosque Redondo, the 16 miles of wooded wetlands along the Pecos River.

Fort Sumner was created because of a horrible American concentration camp experiment that failed. During the Civil War, the US Army in New Mexico and Arizona, feeling they were in constant danger from non-Pueblo tribes living in the territory, built the fort as part of a new million-acre reservation on which to relocate some 450 Mescalero Apaches and more than 8,500 Navajo. Showing remarkable cultural insensitivity, the army forced the nomadic hunter-gatherer Apache and Navajo to build meager shelters along 20 miles of the river and to learn farming, despite the hostile conditions and lack of potable water, which led to illness and death. As many as one-third of the internees died in this shameful but little-known episode in US history, many of them dropping dead of hunger, exhaustion, and illness en route to Bosque Redondo.

STATE PARKS IN SOUTHEASTERN NEW MEXICO

Online at emnrd.state.nm.us/spd

Bottomless Lakes State Park
16 miles southeast of Roswell
(575) 624-6058

Brantley Lake State Park
12 miles northwest of Carlsbad
(575) 457-2384

Living Desert Zoo and Gardens State Park
in Carlsbad
(575) 887-5516

Oasis State Park
6 miles north of Portales
(575) 356-5331

Oliver Lee Memorial State Park
10 miles south of Alamogordo
(575) 437-8284

Smokey Bear Historical Park
Capitan
(575) 354-2247

Sumner Lake State Park
16 miles northwest of Fort Sumner
(575) 355-2541

In 1865, the Mescalero Apache simply up and left the reservation and returned to their nearby homelands, but the Navajo, weakened and despondent after having been forced to walk hundreds of miles from the Dinetah in northeastern Arizona and northwestern New Mexico, were forced to endure this misery for three more years. Finally, in 1868, disease and shortages of food and firewood so plagued the reservation that the army admitted failure, and General William T. Sherman sent the surviving Navajos home.

The Navajo were given a reservation that included their traditional homelands; it was expanded several times later on and is now the largest in the country. They have never forgotten this traumatic episode in their history, however, and stories of the Long Walk have been handed down through generations of affected families for nearly 150 years. The memorial at Bosque Redondo was a long time in coming, but the acknowledgment of wrongdoing by the federal government has gone some way toward beginning to heal the trauma of what their ancestors endured.

In 2005, the memorial opened with, at its center, a museum designed by native architect David Sloan and shaped like a Navajo hogan and Apache tepee. It has exhibits on the Bosque Redondo experiment in social engineering and its aftermath; a second phase of construction is in the works. Take time for reflection while here, by walking the Old Fort Site Trail and the ¾-mile River Walk Trail. Visit the Bosque Redondo Memorial, which was dedicated in 1971. The small shrine consists of a pile of rocks carried by relatives of the Navajo from different parts of the Navajo Nation to commemorate the Long Walk.

The monument is open Wed through Sun from 8:30 a.m. to 4:30 p.m. Admission is free.

Back in the modern-day community of Fort Sumner, you'll come across the most fun of this off-the-beaten-track area's unique spots. If you're a true lover of the legend, you might just sate your hunger for Kid artifacts and lore at the **Billy the Kid Museum**. The privately owned facility was opened as a one-building museum in 1953 and now rambles both indoors and out through several structures.

You can spend several enjoyable hours strolling among the more than 60,000 relics—some historic, some pure kitsch—collected over the years by Ed Sweet, former owner of the museum, and his wife, Jewel. Built in the 1950s, this place is a quintessential roadside attraction and just plain smells old—a wonderfully sentimental scent, as if hundreds of grandmothers' houses were combined.

Kid artifacts include his guns, a jail-cell door that imprisoned the outlaw, and even locks of his hair saved by a Las Cruces barber. There's also an original Billy the Kid "Wanted" poster, signed by territorial New Mexico governor Lew Wallace (a Civil War general and author of the novel *Ben Hur*). In addition, you can view a fine selection of antique cars (some of which are usually parked out front, for effect), as well as fossilized dinosaur dung.

The museum is located at 1435 E. Sumner Ave., 2 miles east of downtown; (575) 355-2380; billythekidmuseumfortsumner.com. It's open daily from 8:30 a.m. to 5 p.m., May 15 to October 1, and Mon through Sat (same hours) the remainder of the year. Admission is $5 for adults, $4 for seniors, $3 for children ages 7 to 15, and free for kids age 6 and younger.

Lincoln County

No other town in New Mexico has preserved its past more meticulously than the community of **Lincoln**, nestled in the Bonito Valley. Western history buffs will want to spend the whole day in Lincoln, because the entire town is a National Historic Landmark and commercialization is blessedly absent here. As Bob Hart, formerly of the Lincoln County Heritage Trust, notes, "You will find no rubber tomahawks here." Seventeen of the 48 historic structures in this tiny one-street town are preserved within **Lincoln State Monument**, with six buildings open to the public.

As with many old, remote New Mexico towns, Lincoln is a survivor of some seriously wild days in its storied past. The former county seat achieved its notoriety as the site of one of the Wild West's bloodiest events: the Lincoln County War of 1878. The war was the culmination of a dispute between opposing factions vying for political and economic control—especially of the city's lucrative mercantile business, which included nearby Fort Stanton.

newmexicotrivia

New Mexico's official state song, "O, Fair New Mexico," was written by Elizabeth Garrett, the visually impaired daughter of famed Lincoln County sheriff and Billy the Kid nemesis Pat Garrett.

The February 13, 1878, shooting of young English cattleman John Henry Tunstall by a member of the local Murphy-Dolan ranch syndicate, at Tunstall's ranch near Lincoln, triggered a series of tragic events, involving Billy the Kid, Tunstall's business partner Alexander McSween, and other Tunstall loyalists, who avenged their friend and employer's death by killing Sheriff Bill Brady. A showdown took place on July 14, when the Kid and his Regulators returned to Lincoln for what came to be known as the Five-Day Battle in downtown Lincoln between the Tunstall-McSween and Murphy-Dolan factions, and at one point, soldiers from nearby Fort Stanton. The Kid escaped and went on the run, was captured and held in Lincoln County Courthouse and various Lincoln homes in 1881, then escaped again, only to be tracked down in Fort Sumner by Sheriff Pat Garrett (see the De Baca County entry). The two-story courthouse is part of Lincoln State Monument. It's said that Billy's gun is responsible for a bullet hole visible in the wall at the foot of the stairwell.

Housed in the historic Tunstall Store on Main Street in Lincoln, monument headquarters displays some 1,000 items from Tunstall's original mercantile inventory; the other half of the store was the bank. Buy your ticket, pick up a walking-tour map, and set off.

Your ticket includes entrance to 4 museums open between November 1 and March 31; all 6 museums are open between April 1 and October 31. Sites include the Tunstall Store, Dr. Wood's House, San Juan Mission Church, Lincoln County Courthouse, the Montaño Store, and the Anderson-Freeman Museum, which has exhibits on Lincoln history from the prehistoric Indians to the Lincoln County War and shows a 12-minute film throughout the day. It's open daily year-round from 8:30 a.m. to 4:30 p.m. Tickets are $7 for adults and free for young people age 16 and younger; free for seniors on Wed and for New Mexico residents on Sun. Call (505) 653-4372 for more information.

Right at the western end of Main Street, you'll find the historic **Wortley Hotel** ("No guests gunned down in over 100 years"), which offers bed and breakfast (lunch is available on Wed and Thurs only). The original structure was built in 1874 but burned to the ground in the 1930s. The current replica was constructed in 1960 and feels quite authentic. Under new ownership since 2016, tthe 7 remodeled rooms are simply but freshly done with clean white paint on the walls and period furnishings reflecting Lincoln's heyday in the late 1800s. Each has an antique brass bed with a new mattress, fireplace, and private bath. For a great diversion on a lazy Lincoln afternoon, settle into one of the many old rockers on the porch spanning the Wortley's facade and close your eyes as the *creak-creak* lulls you back to Lincoln's colorful past.

The hotel restaurant is open daily for breakfast for guests only (included in the room rate), and features farm eggs cooked to order by Troy, the owner; lunch is served on Wed and Thurs only, from 11 a.m. to 3 p.m. The menu features classic American and New Mexican comfort foods.

The Wortley is situated along US 380 in Lincoln; (575) 653-4300; wortley-hotel.com. Rates are $110 per night up to double occupancy.

At the eastern end of Lincoln, you'll find a more upmarket bed-and-breakfast, the **Ellis Store**, a country inn that occupies the store where the Kid was once held prisoner. This is a luxurious experience in a beautiful setting of lush grounds with flowers and trellises. It is known for its exceptional six-course gourmet dinners served in the lovely in-house restaurant, Isaac's Table. Meals are personally cooked by owner Jinny Vigil, with her husband, David, serving and regaling you with stories. This is truly like having dinner with friends, a

newmexicotrivia

Former New Mexico territorial governor Lew Wallace wrote his acclaimed novel *Ben Hur*, which was first published in 1880, in Lincoln County.

very intimate experience. There are 3 restored period rooms in the main house and 6 rooms in the Mill House annex. Room rates include a full country breakfast; dinner is extra but well worth the experience. You will need to reserve ahead for the dinner; it is open to nonguests as well. Ellis Store is located at 1435 Calle La Placita; (575) 653-4609 or (800) 653-6460; ellisstore.com. Rates are $89 to $129 per night.

The picturesque mountain resort town of **Ruidoso**, along US 70 just north of the Mescalero Apache Indian Reservation, provides a beautifully polished place to kick back and relax. It's very popular with visitors from West Texas, so don't be surprised to hear some Texas twangs here. There's no shortage of lodging—from luxury condos to rustic cabins and everything in between—and you'll find plenty of fine restaurants, art galleries, and interesting shops. **Ski Apache Ski Area**, operated by the Mescalero Apache tribe, is nearby and provides excellent downhill skiing.

If you're planning on spending time in Ruidoso and happen to be a horse fan, be sure to head a few miles farther east on US 70 to the community of Ruidoso Downs (known for the racetrack of the same name, home of the world's richest quarter-horse race, the All-American Futurity), and stop by the adjoining **Hubbard Museum of the American West**, formerly known as the Museum of the Horse.

This museum, an affiliate of the Smithsonian Institution in Washington, DC, was begun by R. D. and Joan Dale Hubbard and presented to the City of Ruidoso in 2005. It pays tribute to an animal the museum claims has played a dramatic role in the exploration and expansion of the cultures of the world throughout history. The museum was founded on the collection of Anne C. Stradling, a woman born into a wealthy East Coast family who developed a lifelong passion for horses and anything horse-related. Starting with a worn-out stirrup and bit, her collection eventually grew to more than 10,000 pieces—now housed in the handsome museum.

newmexicotrivia

At 12,003 feet, Sierra Blanca Peak, in the Sacramento Mountains near Ruidoso, is the highest point in southern New Mexico. Wheeler Peak, north of Taos in the Sangre de Cristo Mountains (part of the southern Rockies) is the highest peak in the state, at 13,161 feet elevation.

Gracing the entrance of the museum, *Free Spirits at Noisy Water* is billed as the world's largest equine sculpture. *Free Spirits* is the creation of American sculptor Dave McGary, and includes replicas of eight horses, representing all popular breeds, running through a meadow amid falling water. The sculpture is a marvel of engineering, with five of the horses each balanced on one hoof.

The museum is open Thurs through Mon from 9 a.m. to 5 p.m. Admission is $7 for adults, $5 for seniors and active military personnel with ID, $2 for youths ages 6 to 16, free for children age 5 and under. The museum is located 1 mile east of Ruidoso Downs racetrack, at 841 US 70 W.; (575) 378-4142; facebook.com/hubbardmuseum or visitruidoso.com/hubbard-museum.

In the placid Hondo Valley east of Ruidoso, you'll find one of the most tranquil, unaffected spots in southern New Mexico: the tiny community of **San Patricio**, along the Rio Ruidoso. This is a place of horse ranches and apple orchards. It's also a thriving arts community—a well-hidden fact because of its low-profile location. It's neither promoted nor pretentious. San Patricio is where some of the surviving members of the Wyeth-Hurd creative dynasty continue to paint. Though the family tree has many branches of artists, some of the most celebrated members are N. C. Wyeth, Andrew Wyeth, Peter Hurd, and Henriette Wyeth.

The most imposing and beautiful brick structure in San Patricio is on the Wyeth family ranch, which houses the very polished **Hurd–La Rinconada Gallery** (800-658-6912; wyethartists.com). Built by painter Michael Hurd, son of Peter Hurd and his wife, Henriette Wyeth, the gallery features his art and that of his parents. It is open Mon through Sat from 9 a.m. to 5 p.m. This is a beautiful spot, and if you feel like staying longer you can spend the night right here on the Hurd Ranch, in one of several ranch buildings that Michael has converted into elegant guest homes, sleeping 2 to 10 people. Rates range from $125 to $410, depending on the lodging and number of people, with a two-night minimum (one-night stays incur an additional $25 fee).

Note: There are no restaurants in San Patricio, so plan on bringing food with you or eating in Ruidoso, 20 miles west, or, if you are visiting on the weekend, continue an additional 7 miles east, on US 70, to the tiny town of **Tinnie**, home to the **Creperie at Tinnie's Silver Dollar** restaurant, old-time mercantile emporium, and gallery. The red-roofed adobe structure with its wooden bell tower dominates the landscape and provides a wonderful time-travel experience inside.

Alternately a private residence, mercantile company, and post office dating from 1882, Tinnie's Silver Dollar became a restaurant in 1959. After years as a popular steak house and bar, it was recently reopened under new ownership and is slowly evolving. Tinnie's Silver Dollar is only open on weekends, when the restaurant, the Creperie, serves lunch, early dinner specials, and afternoon teas, including green chile stew, pork tenderloin, sandwiches, salads, crepes, and a selection of homemade cakes and brewed looseleaf tea. Unique offerings in the mercantile include natural sodas, jalapeño cotton candy, homemade truffles and chocolates, local pecans, looseleaf tea, clothing, and gifts. The grounds are lovely here and a popular venue for weddings.

Tinnie's Silver Dollar is on US 70 near the intersection of Highway 368; (575) 653-4425; tinniesilverdollar.com. The mercantile is open Fri and Sat from 10 a.m. to 5 p.m. and Sun from noon to 5 p.m.; lunch and tea in the restaurant are served Fri and Sat from 11 a.m. to 5 p.m. and Sun from noon to 3 p.m.

The favorite son of the village of **Capitan** wasn't even human. He was none other than **Smokey Bear**. (No one knows where that pesky middle name "the" came from, but for the record it's not Smokey the Bear; it's Smokey Bear.) Yes, it's a fact: the national symbol of

newmexicotrivia

The tiny village of San Patricio has been home to the following famous New Mexicans: Billy the Kid, actress Helen Hayes, author Paul Horgan, and artists Peter Hurd and Henriette Wyeth and their son Michael Hurd.

forest-fire prevention really did exist. He was born right here in the Capitan Mountains, went on a big adventure back east, and when he died was brought back to Capitan and buried in the backyard of a tiny historical park dedicated to his memory.

The story of Smokey's life is quite extraordinary. In May 1950, a fire crew rescued a black bear cub with badly singed paws that had been clinging to a charred pine tree after devastating human-caused fires destroyed much of the Lincoln National Forest near Capitan. After recuperating at a veterinary hospital in Santa Fe, "Hot Foot Teddy," as firefighters had dubbed him, was flown to the National Zoo in Washington, DC. Here, under his new moniker of "Smokey," he served as a "spokesbear" for a national campaign by the US Forest Service on forest-fire prevention until his death in 1976, whereupon he was flown back to Capitan for burial.

Smokey's remains repose in the grounds of *Smokey Bear Historical Park* (575-354-2748; emnrd.state.nm.us/sfd/SmokeyBear/SmokeyBear), which also includes an interesting exhibit on the life zones you'll find at different elevations in the forest. The visitor center itself is run by the New Mexico Forestry Division and includes a variety of excellent and well-thought-out exhibits about forest-fire ecology and firefighting history.

The park visitor center is open daily from 9 a.m. to 4:30 p.m. Admission is $2 for adults, $1 for children ages 7 to 12.

Smokey Bear Historical Park is run by the state; the delightful *Smokey Bear Museum/Gift Shop* next door is run by the town of Capitan and, as well as offering items for sale, documents Smokey's personal story in more detail. You'll definitely want to spend some time here. The museum contains several scrapbooks filled with photographs and news clippings on Smokey's life and times. The fact that a museum would even make scrapbooks accessible to visitors is odd, but the effect is very personal, down-home, and nostalgic— a detail that adds to the sentimental feeling of this small, rustic 1906 log museum. An exhibit of Smokey Bear toys, books, and comics from the 1950s and 1960s shows how popular culture was used to convey an important message to the youth of the era. Smokey's legacy and message live on. According to the US Forest Service, the Smokey Bear fire-prevention campaign is the longest-running public-service-announcement campaign in the history of the Ad Council.

The Smokey Bear Museum/Gift Shop (575-354-2298) is open daily from 8:30 a.m. to 4:30 p.m. except during the summer, when it stays open until 5 p.m. There's no admission charge.

If you visit the park, plan on walking down the quiet street and grabbing lunch or dinner at the chef-owned *Che Palle*, a popular Italian restaurant (formerly known as Renee's Real Food) with a small, changing menu featuring excellent renditions of pizza, meat loaf, pastrami, po'boy and grinder sandwiches, fish-and-chips, and brunch items like home-baked bagels, crème brûlée french toast, and the crowd favorite, chicken and waffles. People come from throughout Lincoln County to eat Renee's lovingly prepared food and are rarely disappointed. It's all made from scratch daily using local sources, including organic produce from the hydroponic greenhouse of a former Capitan chef and restaurant owner. It's a funny thing: This little village in the middle of nowhere seems to attract seasoned chefs keen to start their own restaurants. Renee and her husband are firmly in that tradition—to the benefit of all.

Renee's Real Food changed its name to Che Palle when it moved into a larger, purpose-built space next door. It now is open for dinner four days a week, as well as lunch. Che Palle is at 433 Smokey Bear Blvd.; (575) 973-0933. Open Wed through Sat from 11 a.m. to 9 p.m. and Sun from noon to 6 p.m.

Farther north in Lincoln County, you'll find the remains of New Mexico's most raucous mining town in the form of the ghost town of **White Oaks**. One version of White Oaks's birth in the 1870s says that the discoverer of the North Homestake mine sold it to a friend for $40, a pony, and a bottle of whiskey. He probably lived to regret that decision when the mine eventually produced $500,000 in gold.

Along came other mines with names like Rip Van Winkle, Large Hopes, Little Hell, and Smuggler, and the boomtown was under way with a population that swelled to 4,000. The town became a hangout for cattle rustlers and outlaws, including Billy the Kid. Saloons, gambling houses, and "houses of another sort" took hold as White Oaks entrepreneurs thought of quick ways to wheedle away the day's take from area miners.

White Oaks faded when a planned railroad link with El Paso went instead to the New Mexico town of Capitan. The gold played out at about the same time.

A simple historical marker, a cemetery, and many abandoned buildings are all that's left of old White Oaks. A few hardy folks have rediscovered the town, elevating its status to semi–ghost town. An impressive building is Hoyle's Castle, a brick Victorian mansion that looms over the town from its hilltop site. A retired schoolteacher from Carrizozo lives in the structure, which resembles a classic haunted house out of an old movie. It's not open to visitors.

White Oaks does have a bar—the **No Scum Allowed Saloon** (933 White Oaks Ave.; 575-648-5583; noscumallowedsaloon.com)—and the **Miner's Home and Toolshed Museum** (575-648-2363; summer only), a tiny wooden shack near the center of town. A Miners' Day celebration takes place the first week in June each year.

Starting in the late 1990s, White Oaks has become one of the state's newest artists' communities, featuring several nice galleries, which participate in a studio tour each April. Among them is **Ivy Heymann's White Oaks Pottery**, where Ivy Heymann creates simple, elegant ceramics in spare blues, grays, and whites reminiscent of the landscape. For more information and studio information, contact her at (575) 648-2985; whiteoakspottery.com; open daily from 10 a.m. to 5 p.m.

White Oaks is 9 miles off US 54, on Highway 349, 11 miles northeast of Carrizozo. About 5,000 years ago, Little Black Peak north of Carrizozo erupted, spilling red-hot molten lava that flowed for 44 miles, filling much of the Tularosa Basin, before it solidified into black rock. Today, the lava flow—which has been set aside as the **Valley of Fires Recreation Area**—is jagged, jet-black rock twisted into strange formations, split by chasms and undermined by lava tubes. The lava flow is 4 to 6 miles wide and covers 125 square miles in a layer 160 feet thick.

From the parking area and campground, the paved, wheelchair-accessible Malpais Nature Trail loops for 1½ miles, with interpretive plaques pointing out the main features of the strange landscape. Although it looks totally barren from a distance, visitors who take the trail soon discover that pockets of soil have accumulated in the lava over millennia, and many kinds of cacti, bushes, and flowers grow there. Except for the nature trail, the vast expanse of the lava field is so rough that it is virtually inaccessible to humans. Thanks to this protection, animal and bird life is amazingly abundant. You may spot anything from lizards to Barbary sheep, as well as owls, vultures, and golden eagles. The south end of the lava flow meets the northern extent of the White Sands dune field. The sharp contrast of black and white makes it so highly visible from space that it is used as a landmark for visual calibration of satellites.

The Valley of Fires Recreation Area, located 4 miles west of Carrizozo off US 380, is administered by the Bureau of Land Management (575-648-2241; blm.gov/nm/st/en/prog/recreation/roswell/valley_of_fires.html). Hunting and off-road vehicles are prohibited. It is always open, with quiet hours from 10 p.m. to 7 a.m. Fees for day use are $3 per person or $5 per vehicle ($15 for tour buses with 15 or more people on board). You'll find 19 campsites alongside the parking area with water, picnic shelters and tables, and grills. Fees are $7 for tent camping, $12 for RV campsites without electricity, and $18 for RV campsites with full hookups.

Otero County

Driving into Otero County from the north along US 54, observant motorists and spider fanciers should be on the lookout for the brave tarantulas that cross the highway on warm summer days. Highway department tarantula crossing signs wouldn't last out here, as less-than-honest souvenir seekers would pick them off as fast as they could be placed. Tarantulas aside, Otero County offers weekend adventurers several special spots. Though much of the county is off-limits (White Sands Missile Range, Fort Bliss Military Reservation, and the Mescalero Apache Indian Reservation), the parts that are accessible make up for it.

As you head south along US 54, midway between Carrizozo and Tularosa a paved road turns off to the left and takes you to ***Three Rivers Petroglyph Site***, which few travelers stop to visit, even though it's less than a mile off the main highway. This long ridgeline in the northern Chihuahuan Desert is strewn with large, dark basaltic boulders, which, beginning in AD 900 and continuing until AD 1400, proved to be the ideal material for more than 21,000 incised rock art (petroglyphs) made by the Jornada Mogollon branch of the Ancestral Pueblo culture. Indeed, these rock images, much different from the ones at Petroglyph National Monument near Albuquerque, bear a strong resemblance to the distinctive Mimbres painted pottery on display at the Western New Mexico University Museum in Silver City, the work of the Mimbres Mogollon people.

As you walk along the hot, rocky ¾-mile trail along the ridge, you'll discover an amazing array of animal and human figures, along with symbols associated with agriculture, nature, and spirituality. The exact meaning and purpose of these carvings are unknown, and your speculations are as good as those of "experts." You may wonder, as many do, why the Jornada Mogollon went to the effort of making such a huge number of petroglyphs at this particular spot, over a period of some five centuries, while no rock carvings are found elsewhere in the area. Perhaps this was considered a magical spot; it certainly is today.

Three Rivers Petroglyphs is administered by the Bureau of Land Management office in Las Cruces (1800 Marquess St.; 575-525-4300; blm.gov/nm/st/en/prog/recreation/las_cruces). It is open year-round. Admission is $5 per person. Tent camping in the 9-site campground costs $7; RV campsites with hookups are $18. (***Note:*** This area is very hot, dry, and exposed. Prepare accordingly. Wear a hat and sunscreen, eat salty nutritious snacks, and drink plenty of water as you walk around—and avoid midsummer.)

The missile range isn't the only place that's privy to the soft, snow-white gypsum dunes just southwest of the city of Alamogordo. Adjacent to the range is ***White Sands National Monument***—part of the largest gypsum dune field in the world—whose majesty you're welcome to explore.

This extremely stark national park unit, one of the most popular in the state, is the perfect place for uninhibited barefoot frolicking. It's also the place for people who are afraid of the water—lots of beach, no ocean. Pack plastic sleds and snowboards to slide down sand dunes that are up to 60 feet tall. During the height of summer, the sand tends to get quite hot, but since summer is popular with tourists, it's best to avoid that time and plan, instead, a late autumn visit. Better yet, camp out during a full moon (allowed at a backcountry campsite only; registration required)—the reflection of moonlight from the sand provides an unearthly adventure you won't soon forget. It's bright enough to read by!

A Works Progress Administration–era visitor center and museum in the park's historic district has exhibits interpreting how the dunes were formed, including one on those species of plants and wildlife hardy enough to thrive in such a harsh environment. The "sands" behave like a living entity, constantly shape-shifting with the winds and transforming. Gusting winds cause them to shift, which makes keeping the roads clear a full-time chore. The 16-mile Dunes Drive loop is the highlight of a visit to White Sands. Occasionally, it is closed due to nearby missile-range testing, so call ahead. Attractive picnic shelters are available.

White Sands National Monument is 15 miles southwest of Alamogordo, just off US 70; (575) 675-2599; nps.gov/whsa. It's open daily, with hours as follows: in summer (Memorial Day through mid-August), visitor center 8 a.m. to 7 p.m. and Dunes Drive 7 a.m. to 9 p.m.; in winter, visitor center 9 a.m. to 5 p.m.

newmexicotrivia

Director Nicholas Roeg's 1976 film *The Man Who Fell to Earth*, starring the late music icon David Bowie at the height of his 1970s fame, was filmed in various locations in New Mexico. It was based on Walter Tevis's sci-fi novel about an alien, Thomas Jerome Newton, who crash-lands his spaceship on Earth, desperately seeking water to save his parched planet, but becomes addicted to earthly pleasures. Despite achieving wealth and fame, Newton is treated as a freak and is stranded on Earth as his family dies back home. The gypsum dunes stood in for Newton's home planet; Fenton Lake, near Jemez Springs, is where he crash-lands his craft and later builds a retreat. Artesia, a homely oil and gas town in southeastern New Mexico, is where he holes up, meets a waitress, Mary-Lou, and begins creating his science-based empire. The present-day Hotel Andaluz and the plaza in downtown Albuquerque also appear in the film.

and Dunes Drive 7 a.m. to sunset. There's a $5 fee per person for the Dunes Drive, with children age 15 and younger admitted free. (**Note:** There is no restaurant or cafe in the monument; the closest is in Alamogordo, 15 miles to the northeast, and Las Cruces, 50 miles southwest. The park's gift shop sells prepackaged sandwiches and other snacks and bottled water. Carry everything you need with you.)

Just north of Alamogordo you'll find **Heart of the Desert at Eagle Ranch**, producer of Heart of the Desert pistachio nuts. Although the bulk of domestic pistachio farming occurs in the fertile San Joaquin Valley in California, pistachio growing has emerged as a successful agricultural enterprise in this southwestern New Mexico town, after a little research showed that climate and elevation were nearly perfect in Alamogordo for growing the fickle nut.

Never dyed red to appeal to consumers or to cover blemishes, Eagle Ranch's off-white and green nuts are available only by mail, at the ranch store, and in selected farmers' markets and supermarkets in New Mexico. The Alamogordo ranch store offers red chile pistachios for die-hard New Mexican chileheads who need an extra kick to everything they eat. There are other Heart of the Desert outlets on the historic plaza in Mesilla and, in Las Cruces at the Farm and Ranch Heritage Museum.

Marianne Schweers, who owns the groves with her husband, George, shared an interesting bit of pistachio lore: When the Shah of Iran was overthrown in 1979, not only was the world oil market affected but the Middle Eastern country's other principal export also suffered when its markets were cut off. Yes, until that time Iran was the world's premier pistachio supplier. The situation was a big boost to American pistachio production, and the timing couldn't have been better for fledgling Eagle Ranch. Marianne summed up the situation by saying, "The Ayatollah was the best friend that [US] pistachio growers ever had."

Eagle Ranch offers fascinating, free 45-minute farm tours of the pistachio groves year-round. Sept through May, tours take place Mon through Fri at 1:30 p.m.; June through Aug, tours are Mon through Fri 10 a.m. and 1:30 p.m. Groups of 10 or more can call and arrange a special tour in advance, if they wish. The popular Eagle Ranch store, which also sells other southwestern food and gift items, is located 4 miles north of Alamogordo at 7288 US 54/70; (575) 434-0035 or (800) 432-0999; heartofthedesert.com. The store is open Mon through Sat from 8 a.m. to 6 p.m. and Sun from 9 a.m. to 6 p.m. Wine tastings are also held in the store.

In Alamogordo ("Fat Cottonwood"), you'll find the **New Mexico Museum of Space History**, nestled in the foothills of the Sacramento Mountains. This shimmering, massive gold cube of a building houses four levels of museum-like exhibits in the Museum of Space History and the International Space Hall of Fame (annual induction ceremony held the last Saturday in September).

You start on the top floor and work your way down ramps through exhibits like the "There's Space in New Mexico" room, which combines traditional New Mexico ambience—adobe walls, pine-planked floor, vigas (ceiling beams)—with the state's cutting-edge research and contributions to the nation's space program. You can also step inside the interactive "Space Station 2001" exhibit for an astronaut's view of space travel in the future, view exhibits on Robert Goddard's early rocket experiments near Roswell, as well as examine a Skylab space suit and even Soviet space food.

For those who want to take a load off, the Space Center is also home to the *New Horizons Dome Theater*, featuring the world's first Spitz Scidome 4k Laser full-dome planetarium projection system and named after the NASA spacecraft that recently flew by Pluto. IMAX films and live star shows are offered several times a day. Outside, on the grounds of the Space Center, you'll find the *Astronaut Memorial Garden*, a tribute to the Apollo 1 and Space Shuttle Columbia astronauts, and the *John P. Stapp Air and Space Park*, which is filled with actual space hardware and rocket equipment. The *Daisy Track* commemorates tests that were crucial in developing elements of NASA's Project Mercury orbital tests and Apollo moon landings. This is also a good place to get a broad view of White Sands in the distance.

To get to the Space Center, turn east on Indian Wells Road off US 54/70/82 in Alamogordo and follow the signs; (575) 437-2840; nmspacemuseum.org. It's open Wed through Sat from 10 a.m. to 5 p.m., Sun from noon to 5 p.m. The New Horizons Dome Theater and Planetarium is open from 11 a.m. to 5 p.m. Separate admission charges for the museum and giant-screen films in the theater are $7 for adults, $6 for seniors and military, and $4 for young people ages 4 to 12; the planetarium costs an additional $5 for adults, $4 for seniors and children. The best buy is a combination ticket to all three venues that costs $15 for adults, $12 for seniors and military, and $10 for children. *Note:* Admission for all attendees is free to the Hall of Fame on the day of the annual induction ceremony.

newmexicotrivia

Ham, the first chimpanzee in outer space, and Minnie, the longest-surviving "astrochimp," are both buried at the International Space Hall of Fame in Alamogordo.

US 82, from Alamogordo to the village of *Cloudcroft*, is one of southern New Mexico's most beautiful drives. In just 16 miles you'll climb nearly 5,000 feet, passing through all the climatic zones from the Lower Sonoran Desert region of Mexico to the Hudson Bay tundra region of Canada. As the road winds through the forested Sacramento Mountains, you'll come across many scenic overlooks, as well as roadside stands selling apples, cider, and various other forms of produce. New Mexico's only highway tunnel is also on this route.

Once you experience the breathtaking setting of Cloudcroft high in the Sacramentos, you'll understand why getting here is worth the effort. The small town is a year-round playground where you can beat the heat in summer and marvel at the turning of the aspens in fall. And Cloudcroft's magical winters bring downhill skiing at Ski Cloudcroft (see appendix, page 231), the southernmost ski area in the US, and ice-skating at Sewell Skate Pond, one of only a few outdoor places in the state where you can pursue this sport.

Cloudcroft is also home to **The Lodge Resort and Spa**, a romantic mountain getaway. This place has quite a history. Built as a company resort for Alamogordo railroad workers in 1899, the inn was reconstructed after the original lodge burned in 1909. Famous guests include Judy Garland and Clark Gable. Conrad Hilton, founder of the hotel chain that bears his name, owned the place in the 1930s.

The Lodge's European-style architecture, with its four-story copper tower, adds to a mood of romantic seclusion in a chalet high in the Alps. Inside, Victorian ambience takes over in the 59 high-ceilinged guest rooms outfitted with antique furnishings and down comforters. Select a stay when your weary bones need a rest and you couldn't care less about roaming the byways for further adventure.

newmexicotrivia

Alan Hale, codiscoverer of the much-celebrated Hale-Bopp comet, lives and watches the sky near Cloudcroft in the Sacramento Mountains of Otero County in southeastern New Mexico.

Because it's usually chilly at this altitude (9,200 feet), expect a cozy fire in the lobby fireplace any time of year. Just off the lobby is Rebecca's, the lodge's excellent dining room, named after the ghost who is said to roam the inn's halls; Rebecca, the story goes, was a flirtatious, redheaded chambermaid who in the 1930s was killed by a jealous lover.

The Lodge is just off US 82 at 601 Corona Place; (800) 395-6343; thelodgeresort.com. Room rates range from $125 to $235, depending on the particular room and season.

The **National Solar Observatory at Sacramento Peak** (575-434-7000; nso.edu/visit) in the village of **Sunspot** offers visitors a chance to learn why and how astronomers study the sun from this 9,200-foot-elevation vantage point in the Sacramento Mountains. All tours of the observatory are currently suspended; however, the observatory's visitor center (575-434-7190), a co-venture of the NSO, the Apache Point Observatory, and the US Forest Service, has astronomy exhibits and a gift shop, and the observatory grounds are open for self-guided tours daily from dawn to dusk. The visitor center is open daily from 9 a.m. to 5 p.m., Mar through Jan; call for winter hours.

Even if you're not into astronomy, the setting in the Lincoln National Forest is quite awe inspiring. In addition to the million-dollar views of the Tularosa Basin (including the gleaming gypsum sands in White Sands National Monument), you'll find plenty of hiking trails and remote picnic spots.

To get to Sunspot from Cloudcroft, take Highway 130 East to its junction with Highway 6563 (a designated scenic byway). Follow Highway 6563 to its end, about 15 miles, at Sunspot. Admission to the museum is $3 for adults, $1.50 for seniors and active-duty military, and $1 for children ages 11 to 17; $10 family rate.

There's a chance you may be able to combine your visit to the solar observatory with a tour of neighboring ***Apache Point Observatory*** (575-437-6822; apo.nmsu.edu), offered only by advance reservation. Unlike the former, the latter is oriented toward nighttime astronomical observation, and access is aimed toward scientists and their guests. Owned by a private consortium and operated by New Mexico State University, the observatory is home to the Sloan Digital Sky Survey III, a project that is mapping 100 million celestial objects in one-quarter of the earth's sky, using a 2.5-meter telescope.

Chaves County

The largest city in southeastern New Mexico, ***Roswell*** is one of those old-fashioned all-American cities that almost seem caught in a time warp. Cited by national publications as one of the 10 best small cities in the country, this rather homely desert city, facing out to the long distance of the oil-rich Permian Basin and historic cowboy trails to Texas, has also been included in the list of "Ten Peaceable Places to Retire" in *Money* magazine. You are more likely to know it, though, as the "UFO capital of the world."

Roswell may be best known for UFOs and the century-old New Mexico Military Institute, but for visitors by far its most impressive cultural attraction is the Works Progress Administration–era ***Roswell Museum and Art Center***, quite possibly the best small community art museum in the state.

With 11 galleries in the grand 1930s adobe structure, the museum focuses on art, history, and science. Its focal point is the extraordinary Aston Collection of Plains Indian, Pueblo, Spanish Colonial, and early American artifacts, and superb examples of traditional New Mexican arts and crafts made by local artists who were funded by New Deal–era WPA programs. The museum has one of the finest collections of New Mexico art in the state. Period. It should be on every art lover's list. Featured New Mexico artists include Georgia O'Keeffe, Ernest Blumenschein, Henriette Wyeth, Andrew Dasburg, and Fremont Ellis. The nationally acclaimed Hurd Collection, which occupies a separate room, is the most extensive collection of Roswell native Peter Hurd's works.

A special wing of the museum displays the actual engines and rocket assemblies developed by Dr. Robert H. Goddard, who worked in Roswell from 1930 to 1942. The Goddard Wing also has a replica of the early space scientist's laboratory, where he built the world's first liquid-fuel rockets. In addition, the **Robert Goddard Planetarium** on-site presents various programs, for which fees are generally $2 to $5 per person.

The "art center" in the museum's name is the tipoff that this dynamic museum is very involved in arts education. It offers a great many classes and workshops and is well-known for its Artist-in-Residence (AIR) program, founded by artist Donald Anderson, which nurtures emerging artists. Chiricahua Apache sculptor Bob Haozous, son of famed sculptor Allan Houser, and the late Luis Jimenez, a Mexican American sculptor from the Hondo Valley known for his vibrant, contemporary fiberglass sculptures, are both graduates of the AIR program. Both offer powerful contemporary artistic statements about life in America for native and Mexican people.

newmexicotrivia

Actress Demi Moore was born in Roswell.

The museum is located at 100 W. 11th St.; (575) 624-6744; roswell.nm .gov/308/roswell-museum-art-center. It's open Mon through Sat from 9 a.m. to 5 p.m. and Sun and holidays from 1 to 5 p.m. Admission is free; donations are welcome.

To see more contemporary art pieces by Haozous, Jimenez, and others, check out the **Anderson Museum of Contemporary Art** (409 E. College Rd.; 575-623-5600; roswellamoca.org), a less-well-known art museum in artsy Roswell but one that makes a great companion destination to Roswell Museum and Art Center. It was founded in 1994 by artist Donald Anderson, creator of AIR, and makes the most of its light, bright, warehouse-style location, a perfect exhibit space for large-scale art installations.

Anderson Museum of Contemporary Art is open weekdays from 9 a.m. to 4 p.m. and weekends from 1 to 5 p.m. Admission is free.

People take UFO sightings seriously in Roswell—people like Walter Haut, president of the **International UFO Museum and Research Center**

(575-625-9495 or 800-822-3545; roswellufomuseum.com). Haut has reason to believe. In 1947, he made national headlines when, as a public relations officer for the former Roswell Army Air Field, he announced the recovery of a crashed flying saucer at a nearby ranch. The increasingly known museum features interesting displays and published accounts of reported UFO sightings from all over the world.

newmexicotrivia

The Bottomless Lakes area near Roswell, the location of several popular swimming holes named by cowboys in the 1880s, was set aside as New Mexico's first state park in 1933.

Though the army later denied that extraterrestrial matter was found from what is often known as "the Roswell Incident," claiming the debris came from a downed weather balloon, Haut remains convinced that aliens have visited earth. He wants museum visitors to decide for themselves, however. Volunteers staff the nonprofit museum to answer questions and help interpret displays.

The museum is located at 114 N. Main St. (US 70) in downtown Roswell. It is open daily from 9 a.m. to 5 p.m. Admission is $5 for adults, $3 for seniors and active-duty military, and $2 for children ages 5 to 15.

Roswell's notoriety as a mecca for those who believe in UFOs—especially after the release of the 1996 sci-fi blockbuster film *Independence Day* and the acclaimed 1997 film *Contact*, plus an appearance by Roswell's mayor on *The Late Show with David Letterman*—has led the city to hold the annual ***Roswell UFO Festival***, which takes place during the July Fourth weekend. The event includes talks by well-known conspiracy theorists and other UFOlogists, a fireworks display, a nighttime golf tournament (complete with glow-in-the-dark balls), an alien costume contest, and a UFO Crash and Burn Expo, a nonmotorized vehicle competition.

For information on the festival and guided tours of the alleged crash site (complete with an area rancher as the unlikely guide), call the ***Roswell Chamber of Commerce*** at 131 W. Second St.; (575) 623-5695; roswellnm.org.

Anyone interested in military history will want to stop by the ***Gen. Douglas L. McBride Museum***, a US military history museum located at the New Mexico Military Institute. It's located in the 1918 Luna Natatorium, a building that originally housed the first swimming pool west of the Mississippi River. It became a museum in the 1980s, after another pool was built on campus, and was renovated again in 2006 and renamed Luna Hall in 2009.

The museum is on the second floor of Luna Hall at the New Mexico Military Institute, 101 W. College Blvd; (800) 421-5376; nmmi.edu/museum. It is open Mon through Fri from 8 a.m. to 4 p.m. Admission is free.

Also of interest to historians is the ***Historical Center for Southeastern New Mexico***, formerly the Chaves County Historical Museum, which occupies a 1912 mansion at 200 N. Lea Ave.; (575) 622-8333; roswellnmhistory.org. The century-old home, built for a local rancher, retains most of its original fixtures and fittings and furnishings, which makes just visiting the home a nice step back into the past. Exhibited are some of the more than 11,000 historical photographs of the area, collected between 1943 and 1982; you will also find gramophone records and other memorabilia of the early 20th-century Roswell band Louise Massey and the Westerners, pioneers in recorded country and western music. It is open Mon through Fri from 10 a.m. to 4 p.m. Admission is free.

newmexicotrivia

Bitter Lake National Wildlife Refuge near Roswell is one of the most biologically significant wetland areas in the Pecos River watershed. It is a haven for several species of dragonfly and holds a Dragonfly Festival in spring.

Eddy County

Eddy County should probably be called Cave County. In addition to containing world-famous ***Carlsbad Caverns***, the county has untold numbers of other caves, most of them patiently waiting to be discovered by some daring young spelunker. And if the name changed to Cave County, the county seat would undoubtedly be ***Carlsbad Caverns National Park***, probably the single most-visited spot in New Mexico and certainly one of the best known.

Despite its name, the park is located not in Carlsbad but, rather, 26 miles southwest of the city, adjoining ***Whites City***, named after cowboy Jim White, who discovered this underground fantasyland in 1901. Because you'll be underground in a constant-temperature (read: quite cool) environment during most of your visit, pleasant weather is not a major factor for enjoyment. Therefore, it's a good idea to avoid the crowds of summer, when the above-ground temperatures can soar.

From late May through October the park offers visitors the fun of viewing mass bat flights. After dusk almost a million Mexican free-tailed bats swirl out of the cave's entrance for their nightly escapades and insect-feeding frenzies. The bat flight is preceded by informative—and humorous—talks by rangers about the tiny winged mammals. Though it's true that these same bats are in the cave during the day, don't worry: The caverns are enormous, and you won't even notice the slumbering bats.

Though the park is decidedly remote, access is no problem. The main attraction is the famed stalactites and stalagmites decorating the Big Room, one of the world's largest chambers and the centerpiece of Carlsbad. You can either walk down through the Natural Cave entrance, the original opening to the caves discovered by Jim White, or take an elevator down. But as a true adventurer you'll also be drawn to exploring Carlsbad's wild cave tours, including Slaughter Canyon Cave, Spider Cave, Lower Cave, and Hall of the White Giant.

These wild caves preserve some of the thrilling sights that cavers experience when exploring a new find. Guided lantern tours take you through the undeveloped caves in all their eerie, dark splendor. You'll need to bring along a flashlight, water, and nonslip shoes. Make advance reservations for wild cave tours; they are limited and very popular; call (877) 444-6777. Tour fees range from $7 to $20. **Note:** Don't attempt this type of cave adventure unless you're in reasonably good physical shape and comfortable doing minor crawling, squeezing, and ladder and rope work.

Although you can't visit it, the deepest known cave in the US, **Lechuguilla Cave**, is located in a remote part of the park. Its magnitude was discovered only in 1986. It's designated a "wild" cave and only open to experienced cavers in organized expeditions (park permit required). The National Park Service does not plan to develop Lechuguilla; it, along with several other wild caves, may be designated the world's first cave wilderness.

The park entrance is located just west of Whites City on Highway 7; park: (575) 785-2232; nps.gov/cave; tour reservations: (877) 444-6777; recreation.gov. Carlsbad Caverns is open daily with continuous self-guided tours; however, other ranger-led caving experiences are limited and require reservations. Be sure to plan ahead and reserve the tours you wish to take. Park entrance fees are $10 for adults, free for children age 15 and under for the normal self-guided tour. Ranger-guided cave tour fees are currently $8 for Kings Palace Tour, $7 for the candlelit Left Hand Tunnel Tour, $15 for the Slaughter Canyon Tour, and $20 for each of the Lower Cave, Hall of the White Giant, and Spider Cave guided tours; children are half price. Visitor center hours are daily from 8 a.m. to 7 p.m. in summer and 8 a.m. to 5 p.m. the rest of the year. Hours for self-guided tours in summer are 8:30 a.m. to 5 p.m. via elevator, until 3:30 p.m. hiking in via the Natural Entrance, 4 p.m. hiking out; the rest of the year, hours are 8:30 a.m. to 3:30 p.m. via elevator, and until 2:30 p.m. hiking in via the Natural Entrance, 3 p.m. hiking out.

Closer to the city of Carlsbad, you'll find **Living Desert Zoo and Gardens State Park**, which interprets the flora and fauna of the surrounding Chihuahuan Desert. This unique park atop the Ocotillo Hills combines botanical gardens and a zoo in a natural setting. The zoo cares for more than 200

The Goodnight-Loving Trail

Nineteenth-century cattle trails were just about as important to the settlement of the American West as were the celebrated commerce trails like the Santa Fe Trail and the Oregon Trail. The Chisholm Trail may have more name recognition as a cattle trail, but it was the trail with the soothing name, the Goodnight-Loving Trail, that made its mark on southeastern New Mexico.

The Goodnight-Loving Trail adventure began because two particularly ambitious ranchers, like many southern ranchers, had experienced problems selling "recovered" cattle (those that had scattered during the Civil War) in war-ravaged markets. In 1866 Charles Goodnight and Oliver Loving set out from the northwest-Texas frontier to blaze a trail that would allow them to seek out more lucrative markets to the west. They hooked up with Texan rancher John Chisum, who ran cattle in New Mexico on large ranches in Bosque Redondo and south of Roswell. The Goodnight-Loving Trail led for hundreds of miles, looping up into New Mexico near present-day Carlsbad and Roswell, and ended in Fort Sumner, where Goodnight and Loving separated. Loving continued north to Colorado, and Goodnight returned to Texas for another herd of cattle.

That lucrative first trip started a new industry in New Mexico. Cattle ranching and beef processing continue the legacy of the Goodnight-Loving Trail in eastern New Mexico to this day.

animals representing 40 species that have been rescued and rehabilitated after injury in the wild, including mountain lions, bobcats, black bears, bison, and antelope. Endangered Mexican wolves here are part of a captive breeding program designed to introduce the wolves to the Southwest. The gardens include an excellent collection of exotic cacti and succulents from around the world. The views of Carlsbad and the Pecos River valley from parts of the trail are spectacular.

The park is located just off US 285 at 1504 Miehls Dr., on the northwest edge of Carlsbad; (575) 887-5516; emnrd.state.nm.us/spd/livingdesertstatepark .html. It's open daily from 8 a.m. to 5 p.m. (last entry at 3:30 p.m.) in summer and 9 a.m. to 3:30 p.m. the rest of the year. Admission is $5 for adults, $3 for children ages 7 to 12, and free under age 7. Camping is available at both developed and primitive sites: $10 for developed tent sites, $14 for RV sites with electric or sewage hookups, $18 for RV sites with both electric and sewage hookups, and $8 for primitive sites.

This area of New Mexico in the Permian Basin is often dubbed "Little Texas," for obvious reasons—its oil pumps, windmills, cattle, antelope, and far-flung ranches do indeed blur the boundaries between the states. Texas cattle baron John Chisum, along with his partners Charles Goodnight and Oliver Loving, blazed the famed Goodnight-Loving Trail through the Pecos River valley from New Mexico to Texas in the 1860s and built huge ranches south of Roswell.

The small southeastern community of **Artesia** is named for the artesian water that, when it was discovered in the early 1900s, led to a boom in irrigated agriculture here. It often gets shortchanged, due to its convenient location halfway between the larger and more well-known cities of Roswell and Carlsbad, and it's a homely town that is certainly no oil painting; however, in Artesia you'll find authentic small-town hospitality and a leisurely pace, very welcome on long, dusty drives through the desert. You may recognize the town from the 1976 Nicholas Roeg film *The Man Who Fell to Earth*, starring David Bowie. The hotel that featured prominently in the film is no longer there, though.

Restaurant offerings in Artesia have been improving, and you'll find a good selection of food options here, from upscale dining to brewpub to coffeehouse. If you're a Mexican food aficionado, check out the family-run **La Herradura** (1901 Pine St.; 575-746-0040). The restaurant building itself is nothing to write home about, they don't serve alcohol, and the location is slightly obscure, but the authentic tacos and *barbacoa* are worth seeking out.

Following in the path of unusual locations of public buildings—Artesia boasts the first underground elementary school, built as a bomb shelter—is an award-winning bed-and-breakfast inn that was the first to open in Artesia, and still ranks as the top choice in Artesia. **Artesia Heritage Inn** is at once one of the most likely places for a small-town inn—in the oldest building on Main Street, built in 1905—yet also in one of the most unlikely: It's perched above a computer store.

You won't even be aware of the steady business of a retail store below as you enjoy the well-insulated country Victorian atmosphere of the inn, with its old 8-foot-high windows, gleaming hardwood floors, and colonial American furnishings and decor. In addition to 11 guest rooms, each with a queen-size bed and its own bathroom (an accessible king-size suite downstairs has a kitchenette), the inn provides a parlor/lounge for its guests, complete with TV/DVD player and a small library. Though the building may be old, the inn is not. The space has been completely renovated, so you can expect the conveniences of a modern boutique hotel: private bathrooms, Wi-Fi, flat-screen TVs, telephones, and refrigerators in every room. A basic continental breakfast is included in the room rate.

You'll find the inn at 209 W. Main; (575) 748-2552 or (866) 207-0222; artesiaheritageinn.com. Rates start at $139 per night; the king-size accessible suite is $149.

Lea County

The Llano Estacado, or "Staked Plains," makes up much of the landscape of New Mexico's southeasternmost county, one of the last major land areas in the continental US to be settled. Homesteading and open-range ranching were a way of life on this often-harsh land during the early part of this century. Today, for the most part, working cowboys have given way to rodeo cowboys in these parts. In fact, Lea County has produced more professional rodeo champions than any other county in the US, starting with Henry Clay McGonagill in 1901. The **Western Heritage Museum and Lea County Cowboy Hall of Fame** was founded in the old Caster Gymnasium in 1978 in the county's largest city, **Hobbs**, to honor this heritage.

As originally envisaged by Dale "Tuffy" Cooper, a local rancher and roper, the museum and cowboy hall of fame celebrates county residents who have distinguished themselves in rodeo, ranching, and the ranching way of life in Lea County. Dioramas bring to life the different eras of settlement, from pioneer to contemporary, and include a pioneer bedroom and kitchen that looks as though someone might return any minute. The museum is also now home to the sizable Virgil and Thelma Collection, a home museum of historic ranch implements and memorabilia collected and displayed by local rancher Thelma Webber and her husband, Virgil, beginning in the 1920s, and donated to the museum. An Eclipse windmill is located at the museum, a distinctive feature in this part of New Mexico.

In 2005 the museum and hall of fame had outgrown their original location and were relocated to the campus of New Mexico Junior College. An attractive, modern stone-and-glass building now houses the complex, and under the college's direction, the museum has now developed into an educational institution, with special programs about women's ranch work and brands. Temporary exhibitions are also regularly mounted here, including a major traveling exhibit looking at modern research into dinosaur fossils, a co-venture of the American Museum of Natural History and other major American natural history museums.

The Western Heritage Museum and Lea County Cowboy Hall of Fame is located at 1 Thunderbird Circle; (575) 492-2678; nmjc.edu/museum. It's open Tues through Sat from 10 a.m. to 5 p.m. and Sun from 1 to 5 p.m. The admission fee is $5 for adults, $3 for seniors and students, and free for children age 5 and under.

Another notable museum in the area is the **Lea County Museum** (575-396-4805; leacountymuseum.org) at 103 S. Love in the town of Lovington (northeast of Hobbs via Highway 18). This local-history museum, situated in a

Traditional Food of New Mexico

Classic Gold Margarita

This *comida* (food) is actually a *bebida* (drink) and the perfect accompaniment or prelude to a traditional New Mexican meal.

1 oz. any premium gold tequila

½ oz. Cointreau (or triple sec, a less expensive orange liqueur)

1 oz. fresh-squeezed lime juice

¼ oz. fresh-squeezed lemon juice

margarita or kosher salt (coarser than table salt)

1 wedge lime and/or 1 wedge lemon

Make a slice in a lime wedge and run it around the rim of a glass (to dampen the edge). Dip dampened glass edge in salt. Fill a large cup with ice and add remaining ingredients. Shake gently. For a margarita "on the rocks," pour ice and drink into the salt-rimmed glass; for a margarita "neat," strain out the ice. Makes 1 margarita. *¡Salud!*

former landmark hotel built in 1918, displays exhibits of pioneer families. It's open Tues through Sat from 9 a.m. to 5 p.m.; donations are welcome.

Roosevelt County

North of the city of **Portales**—the home of Eastern New Mexico University—you'll come across one of the most significant archaeological sites in North America: Blackwater Draw. And the **Blackwater Draw Museum** is on hand to help interpret exactly why this spot is so important. **Note:** The Blackwater Draw site, a designated National Historic Landmark, is actually a little northwest of the museum, but visit the museum first.

The significance of the Blackwater Locality No. 1 site, located within Blackwater Draw in eastern New Mexico, was first recognized in 1929 by Ridgeley Whitman of Clovis. Then, on this site in 1932, A. W. Anderson, also of Clovis, discovered what was then (and remained until recently) the oldest evidence of human existence in the New World, dating to 11,000 BC. Finely worked Clovis spear points, bones, and the fossilized remains of late Pleistocene woolly mammoths, saber-toothed tigers, camels, and an early species of bison have been recovered from the sprawling maze of canyons. The elegant Clovis points predate the spear points discovered in Folsom, just to the north.

At one time Blackwater Draw was a large watering hole used by prehistoric big game, and Clovis hunters used it as an ambush site for cornering and killing their prey. It's thought that Paleo-Indian hunters crossed the Bering Strait from what is now Mongolia and followed big game down through North America, beginning at the end of the Ice Age; the animals made easy targets, as they congregated around water holes in the New World, and increasing numbers of paleo-hunters arrived to hunt them. But as the climate continued to warm and dry, water sources like this one dried up and big game dwindled, their numbers doomed by lack of water and overhunting by a growing though mobile, scattered population.

Eventually the nomadic Archaic hunter-gatherer culture supplanted the Folsom and Clovis hunters. They were forced to hunt much smaller game and, therefore, relied increasingly on seasonal gathering of wild foods that found a foothold in the Southwest—a very successful, millennia-long strategy that continued until agriculture was introduced from Mexico around the time of Christ. The watering hole at Blackwater Draw dried up 7,000 years ago, during the mid-Archaic period, forcing people to move on.

Blackwater Draw Museum displays some of what has been discovered at this hugely important archaeological site, but excavations continue under the aegis of Dr. John Montgomery of ENMU. Over the years, the digs have been funded by the likes of the Carnegie Institute, the National Geographic Society, and the Smithsonian Institution.

The museum is located 7 miles northeast of Portales on US 70; (575) 562-2103; my.enmu.edu/web/blackwater-draw/home. The museum is open Tues through Sat from 9 a.m. to 5 p.m. and Sun from noon to 5 p.m.; open Mon in summer. Admission is $3 for adults, $2 for seniors, $1 for young people ages 6 to 15 and students with ID, and free for children age 5 and younger. A single ticket allows visits to both the museum and archaeological site. Admission is free on the fourth Sun of the month.

What with the huge scientific brain trust in New Mexico (the Sandia and Los Alamos national laboratories, White Sands Missile Range, Intel), it's only fitting that the genre of science fiction would earn a place of respect here as well—and it did, with the opening and dedication of the ***Jack Williamson Science Fiction Library*** in 1982 on the top floor of the Golden Library on the campus of Eastern New Mexico University in Portales. Combine that with all the renewed attention focused on "the Roswell Incident" of 1947 (see International UFO Museum, earlier in this chapter), and you'd imagine the public interest in this little-known specialty library is bound to increase. It is, in fact, one of the top science-fiction libraries in the world.

Begun in 1967, when Dr. Williamson—a Grand Master of Science Fiction and Nebula and Hugo Award–winning pioneer science-fiction writer, teacher, student, and benefactor—first donated his personal collection of materials, the library has grown to house one of the top science-fiction collections in the world, now including more than 30,000 volumes. Among the collection are the manuscripts and papers of noted authors Edmond Hamilton and Leigh Brackett, thousands of issues of science-fiction "pulps" dating back to the early 1900s, and an original copy of Gene Roddenberry's pilot script for the *Star Trek* television series. Among authors collected are Isaac Asimov, Edgar Rice Burroughs, Harlan Ellison, Robert Heinlein, Robert Silverberg, Spider Robinson, Ursula LeGuin, and Gordon Dickson. And the best part is, most of the books can be borrowed, with the exception of autographed or fragile editions.

The library is open Mon through Fri from 8 a.m. to 5 p.m.; (575) 562-2636; my.enmu.edu/web/golden-library/.

Curry County

Clovis, the largest city in Curry County and trade center for nearby Cannon Air Force Base, holds a place in rock 'n' roll history as the home of the famous **Norman Petty Studios**. The old studio is no longer operating as a studio; instead, it is a shrine to Buddy Holly, the pioneering rock 'n' roller who propelled such hits as "That'll Be the Day" and "Peggy Sue" to the top of the charts in the 1950s—hits that were recorded right here at the then state-of-the-art studio.

The studio was founded by producer-arranger-musician Norman Petty, who died in 1984, and his wife, Vi, who later cleaned and restored the studio to its former glory and personally led tours through the place before her death in 1992. She'd point out the drink machine where Holly would buy Cokes, Holly's microphone and Fender guitar amplifier, and the room where Holly and other studio guests stayed, all its furniture intact. Besides Holly, the studio drew other musicians from West Texas and New Mexico, most notably Roy Orbison.

Kenneth Broad, an area minister and executor of the Pettys' estate, feels it's important to keep the restored studio open as a shrine for Holly's fans. Broad and other locals would like to open the studio for regular tours as well as turn it into a working recording studio again. In the meantime, however, the little gray building on 7th Street in downtown Clovis is officially open only during the four-day **Clovis Music Festival** (575-763-3435; clovisnm.com), held each September as an annual tribute to Petty and local musicians.

During other times, anyone wanting to see the place must contact Kenneth Broad at least two weeks in advance at PO Box 926, Clovis, NM 88101; (575) 356-6422; e-mail ksbroad@yucca.net; superoldies.com/pettystudios, to arrange for a tour. There's no admission fee, but donations are accepted.

Like many sizable towns across America, Clovis has a historic theater on its Main Street. A tall, rather ordinary facade, with that familiar vertical neon spelling out *lyceum* in an art deco typeface, belies the grand interior of the town's **Old Lyceum Theatre**. Built in 1919–1920 as a theater that would be used for both live performances and films, the Lyceum has a huge screen that was tailor-made to reflect the glory of early Hollywood, including Tom Mix cowboy movies and films starring Shirley Temple. The vision of the theater's founder, Eugene F. Hardwick, was to create the best performing stage west of Kansas City. Many folks at the time believed that he succeeded.

The Lyceum closed in 1974, and later a group of locals formed to "Save the Lyceum!" and ended up purchasing it for $40,000. A nonprofit group then began restoring and, eventually, operating the theater. The restored Lyceum now serves as the town's performing arts center and is the linchpin of Clovis's Main Street historic preservation program. Guided tours are available upon request. The Lyceum is at 411 N. Main St.; (575) 763-6085; clovismainstreet.org.

Where to Stay in Southeastern New Mexico

DE BACA COUNTY

Billy the Kid Country Inn
1704 E. Sumner Ave.
Fort Sumner
(575) 355-7414
Moderate

Fisherman's Hideaway Restaurant, Resort, and Lounge
Lake Sumner
25 Wild Turkey Ln.
Fort Sumner
(575) 355-2629
Moderate

LINCOLN COUNTY

Ellis Store
Highway 380 at mile marker 98
Lincoln
(800) 653-6460
ellisstore.com
Moderate

Forest Home Cabins
436 Main Rd.
Ruidoso
(575) 257-4504
foresthomecabins.com
Moderate to very expensive

Holiday Inn Express
400 W. US 70
Ruidoso
(575) 257-3736
hiexpress.com
Moderate

Shadow Mountain Lodge
107 Main Rd.
Ruidoso
(575) 257-4886
smlruidoso.com
Moderate to expensive

Swiss Chalet Inn
1451 Mechem Dr.
Ruidoso
(575) 258-3333
(866) 322-0333
sciruidoso.com
Inexpensive

Wortley Hotel
US 380
Lincoln
(575) 653-4300
wortleyhotel.com
Moderate

OTERO COUNTY

Cloudcroft Mountain Park Hostel
1049 US 82
High Rolls Mountain Park
(575) 682-0555
cloudcrofthostel.com
Inexpensive

Inn of the Mountain Gods
(resort and casino)
287 Carrizo Canyon Rd.
Mescalero
(575) 464-5141
(888) 324-0348
innofthemountaingods.com
Moderate to very expensive

The Lodge Resort and Spa
Just off US 82
Cloudcroft
(800) 395-6343
thelodgeresort.com
Expensive to very expensive

Satellite Inn
2224 N. White Sands Blvd.
Alamogordo
(575) 437-8454
(800) 221-7690
satelliteinnnm.com
Inexpensive

White Sands Motel
1101 S. White Sands Blvd.
Alamogordo
(575) 437-2922
Inexpensive

CHAVES COUNTY

Best Western El Rancho Palacio
2205 N. Main St.
Roswell
(575) 622-2721
(800) 780-7234
bestwestern.com
Inexpensive

Budget Inn
2101 N. Main St.
Roswell
(575) 623-6050
(800) 637-5956
budgetinn.com
Inexpensive

Days Inn
1310 N. Main St.
Roswell
(575) 623-4021
(800) 329-7466
wyndhamhotels.com/days-inn/roswell-new-mexico
Inexpensive

Holiday Inn Roswell
2620 N. Main St.
Roswell
(877) 859-5095
holidayinn.com/roswell
Expensive

Hurd–La Rinconada Gallery and Guest Homes
PO Box 100
San Patricio
(800) 658-6912
wyethartists.com
Expensive to very expensive

EDDY COUNTY

Best Western Cavern Inn
17 Carlsbad Caverns Hwy.
Whites City
(575) 785-2291
(800) 780-7234
bestwestern.com
Moderate

Best Western Pecos Inn
2209 W. Main
Artesia
(575) 748-3324
Moderate

Best Western Stevens Inn
1829 S. Canal St.
Carlsbad
(575) 887-2851
Expensive

Fiddler's Inn Bed and Breakfast
705 N. Canyon St.
Carlsbad
(575) 303-0755
fiddlersinnbb.com
Expensive

Heritage Inn Bed & Breakfast
209 W. Main
Artesia
(505) 748-2552
(866) 207-0222
artesiaheritageinn.com
Moderate

The Trinity Hotel
201 S. Canal St.
Carlsbad
(575) 234-9891
thetrinityhotel.com
Moderate to expensive

LEA COUNTY

Best Western Executive Inn
309 N. Marland Blvd.
Hobbs
(575) 397-7171
(800) 780-7234
Inexpensive

Comfort Inn and Suites Lovington
1202 N. Main Ave.
Lovington
(855) 849-1513
choicehotels.com/new-mexico/lovington/comfort-inn-hotels
Moderate

En Sueno Bed and Breakfast
3505 W. Alabama St.
Hobbs
(575) 392-9347
ensuenobnb.com
Moderate

Hilton Garden Inn
4620 N. Lovington Hwy.
Hobbs
(855) 618-4697
hiltongardeninn.3hilton
.com/en/hotels/new-
mexico/hilton-garden-inn
-new-mexico
Moderate

Lea County Inn
5412 Lovington Hwy.
Hobbs
(575) 408-8793
leacountyinn.com
Inexpensive

ROOSEVELT COUNTY

Almost Home Bed and Breakfast
8168 Hwy. 206
Portales
(575) 356-0011
almosthomebedand
breakfast.com
Moderate

Holiday Inn Express Portales
1901 W. Second St.
Portales
(877) 859-5095
lhg.com/holiday-inn-
express/hotels/us/en/
portales
Expensive

Super 8 Portales
1895 W. Second St.
Portales
(800) 536-1211
wyndhamhotels.com/
super-8/portales-new
-mexico
Moderate

CURRY COUNTY

Days Inn and Suites Clovis
2700 Mabry Dr.
Clovis
(575) 762-4491
wyndhamhotels.com/days
-inn/clovis-new-mexico
Inexpensive

Super 8 Clovis
2912 Mabry Dr.
Clovis
(800) 536-1211
wyndhamhotels.com/
super-8/clovis-new-mexico
Inexpensive

Where to Eat in Southeastern New Mexico

DE BACA COUNTY

Fred's Restaurant & Lounge
1408 E. Sumner Ave.
Fort Sumner
(575) 355-7500
Inexpensive
American and New
Mexican

Mill Iron Coffee Bar
801 N. 4th St.
Fort Sumner
(575) 355-2622
facebook.com/
MillIronCoffeeBar
Locally roasted coffee,
tea, and homemade
daily breakfast and lunch
specials; also sells fresh
flowers, handmade cards,
candles, country antiques,
and gifts

Rodeo Grill
715 E. Sumner Ave.
Fort Sumner
(575) 355-8000
Inexpensive
American; known for its
brisket, burgers, and hand-
cut fries

LINCOLN COUNTY

Cafe Rio Pizza
2547 Sudderth Dr.
Ruidoso
(575) 257-7746
Inexpensive to moderate
Pizza, sandwiches, as well
as Greek, Portuguese, and
Cajun classics

Che Palle
433 Smokey Bear Blvd.
Capitan
(575) 973-0933
facebook.com/Che-
Palle-117802376558316
Inexpensive to moderate
Fresh pizza, po'boys, meat
loaf, and salads made
with locally grown organic
produce

The Creperie at Tinnie's Silver Dollar
US 70
Tinnie
(575) 653-4425
tinniesilverdollar.com
Moderate to expensive
Under new ownership, with lighter homemade lunch and afternoon tea fare including crepes, pie, cakes, and blended teas

El Paisano Restaurant
442 Smokey Bear Blvd.
Capitan
(575) 354-2206
Inexpensive to moderate
New Mexican

Ellis Store
Highway 380 at mile marker 98
Lincoln
(575) 653-4609
(800) 653-6460
ellisstore.com
Very expensive
Six-course dinners in a unique historic inn for guests and nonguests by advance reservation

Smokey Bear Restaurant
310 Smokey Bear Blvd.
Capitan
(575) 354-2257
Inexpensive
American

Wortley Hotel Dining Room
Main Street (US 380)
Lincoln
(575) 653-4300
wortleyhotel.com
Inexpensive
New Mexican and American (seasonal hours)

OTERO COUNTY

Mad Jack's
105 James Canyon Hwy.
Cloudcroft
(575) 682-7577
Inexpensive
Authentic Central Texas–style barbecue; wildly popular—get there early

Memories
1223 New York Ave.
Alamogordo
(575) 437-0077
memories-restaurant.com
Moderate
Steak, seafood, pasta

Rebecca's at the Lodge
The Lodge Resort and Spa
Cloudcroft
(575) 682-1680
(800) 395-6343
thelodgeresort.com
Moderate to very expensive
Continental

Spaghetti Western of High Rolls New Mexico
(inside High Rolls General Store)
845 US 82
High Rolls Mountain Park
(575) 682-6653
Inexpensive to moderate
Homemade pizza, salads, sandwiches, and pies

Western Bar and Restaurant
304 Burro Ave.
Cloudcroft
(575) 682-2445
Inexpensive
New Mexican and American

CHAVES COUNTY

Big D's Downtown Dive
505 N. Main St.
Roswell
(575) 627-0776
facebook.com/bigdsdowntowndive
Moderate
Top-rated, locally sourced grass-fed burgers at this quirky chef-owned spot

Cattle Baron
1113 N. Main St.
Roswell
(575) 622-3311
cattlebaron.com
Moderate
Leading contender for steaks, seafood
(branches in Hobbs and Portales)

Cowboy Café
1120 E. 2nd St.
Roswell
(575) 622-6363
facebook.com/cowboycaferoswell
Inexpensive
Local hot spot for homestyle breakfast and brunch and homemade pies
(sister restaurant to Black Betty BBQ)

La Posta
2103 N. Main St.
Roswell
(575) 622-4919
Inexpensive
Mexican fare in a quaint postage-stamp-size building

Pasta Cafe
1208 N. Main St.
Roswell
(575) 624-1111
pastacafeitalianbistro.com
Moderate
Authentic Italian entrees
and New York–style hand-
thrown pizza

EDDY COUNTY

**Blue House Bakery and
Café**
609 N. Canyon St.
Carlsbad
(575) 628-0555
Inexpensive
Lovely little cafe in a
residential neighborhood
serving fresh breakfasts
(guests of nearby Fiddler's
Inn Bed and Breakfast eat
breakfast here for free)

Flume Restaurant
in Best Western Stevens
Inn
1829 S. Canal St.
Carlsbad
(575) 887-2851
Moderate to expensive
Prime rib, steaks

La Herradura
1901 Pine St.
Artesia
(575) 746-0040
Inexpensive
Mexican

Trinity Hotel Restaurant
201 S. Canal St.
Carlsbad
(575) 234-9891
thetrinityhotel.com
Moderate to expensive
Gourmet Italian

Yellow Brix Restaurant
201 N. Canal St.
Carlsbad
(575) 941-2749
yellowbrixrestaurant.com
Former coffee shop in
an artsy 1920s building
serving gourmet New
American fare with global
influences

LEA COUNTY

Pacific Rim
in Comfort Suites
1309 W. Joe Harvey Blvd.
Hobbs
(575) 392-0030
Moderate to expensive
Pan-Asian

Saxony Steakhouse
in Hobbs Family Inn
501 N. Marland
Hobbs
(575) 397-3251
hobbsfamilyinn.com
Moderate to expensive
Popular chef-owned steak
house inside an older inn

ROOSEVELT COUNTY

Do Drop In
123 S. Main St.
Portales
(575) 226-5282
Inexpensive
Old-timey place for coffee,
soup, and sandwich
specials and homemade
pies and cakes

**Juanito's Mexican
Restaurant**
813 S. Avenue C Place
Portales
(575) 359-1860
Inexpensive to moderate
Mexican

**Roosevelt Brewing
Company**
201 S. Main Ave.
Portales
(575) 226-2739
rooseveltbrewing.com
Inexpensive to moderate
Popular microbrewery
serving pub grub

Something Different Grill
805 W. 2nd St.
Portales
(575) 356-1205
Inexpensive
Eclectic deli sandwiches,
salads, and entrees on the
healthy side
(second branch in Clovis)

CURRY COUNTY

Gallery 15 and Bistro
(inside an antiques store;
watch for signs)
422 US 60 (between Clovis
and Texico)
Clovis
(575) 482-9090
Inexpensive
Bistro serving homemade
soups, salads, paninis,
wraps, and pies

**Leal's Mexican Food
Restaurant**
3100 Mabry Dr.
Clovis
(575) 763-4075
Inexpensive to moderate
Tex-Mex

Appendices

NEW MEXICO INDIAN PUEBLOS

(Listed by county in which most of the Indian reservation land is located.)

BERNALILLO COUNTY

Isleta Pueblo
PO Box 1270
Isleta, NM 87022
(505) 869-3111
isletapueblo.com

CIBOLA COUNTY

Acoma Pueblo
PO Box 309
Acomita, NM 87034
(800) 747-0181
acomaskycity.org

Laguna Pueblo
PO Box 194
Laguna, NM 87026
(505) 552-6654
lagunapueblo.nsn.gov

MCKINLEY COUNTY

Zuni Pueblo
PO Box 339
Zuni, NM 87327
(505) 782-7000
ashiwi.org

RIO ARRIBA COUNTY

Ohkay Owingeh Pueblo
(formerly San Juan Pueblo)
PO Box 1099
San Juan, NM 87566
(505) 852-4400
indianpueblo
.org/19pueblos/
ohkayowingeh.html

Santa Clara Pueblo
PO Box 580
Española, NM 87532
(505) 753-7326
newmexico.org/
santa-clara-pueblo

SANDOVAL COUNTY

Cochiti Pueblo
PO Box 70
Cochiti, NM 87072
(505) 465-2244
pueblodecochito.org

Jemez Pueblo
PO Box 100
Jemez, NM 87024
(575) 834-7235
jemezpueblo.org

Kewa Pueblo
(formerly Santo Domingo
Pueblo)
PO Box 99
Santo Domingo, NM 87052
(505) 465-2214
indianpueblo
.org/19pueblos/
santodomingo.htm

Sandia Pueblo
Box 6008
Bernalillo, NM 87004
(505) 867-3317
sandiapueblo.nsn.us

San Felipe Pueblo
(Katishtya)
PO Box 4339
San Felipe, NM 87001
(505) 867-3381
newmexico.org/
san-felipe-pueblo

Santa Ana Pueblo
(Tamaya)
2 Dove Rd.
Bernalillo, NM 87004
(505) 771-6700
santaana.nsn.gov

Zia Pueblo
Pueblo of Zia
Administration Building
135 Capital Square Dr.
Zia Pueblo, NM 87053
(575) 867-3304
zia.com/home/zia_info.html

SANTA FE COUNTY

Nambé Pueblo
Route 1, Box 117-BB
Santa Fe, NM 87501
(505) 455-2036
nambepueblo.org

Pojoaque Pueblo
Route 11, Box 71
Santa Fe, NM 87501
(505) 455-2278
pojoaque.org

San Ildefonso Pueblo
Route 5, Box 315-A
Santa Fe, NM 87501
(505) 455-3549
indianpueblo
.org/19pueblos/
sanildefonso.html

Tesuque Pueblo
Route 5, Box 360T
Santa Fe, NM 87501
(505) 983-2667
(800) 483-1040
newmexico.org/
tesuque-pueblo

TAOS COUNTY

Picuris Pueblo
PO Box 127
Peñasco, NM 87553
(575) 587-2519
picurispueblo.org

Taos Pueblo
PO Box 1846
Taos Pueblo, NM 87571
(575) 758-1028
taospueblo.com

NON–PUEBLO INDIAN TRIBES IN NEW MEXICO

Alamo Chapter Navajo Nation
Alamo Route
Magdalena, NM 87825
(575) 854-2686
alamo.navajochapters.org
(Socorro County)

Jicarilla Apache Nation
PO Box 507
Dulce, NM 87528
(575) 759-3242
newmexico.org/jicarilla-apache-nation
(Rio Arriba County)

Mescalero Apache Tribe
PO Box 176
Mescalero, NM 88340
(575) 464-4494
mescaleroapachetribe.com
(Otero County)

Navajo Nation (Dine)
Tourism Department
PO Box 663
Window Rock, AZ 86515
(928) 871-6647
discovernavajo.com
(San Juan and McKinley Counties in New Mexico but also in northeast Arizona and southeast Utah)

Ramah Chapter Navajo Nation
PO Box 308
Ramah, NM 87321
(505) 775-7140
ramahnavajo.org
(Cibola County)

To'hajiilee Chapter Navajo Nation
PO Box 3398
To'hajiilee, NM 87026
(505) 836-4221
tohajiilee.navajochapters.org
(Bernalillo County)

NEW MEXICO WINERIES

Acequia Winery
240 Reclining Acres Rd.
Corrales, NM 87408
(505) 264-1656
acequiawinery.com

Amaro Winery
402 S. Melendres St.
Las Cruces, NM 88005
(575) 527-5310
amarowinerynm.com

Anasazi Fields Winery
26 Camino de los Pueblitos
Placitas, NM 87043
(505) 867-3062
anasazifieldswinery.com

Arena Blanca Vineyards
7320 US 54/70 N.
Alamogordo, NM 88301
(575) 437-0602
(800) 368-3081
pistachioland.com

Black Mesa Winery
1502 Hwy. 68 (mile marker 15)
Velarde, NM 87582
(800) 852-2820
blackmesawinery.com

Black Range Vineyards
10701 Hwy. 152
Hillsboro
(575) 895-5000
blackrangevineyards.com

Camino Real Winery
13 Tomes Hill Rd.
Las Lunas, NM 87031
(505) 307-0469
caminorealwinery.com

Casa Abril Vineyards and Winery
01 Camino Abril
Algodones, NM 87001
(505) 771-0208
casaabrilvineyards.com

Casa Rondeña Winery
Rondeña Way
733 Chavez Rd. NW
Albuquerque, NM 87107
(505) 344-5911
(800) 706-1699
casarondena.com

Corrales Winery
6275 Corrales Rd.
Corrales, 87048
(505) 898-1819
corraleswinery.com

Don Quixote Distillery and Winery
18057-A US 285/84
Pojoaque, NM 87506
(505) 695-0817
dqdistillery.com

Dos Viejos Winery
69 Pecos Rd.
Tularosa, NM 88352
(575) 585-2647
dosviejoswines.com

Estrella del Norte Vineyard
106 N. Shining Sun
Santa Fe, NM 87506
(505) 455-2826
estrelladelnortevineyard
.com

Gruet Winery
8400 Pan American
Freeway NE
Albuquerque, NM 87113
(505) 821-0055
(888) 857-9463
gruetwinery.com

Guadalupe Vineyards
188 San Jose Loop
San Fidel, NM 87049
(505) 552-0082
guadalupevineyards.com

La Chiripada Winery
Highway 75
PO Box 191
Dixon, NM 87527
(575) 579-4437
(800) 528-7801
lachiripada.com

La Viña Winery
4201 S. Hwy. 28
La Union, NM 88021
(575) 882-7632
lavinawinery.com

Los Luceros Winery
PO Box 1100
Alcalde, NM 87511
(505) 852-1085

Luna Rossa Winery (also Mesilla)
3710 W. Pine St.
Deming, NM 88030
(575) 544-1160
lunarossawinery.com

Madison Vineyards and Winery
HC 72, Box 490
Ribera, NM 87560
(505) 421-8028
madisonvineyards.com

Matheson Winery
103 Pat D'Arco Hwy. B3
Rio Rancho, NM 87124
(505) 350-6557
mathesonwines.com

Milagro Vineyards
985 W. Ella
PO Box 1205
Corrales, NM 87048
(505) 898-3998
milagrowine.com

Pasando Tiempo Winery
277 Dandelion Rd.
Corrales, NM 87048
(505) 228-0154
pasandotiempowinery.com

Ponderosa Valley Vineyards and Winery
3171 Hwy. 290
Ponderosa, NM 87044
(575) 834-7487
ponderosawinery.com

Rio Grande Winery
5321 Hwy. 28 (mile marker 25)
Las Cruces, NM 88005
(575) 524-3985
riograndewinery.com

Sombra Antigua Winery
430 La Vina Rd.
Anthony, NM 88027
(915) 241-4349
(915) 471-5113
sombraantigua.com

St. Clair Winery
1325 De Baca Rd.
Deming, NM 88030
(888) 799-4637
stclairwinery.com

Tularosa Vineyards & Winery
23 Coyote Canyon Rd.
Tularosa, NM 88352
(575) 585-2260
(800) 687-4467
tularosavineyards.com

Vivac Winery and Art Gallery
2075 Hwy. 68
Dixon, NM 87527
(505) 579-4441
vivacwinery.com

Wines of the San Juan
233 Hwy. 511
Blanco, NM 87412
(505) 632-0879
winesofthesanjuan.com

NEW MEXICO SKI AREAS

As part of the southern reaches of the Rocky Mountains, New Mexico's mountain ranges are home to many downhill and cross-country ski areas. During ski season, which is roughly late November or early December through mid-March or early April, most ski areas are open from 9 a.m. to 4 p.m. For New Mexico road conditions, call (505) 827-5213 or (800) 432-4269 (out of state), or check online at nmroads.com; and for detailed or updated information on the downhill ski areas listed below, or for information on cross-country ski areas, please call Ski New Mexico at (505) 858-2422; skinewmexico.com. (***Note:*** Lift fees are included for comparison purposes only; they are subject to change from season to season. Fees for half-day lift tickets and those for children and seniors are lower.)

Angel Fire
Angel Fire
(575) 377-6401
angelfireresort.com
Number of trails: 80
Adult full-day lift ticket: $75

Pajarito
Los Alamos
(505) 662-5725
skipajarito.com
Number of trails: 40
Adult full-day lift ticket: $49

Red River
Red River
(575) 754-2223
redriverskiarea.com
Number of trails: 60
Adult full-day lift ticket: $73

Sandia Peak
Albuquerque
(505) 242-9052
sandiapeak.com
Number of trails: 25
Adult full-day lift ticket: $55

Sipapu
(outside of Peñasco)
(800) 587-2240
sipapunm.com
Number of trails: 41
Adult full-day lift ticket: $45
(special deals on lodging in Santa Fe with 2-day passes)

Ski Apache
Ruidoso
(575) 464-3600
skiapache.com
Number of trails: 55
Adult full-day lift ticket: $40.99

Ski Cloudcroft
Cloudcroft
(575) 682-2333
skicloudcroft.net
Number of trails: 25
Adult full-day lift ticket: $45

Ski Santa Fe
Santa Fe
(505) 982-4429
skisantafe.com
Number of trails: 79
Adult full-day lift ticket: $75

Taos Ski Valley
Taos
(575) 776-2291
(866) 968-7386
skitaos.org
Number of trails: 110
Adult full-day lift ticket: $98

Index